SEIZED

SEIZED

A Sea Captain's Adventures

Battling Scoundrels and Pirates

While Recovering Stolen Ships in the

World's Most Troubled Waters

WITHDRAWN

MAX HARDBERGER

BROADWAY BOOKS
NEW YORK

BROADWAY

Copyright © 2010 by F. Max Hardberger

Published in the United States by Broadway Books, an imprint of
the Crown Publishing Group, a division of Random House, Inc., New York.

www.crownpublishing.com

BROADWAY BOOKS and the Broadway Books colophon
are trademarks of Random House, Inc.

Library of Congress Cataloging-in-Publication Data

Hardberger, Max.
Seized: a sea captain's adventures battling scoundrels and pirates while recovering
stolen ships in the world's most troubled waters / Max Hardberger.
p.   cm.
1. Pirates.   2. Maritime terrorism—Prevention.   3. Hijacking of ships—
Prevention.   I. Title.
G535.H28 2010
364.16'4—dc22   2009040930

ISBN 978-0-7679-3138-0

Printed in the United States of America

Design by Leonard W. Henderson

10 9 8 7 6 5 4 3 2 1

First Edition

To my brother, Karl, and my sister, Dotty

CONTENTS

FOREWORD

THE AUTHOR OF A memoir is expected to tell the truth, as best as he or she can recollect it. However, a writer who intends to entertain as well as inform must do more than recount mere facts; even the teller of truth may have to reconstruct dialogue for those words lost in the mists of time. In addition, I have changed the names of locations and ships to protect the innocent—and the guilty; in a few instances, for the purposes of pacing and narrative, I have combined elements of two or more separate experiences into one. Otherwise, all the experiences described in the book are recounted as I remember them.

During the years covered by this book, I and my associates made many enemies—some still living and preying on the unwary. So while I've recounted my own actions, and stand behind them, I've no wish to force my friends to do the same. I've therefore changed the names and descriptions of the people in the book, except those previously revealed in public records. If some of the villains I've encountered escape censure as a result, I'll be content to let them be judged by their Maker.

In spite of the above, this work is essentially true to my life, and to the stories of the many men and women who, for better or worse, came and went during those turbulent days.

SEIZED

THROUGH THE REEFS ON THE *NARUDA*

T HE FIRST TIME I ever stole a ship out of port was on the sturdy old
bulk carrier *Naruda,* lying at anchor in Cap Haitien Bay, Haiti, at the
end of May 1987. We had finished discharging our cargo of rice
the previous day, and on Friday afternoon I was sitting in the wheelhouse,
waiting for a clearance to leave, when I noticed a gang of soldiers with
automatic weapons coming out of the customs building on the waterfront.
They climbed down into a rough-hewn dory bobbing against the dock.

My first officer, a heavyset Dominican named Arturo Robles, appeared
at the door to the starboard wing of the bridge, his shirt unbuttoned and
his round brown belly streaked with sweat. "Hold is clean, Cap," he
announced. "Can we let the Haitians have the rice?"

"Sure," I said. "Looks like we're going to have visitors, First." I nodded my chin toward the dory, now pulling steadily toward us through the
low Atlantic swells that rolled in past the reefs. The boatman sculling on
the stern was helped by a gentle breeze that whispered down from the western mountains and carried the smells of rotten fruit and sunbaked dirt from
the slums that ring the bay.

Arturo crossed to the port side. "That boat's full of soldiers," he said.
"Trouble for us, Captain?"

"Yeah. I knew when the agent couldn't get us a clearance yesterday that
something bad was going to happen. We should've upped anchor and
steamed out last night."

The boat sped across the cloud-dappled water and pulled up at the pilot
ladder on the ship's port side. I went down on deck to meet the soldiers as
they climbed up one by one. The first man up was a short, stocky officer
with a Colt automatic in a scarred black holster.

"You captain?" he demanded in a gravelly voice.

"Yes," I said, "I'm the captain. How may I help you?"

He thrust a grimy, badly photocopied paper into my hand. It said that the ship was seized *"pour les dettes."*

"What's this about?" I asked in French. "What debts are these, eh?"

He shrugged. His men crowded on deck behind him and stared at me sullenly. "It's a matter for the court," he said. "You are required to go to court on Monday." He waved two of the men forward, thin young men in faded uniforms, one light-skinned and the other black as jet. They carried submachine guns slung over their shoulders. "These men will stay on board until then," the officer said. "You will feed them and treat them properly."

I bowed toward them. "Of course," I said. "They will be our guests on board."

"You will give them a radio," the officer said. *"Une radio portative.* So they can call the port office if anything goes wrong."

"Yes, of course," I said.

His muddy little eyes glinted with hostility. "You will give it to them now, before I leave."

I shrugged and turned to Arturo. "First, please go get one of the walkie-talkies and bring it down. The yellow one."

He hesitated. Of the four walkie-talkies on board, the yellow one had the worst battery. It wouldn't stay charged more than a couple of hours. I gave him a look. He said "Yessir" and hurried to the accommodations.

The officer and I regarded each other without talking. A few minutes later Arturo returned and gave the officer the walkie-talkie. He held it to his ear and said, *"Capitaine du port, capitaine du port, le bâtiment appelle."*

After a few seconds, the port office answered. The officer handed the walkie-talkie to the light-skinned soldier. "Call the captain of the port if the ship tries to leave," he told him. "Do you understand?"

"Oui, Colonel," the man said. The colonel herded the rest of his men down the pilot ladder and the dory swung away from the ship's side, the boatman's black, muscular back working as he sculled against the wind.

"Please," I said to the soldiers, "you can relax in the messroom if you wish. The cook will bring you drinks."

The black man started toward the accommodations without speaking, but the brown man ducked his head and murmured, *"Merci, Capitaine."*

I went with them to the crew's mess on the starboard side and told Cookie, hovering unhappily in the galley, to bring them Cokes with ice. Lunch was over, but I told him to fix them something to eat.

Back on the bridge, Arturo said, "Why are you treating those men so well, Captain? You will not get them to disobey their orders."

I chuckled. "No, but maybe I can get them to drop their guard."

"What do you have in mind?"

I went up close and lowered my voice. "We're not waiting until Monday. The judge will probably order us off the ship, and might even put us all in jail. I'm taking this ship out tonight."

His brown eyes widened. "Put us in jail? What for? What have we done?"

"We've done nothing wrong. But you know that the receiver—that little fat man who came on board when we first arrived—is claiming a short shipment. It's not the ship's fault that the shipper didn't load as much cargo as the Haitian paid for, but that won't matter to a Haitian court. The only thing we can do is get out."

"What about the guards? You're not going to . . ."

"No, no," I said hurriedly. "I won't hurt them. *Pero cada quien tiene su manera de matar pulgas, seguro?*"

He nodded. "Everybody kills fleas in his own way" is the Spanish equivalent to "There's more than one way to skin a cat." I clapped him on the shoulder. "Don't say anything to the crew. I haven't got a plan yet, but I can promise you this: We won't be here Monday morning."

He went down and I called the ship's owner—a middle-aged Greek living in Miami with his young American wife—on the SSB radio. He was at home and accepted the collect call.

"But, Captain," he cried, "the ship's not responsible for short-loading. Surely the judge will let the ship sail."

"I think the receiver is trying to steal the ship. This is an outlaw port, you know. He can do what he wants here."

"Sacred Mary! What can we do, then?"

The whole world can listen in on radio communications. "I don't want to say too much," I said carefully. "I just want your permission to do what has to be done."

"You have it, of course," he said fervently. "Just keep me advised when you can."

We hung up and I dragged a stool out on the port wing of the bridge. The sun was dropping toward the western mountains, low over the ruins of the mountaintop castle that the slave-king Henri Christophe had built to guard the entrance to the bay. Far below its ramparts, fishing boats with long, willowy booms ghosted into the bay. There were no buoys or other navigation aids marking the entrance, and the rusty hulk of a freighter that had missed the channel lay a mile to the east, broken on the reef that stretched out of sight toward the Dominican border.

We'd come in through the reef only three days earlier, but I hadn't marked any of the waypoints. Loran—the only positioning equipment we had—wasn't accurate enough for this kind of navigation at night. I went into the chart room and studied the chart. The passage through the reef had a dogleg in the middle; we would have to bear northeast until we reached it, then make a hard left for five hundred yards before turning back to the northeast. At night, with nothing marking the channel, getting out would be a crapshoot, and the penalty for failure would be the loss of the ship and a long stint in a Haitian prison.

I found the chief engineer in his cabin, a muscular Honduran in his late forties with gray hair that bristled up from his square head like iron filings. He'd come aboard only two weeks earlier, in Miami, but he seemed to be a good, competent engineer. He was sitting in front of the fan on his desk, reading a Spanish paperback. He put it down and stood up when I knocked on his doorframe.

"Keep your seat, Chief," I said, sitting on his bunk. "I'm going to need some help from you tonight."

He raised an eyebrow. "To do what?"

I leaned close. "We're going to take the ship out. You know the receiver's had the ship seized on a bogus claim. Now listen . . . I want the guards on board to think we can't sail, so they won't be suspicious."

"What can I do to help?"

"While we're at supper, I want you to come into the mess and tell me that the main engine's broken. Bring some broken part to show me. Can you do that?"

"Of course. But what will the guards do when they find out we're sailing?"

I stood up. "I'm still working on that."

"Are you going to force them off the ship?"

I patted his shoulder and went to the door. "By the time I'm finished with them, they'll be glad to get off."

He wasn't convinced, but he shrugged and picked up his book. I went out and up to the bridge.

As I pushed open the heavy steel door to the wheelhouse, I stopped and examined its lock. Then I went back down and checked the doors leading from the landings in the companionway to each deck. The *Naruda* was a small ship, with only three levels above the main deck. International safety standards require steel doors on any passageway that could let fire travel from deck to deck, and although she was old and tired, the *Naruda* had been well built. I went down and found Arturo and the ABs—the ship had two able-bodied seamen to work the deck—dogging down the hatch covers.

The hold had been swept free of spilled cargo, and the Haitians I'd hired to clean it were climbing down to a waiting dory, holding their pitiful little bags of salvaged rice mixed with dust and rust chips. I led Arturo aft to the port passageway.

"I've got an idea, First," I said. "It's going to take some tricky timing, but it might work." I explained my plan.

He grimaced. "Sounds pretty risky, Captain."

"They won't be suspicious." I told him about the chief engineer's story of a broken main engine. "Plus, they'll have a big supper and a lot of rum in them."

"Rum? You're going to give them rum?"

"You will. I'm sure they speak Spanish . . . This close to the border, almost all Haitians speak Spanish."

"True enough."

"Do you have some rum?"

"*Sí*, I have a *botella* in my cabin, almost full."

"Good. The ship'll buy it from you. I want you to take it to the crew's mess after supper and get them drinking. Since they'll think the ship can't sail, they'll probably take a few drinks."

"And if they don't?"

I shrugged. "Then they don't. The plan might work anyway."

"How can we put them ashore? Nobody in the crew will want to take them in the boat."

"They can go by themselves. It's worth losing the boat to get rid of them."

He looked at me for a long time, then said, "Well, I don't like it, but you're the captain. I'll do as you say."

"Thanks, First. Now go get some pieces of wood. Measure the distances between the doors and the hallway bulkheads and cut them to fit. Check the rescue boat's engine and put gas in the tank. And put a couple of life jackets in it."

He nodded and went forward to help the ABs finish securing the hatch covers. I glanced in the crew's mess as I went past, and saw the guards sitting at one of the tables with their guns in their laps, watching television. It was tuned to a Haitian station, and I could hear a snatch of a news broadcast. There was another revolution under way, and the rebels were marching on Port-au-Prince.

I went in the galley, where Cookie was frying chicken in a heavy skillet. The door to the crew's mess was open, so I drew him out onto the afterdeck. "Fix the best food you have, Cookie," I whispered into his ear. "Make a lot of it, and keep serving the guards food until they can't eat any more."

He was a rotund, pleasant-faced Nicaraguan who'd been on the ship since before I joined, six months earlier. He didn't ask any questions. "*Sí, Capitan,*" he said, and went back in the galley.

At 1800 hours, the ship's normal suppertime, I went down to the crew's mess and took a seat at one of the tables. I would normally eat in the officers' mess, but the guards couldn't know that. They were already eating, their submachine guns in their laps, but they nodded when I came in. A few minutes later Arturo came in and sat across from them.

"How is supper?" he asked them in Spanish. "Good?"

"Very good," the brown man replied. "*Muy sabroso.*"

Cookie brought my plate. There was a French soap opera showing on the television, and the guards watched it intently while they ate. Arturo caught my eye and gave me a fleeting smile.

On cue, the chief engineer came in, his T-shirt limp with sweat; he was holding a bearing in a greasy rag. "We have a problem, Captain," he said in Spanish. The guards looked around.

He showed me the bearing. "The lube-oil pump bearing has frozen up. We can't start the main engine."

The bearing could have come from any of a dozen pumps on board, but neither I nor the guards could have told it from any other. "Got a spare on board, Chief?"

He shook his head. "No, Captain. No spare on board."

"So we can't use the main engine?"

"I'm afraid not."

I shrugged. "Well, we can't leave before Monday anyway. I'll call the owner and get a replacement shipped down. How long to install it?"

"Only a couple of hours."

"Everything else okay in the engine room?"

He made a disgusted sound. "We need plenty things, Captain. You know I order parts and the owner never sends them. But if we can get this replaced, we can sail."

"Thanks, Chief."

He went out and the guards went back to their meal. Cookie came in with another platter of fried chicken, and the guards heaped their plates anew. I wasn't surprised. A private in the Haitian army would have a hard time getting enough to eat, so this would be a feast to them.

I declined the bread pudding, but the guards accepted their bowls gladly. The oilers—the engineers' assistants in the engine room—and the ABs came in and took their seats. They looked surprised to see the captain and first officer eating in the crew's mess, but I gave them a tiny shake of the head and they didn't say anything. After I finished eating I went up to the bridge to wait.

Dark was a long time coming. Finally, when the last pink rays of sunlight had faded from the sky above the ruined fort, I crept down the outside companionway aft of the house and eased up under one of the open ports of the crew's mess.

I could hear the first officer and the guards talking, and from the sound of it, they were getting along just fine. Arturo said, his speech slightly slurred, "We don't care about that owner. He doesn't treat us right. I tell you, the captain is happy to stay here. He has a Haitian girlfriend in Port-au-Prince. If the judge says the ship can't leave, he'll get her to come up and stay on board."

The guards laughed. One of them said, "And you, *Primer Oficial*? Do you have a Haitian girlfriend?"

"Not yet, but if we have to stay, perhaps I can find one."

The same guard said, "Oh, you will have no trouble with that. Come to my house and we will have a party. Plenty girls will be there."

They laughed and glasses clinked. I crept aft and went back up to the bridge. Now the night was full dark, and the *terral*, the nightly land breeze, was starting to build from the south. I'd already checked the moon phase, and although the night was clear, the moon wouldn't rise until eleven. I intended to have the ship well on her way by then.

It would take luck as well as skill, but I wasn't going to let that scumbag Haitian receiver have my ship. If we went up on the reef, I would take to the lifeboat and try to make it to the Turks and Caicos islands, two hundred miles to the north. The crew could come with me if they wished.

I went down to the lower accommodations deck and visited the ABs and oilers in their cabins. They weren't happy about my plan, but they were good crewmen and promised to do their best. Back on deck, I crouched below one of the crew's mess ports and listened to Arturo and the guards laughing and joking. I risked a glance through the open porthole and saw that the rum bottle was almost empty.

On the way to the bridge, I checked on the timbers lying by the companionway doors on each deck. They were ready.

At ten-thirty, Arturo appeared on the bridge from the companionway, damp strands of black hair plastered to his sweaty forehead. "They're pretty drunk, *Capi*," he said. "Maybe if we wait, they'll go to sleep on their own."

I shook my head. "Then we'd just have to wake them up to get their guns. Let's go ahead with the plan."

"What if they call the port on the walkie-talkie?"

"What? You think the battery's still good?"

He chuckled. "No, the battery's dead by now."

"It wouldn't transmit through the steel walls of the companionway anyway. And, remember, the port doesn't have a pilot boat. By the time somebody in the office found a motorboat to chase us, we'd be long gone."

"I guess you're right. So what now?"

"Go back to the mess. I'm going to call you on the intercom and ask you to bring the guards up to the bridge. Tell them I want both of them."

He frowned. "What if one wants to stay behind?"

"I don't know . . . Okay, I got it. Tell them I'm going to give them some money. That way neither one will want to be left behind. But make sure they go into the companionway first."

"I suppose we must try it," he said doubtfully. "Is everything ready?"

"As ready as we can make it. As soon as you get the doors jammed shut, take a gang forward and up anchor."

I gave him enough time to go down to the main deck, then picked up the intercom handset and rang for the crew's mess. When he answered, I said loudly, in Spanish, "*Primer Oficial,* tell the guards to come up to the bridge pronto. I need to talk to them."

"You want both of them?"

"Yes. I have some money for them, but they must both come up."

"*Bien.* I will tell them."

We hung up and I stepped to the companionway door. The cut timber was lying on the deck. I jammed one end against the door and the other against the after bulkhead of the chart room.

I couldn't hear anything through the steel, but two minutes later Arturo appeared in the door from the port wing. "They're in the companionway, Captain. Can you hear them?"

At that moment a yell sounded on the other side of the door, then some shouted words, muffled by the steel. "They're in there," I said. "Are the other doors jammed shut?"

"Yessir."

"Then get the anchor up, *rapido.*"

He grinned, a flash of white teeth in his brown face. "It's working, *Capi.*" He went out.

A minute later he and both ABs were running forward along the port deck, the house's lights throwing long shadows ahead of them. The calls from inside the companionway got louder, yelling in French and Spanish for somebody to open the door. There was a pounding on the door, probably from a gun butt. I hoped they didn't start shooting. Bullets wouldn't penetrate the steel bulkhead, but they themselves could get hit by ricochets.

They didn't shoot. Their voices faded as they went back down, probably to try the other doors. Then I had a brilliant idea and went to the main electrical panel to switch off the companionway lights. That would leave them in total, disorienting darkness, and a panicky man is an irrational man.

The anchor chain clanked in the hawsepipe. I studied the shore with the binoculars. Lights were on in the port office, a small concrete building on the waterfront, but I could see no movement in the windows. I had the VHF radio tuned to channel 16, the frequency the guards' walkie-talkie was set to, but it was silent. If they were trying to call the port office, either the battery was too run-down or the companionway's steel walls blocked the transmission.

The ship wasn't bridge-controlled, so I had to signal the engine room for half ahead. The chief was already at the engine controls, and two seconds later the main engine started with a heavy rap. I spun the wheel hard a-starboard. The lights of the port began to swing to port.

A few minutes later we were beyond the port's lights. I turned the bow toward the invisible break in the reef. Arturo rushed in and took the wheel. "All okay, Captain?"

"I think so. Are the guards still in the companionway?"

"The doors are still jammed shut. Can you hear them?"

"Not now."

I had no time to spare for the guards. We felt our way toward the first bend in the channel, running at dead slow ahead, then turned toward the second bend. The reefs glowed faintly in the binoculars, thin lines of white dots where coral heads broke the surface.

By eleven o'clock we had cleared the last reef. Nothing moved in the dark waters behind us. I put the glasses down and went to the console to call for stop engine. The main engine rattled to silence. The ship coasted to a stop with the lights of Cap Haitien rocking slowly off our port stern. "I'm going down to the motor-generator room to talk to the guards," I told Arturo.

He craned around. "How will you do that?"

"There's a vent between the motor-generator room and the companionway. I'll talk to them through that. It's a steel wall, so they can't shoot through it."

"All right, Captain. Be careful."

I went down to the boat deck. The door to the motor-generator room groaned heavily. I threaded my way past the machinery, leaving the light off, and pushed up next to a small metal grating.

"*Messieurs,*" I called in French, "can you hear me?"

They were below me, on the main-deck level. I heard one of them—the same one who'd offered to take Arturo to his house for a party—call up, "Who is that? What do you want?"

"This is the captain. I'm taking this ship to Colombia. We're already out of port."

They came up the companionway. "What are you going to do with us?" the same man asked, his voice shaking.

"If you give up your guns, I'll put you in a boat and you can go home. If you don't, I'll take you to Colombia and tell the police you tried to hijack my ship."

There was a silence as that sank in. They knew that a ship captain's word carries a lot of weight, and the Colombian police—the police in all Latin American countries—have little use for Haitian stowaways. Haitian hijackers could expect even less.

"We will put down our guns, Captain," the other man said. "Please do not mistreat us. We were only doing our job."

"I know that. You will not be mistreated. Now, take your guns down to the main deck—the bottom of the stairway—and leave them there. Then go up to the top and wait there."

"*Oui, Capitaine,*" the man said, then, to his companion, "*allons-nous.*"

They went down. I ran up to the bridge and switched on the companionway lights. "Open the companionway door when I tell you," I told Arturo. "The guards will be ready to come out."

I ran back to the motor-generator room. Now I could see through the grating, but the guards couldn't see me. They came past the second deck without their submachine guns and went up to the bridge deck. I stepped back to the boat-deck door and yelled to Arturo, "Okay, First, let 'em out."

Back at the grating, I could see the wheelhouse door open. The guards went through it. I rushed down to the main deck, yanked the brace from the door, and scooped up the two submachine guns. I stuffed them in a cabinet in the crew's mess and ran up to the bridge.

The guards stood, cowed and helpless, against the after bulkhead. "Men," I told them, "you've done nothing wrong. You were just following orders. I will give you the ship's rescue boat to get home in." I grinned. "That boat's worth plenty of money. You can sell it before you report to your colonel in the morning. Now, do you think you can get through the reef safely?"

The black-skinned guard stepped forward. "I am a fisherman, Captain. I can get through the reef anytime, even at night."

"Good. The moon will be up in a few minutes. You should have no problem. Come with me."

We went to the boat deck, where Arturo had already cast off the rescue boat's lashings. The tank was hooked to the engine and two life jackets lay in the bottom. "Get in the boat and wait for me," I told them. Then I went down and got the two submachine guns. I removed the magazines, emptied the cartridges, then reinserted the magazines and took the guns to the afterdeck.

"Here are your weapons," I told the guards. "I don't want you to get in trouble for losing them." They took them uncertainly and crouched on the floor of the boat, but they must have realized that I wouldn't have left them loaded, so they didn't raise them.

I nodded to Arturo and he cranked the davit, lifting the boat out of its cradle. I helped him push it over the side. When it hit the water and the weight came off the slings, the boat slipped free, and a minute later the black guard got the engine started.

"*Bonne chance,*" I called down. They looked up and waved, then turned toward the lights of Cap Haitien. The boat gained speed and disappeared into the darkness.

"Come," I told Arturo, "let's go to Miami."

I signed off the *Naruda* in Miami and went home to New Orleans. My wife wanted me to give up the sea, so I tried my hand at marine surveying, but shipping was down and work was hard to find. Then, in the fall the owner of a ship named *Erika* persuaded me to take her command, and I shipped out again.

I left the *Erika* the following year to take a job as port captain for a Miami shipping company, Cartones del Sud, loading and discharging ships in Central and South America. Two years later, while I was loading coffee in Buenaventura, Colombia, a small port on the Pacific coast, the company's owner asked me to go to Puerto Cabello, Venezuela, as fast as I could.

A company ship had been seized by a corrupt judge, and he wanted me to steal her out of port.

CHAPTER TWO

THE *PATRIC M*

THE CAPTAIN OF the *Patric M*, a four-thousand-ton general-cargo freighter, stared at me in alarm. "The fishing boats!" he cried. "They will call the police!"

"No, Captain," I replied patiently. "They're too busy fishing to worry about us. They don't even have radios."

We were sitting in a hotel room in Puerto Cabello, Venezuela. The captain and chief engineer were under house arrest, detained on trumped-up charges so a shady receiving company could seize the ship. The captain's head rocked in despair. "They are watching us, I know it."

The walls of the Miramar Hotel were thin. I put a finger to my lips and he shut up. A cigarette lighter snapped behind me. The chief engineer, Namrah Puraji, a short, round man with a ringmaster's mustache and goatee, was leaning against the wall by the window. He blew a plume of smoke toward the ceiling and looked at the captain without expression.

"All right, Captain. Don't worry about it." I went to the door and turned to the chief. "Mr. Maher's at the agent's office now. I'm going to meet him. I'll be back in an hour."

He nodded. The captain stared at his hands.

In spite of its name, the Miramar had no view of the sea. The hall's end window looked westward toward a brooding line of mountains, now blue-black under the setting sun. The hallway was cold. I rubbed my arms and hurried toward the stairs. The desk clerk knew I was on the sixth floor, and he knew that the two foreigners on the fourth floor weren't supposed to have visitors. Since I was the only other foreigner in the hotel, I never took the elevator down from the fourth floor.

I needn't have bothered. The reception desk was empty. The guard was at his usual table in the café, toying with some coins on the shiny black tabletop. He had a cup of *tinto* in front of him. It looked like it'd been there awhile. He paid no attention to me.

Two days earlier, when I'd first gotten the captain and chief engineer released into house arrest, the guard had taken a folding chair up to the fourth floor and set it down next to their room, but yesterday he and his relief had started keeping watch from the café. It was open to the lobby, and by sitting at the front table they could watch the doors in case the prisoners tried to escape. The guards wore gray Naval Police uniforms, with white canvas leggings and automatic pistols in white, patent-leather holsters. Neither had impressed me as being particularly curious. This one didn't look at me once.

I went out under the portico. A parched wind scurried across the empty field on the other side of the road and brought the smell of dust and bitterweed. A pair of headlights appeared from the south and the doorman leaped into the road waving his arms.

I told the driver to take me to the Edificio Marítimo, on the waterfront. It was the end of siesta, still quiet, and the beachfront cafés were in that slack time between the sunbathers of the afternoon and the drinkers of the night. The road turned away from the water, toward the port. The small shops and warehouses were now shuttered.

The shipping agent's office was in a square, two-story building with long, black-tinted windows. Lights glowed dimly on the second story. I went up the outside staircase and rapped on the glass door.

After a moment Jim Maher came out of Gustavo's office, down the hall. He pushed the outside door open, smiling broadly, and clasped my hand with both of his. "Captain, it's good to see you. Thank God you were able to come." He wore a shapeless blue suit and a purple tie festooned with art-deco whales. Gray hair framed his lined face under the hard fluorescent bulbs overhead.

"Come," he said. "Gustavo has news." He gestured for me to go first. "Not good, I'm afraid."

The telephone rang as we got to Gustavo's door. We heard him pick it up and waited in the hallway. "Did you come from Miami?" Jim asked.

"From Buenaventura, through Miami. I met Mr. Gonsalves at the Miami airport."

He looked surprised. "Buenaventura? Loading coffee for us?"

"Yes. For New York."

"You and Charlie Johnson?"

"Yep."

He chuckled. "Is it true Charlie threatened to punch Captain Shrinivas?"

"Yeah, but Charlie was in Colombia and Captain Shrinivas was in Miami, so I wouldn't call it a direct threat."

"Charlie could do it, though."

A couple of months earlier, I'd been with Charlie Johnson in Buenaventura when he'd snatched a pistol away from an unhinged taxi driver. I thought he was going to pop the man, but all he did was throw it in the swamp. Jim hadn't heard about that. "Sure he could," I agreed. "He killed thirty-eight men in 'Nam." I raised a finger. "Captain Shrinivas might want to keep that in mind."

"For some reason he rubs Charlie the wrong way." Jim's faded blue eyes peered at me. "Charlie told you he killed thirty-eight men in Vietnam?"

"Yeah. He was a sniper. He had to keep count."

Inside the office, Gustavo's voice rose and fell in argument. Jim said, "I left Antofagasta this morning at six. Had to go through Rio. I didn't know the situation here until I landed."

Gustavo finally called us in. His office smelled of stale tobacco smoke and fresh coffee. He was a wide, dark man with a perennial three-o'clock shadow, his thick neck supporting a narrow head topped by an old-fashioned flattop haircut. His guayabera shirt was damp under the armpits, and he puffed nervously on his cigarette. "Sit, sit. Captain, I have bad news. Adolfo, my friend the pilot, will not be working tomorrow night. We will have to do it tonight."

Normally, the pilots' job is to guide ships in and out of port, but in Puerto Cabello they also act as de facto traffic control. If a ship gets seized or detained, the *commandante* calls the pilot office, and the pilot on duty makes sure it doesn't leave. Without Adolfo on duty, we'd never get the ship out.

"Is he working Monday?" I asked.

"That's the other bad news," Jim said. "Flete Blanco has gotten a court order taking the crew off the ship. The order won't be made public until Monday, but it's already signed."

"Who's Flete Blanco?"

"The receiver," Gustavo said. "Some Venezuelan company I never heard of."

There are four entities normally involved in a cargo shipment: the shipowner, the charterer, the shipper, and the receiver. The charterer rents the ship from the owner and looks for cargoes to carry. The shipper is the company with the cargo that contracts with a charterer to carry it. The receiver is the company buying the cargo from the shipper. Normally the receiver doesn't have any connection to the charterer, since it's the shipper who contracts to carry the cargo, but this wasn't a normal situation.

"They're tied in with Lineas Andinas," Jim said. "That's the charterer. Captain Shrinivas has seen documents from both Lineas Andinas and Flete Blanco with the same man's name on them. José Maldonado."

Gustavo frowned. "José Maldonado? Is he involved in this?"

"Do you know him?" Jim asked.

Gustavo stubbed out his half-smoked cigarette and pulled another from the pack on his desk. "Yes, from the *Granco Dawn*. She was about ten thousand tons. The same thing happened with that ship two years ago. Let me get the file."

He lit the cigarette and went out. Jim said, "You ever hear of this guy, José Maldonado?"

I shook my head.

"Captain Shrinivas says he's a real pirate. I paid three million dollars for the *Patric M,* and a year later these Peruvian scumbags are trying to steal her from me." His voice shook with anger. "You know, I named her for my father."

That was a mistake, I thought. I once knew a man who named his ship for his daughter, the *Reinelle Rainey*. After she sank with all hands—twelve men went down—poor Reinelle's name was forever linked to death and litigation. But all I said was, "We'll get her out."

Gustavo came back with a fat file. "Yes, that was the ship. The *Granco Dawn*. Vapores Pacifico was the charterer. Same situation. The ship refused to open the hatches and the receiver—let's see, here it is, Empresas

Paraguana—had the ship seized under this 'prejudice against a national company' law." He thumbed the file.

"Were the Maldonados involved with Vapores Pacifico?"

"A fax from Vapores Pacifico was signed by José Maldonado. I knew I remembered that name."

"Same judge?" Jim asked.

More smoking, more flipping. "Yes, here's the order of sale. The same judge, Orestes Blanco."

"Is that the guy we paid?" Jim asked.

"Yeah," I said. "He must've taken money from Maldonado as well. That's why he went on sick leave as soon as we paid him to let the captain and chief out of jail."

Jim stood up and took a couple of paces in the narrow space between the desk and the wall, like a lion in a circus cage. "You didn't know anything about this, Captain?"

"Hell, no," I said. "I've been in Colombia loading coffee."

"Did you know the police put a pistol to the chief engineer's head?"

"Mr. Gonsalves told me."

Gustavo said sadly, "There is a law in Venezuela. If the delay in discharging is prejudicial to a Venezuelan company, it can get a court order forcing the ship to open the hatches. Your chief engineer refused to obey the order."

Jim started pacing again, two steps and turn, two steps and turn. "I'll make sure the international press hears about this," he muttered.

"We've got a more immediate problem," I said. "I don't think Captain Menenzes is going to do it."

He looked at me quizzically.

"Take the ship out," I explained.

"Did he say he wouldn't?"

"Not exactly." I described the captain's paranoia. "Hard to blame him. Nobody wants to spend ten years in a Venezuelan prison."

"What makes him think the fishing boats are watching the ship?" Jim demanded. "That's ridiculous."

"It was just something to say. He's terrified."

He rubbed his face with both hands and looked at me with bloodshot eyes. "Can the first officer take the ship out?"

"I don't know. I don't know the crew at all. I just went on board this afternoon."

"Can you call the chief engineer, see what he thinks?"

I shook my head. "The hotel switchboard's got orders not to put calls through to 'em."

"Then how do you communicate?"

"I go to their room."

"I thought they were under guard."

"The guards quit standing watch in the hallway yesterday. Now they stay in the hotel café."

"Can they get out?"

"Not through the front door. But there's an exit from the stairwell, through the laundry room."

"Good." He reached for Gustavo's desk phone. "Let me call Captain Carvalho."

Dolores answered the phone—I could hear her musical Spanish voice—and put him through to Captain Carvalho, the man in our Miami office who managed the *Patric M*. He and Captain Menenzes were both from Goa, India, which was why they had Portuguese names. Captain Carvalho was a light-skinned man of about thirty with a neatly trimmed mustache who, from certain angles, looked like Omar Sharif. For some reason, though, he wasn't popular with the girls in the office.

"Captain Carvalho," Jim said, "we've got a problem here. The *Patric M*'s captain is afraid to take the ship out. Can the first officer do it?" He glanced at me. "Ah, hah. Yes, he's here in the office." His voice became guarded. "I'm not sure. I'll see. I'll call you later."

He hung up. There was a silence, broken only by the soft hissing of the air conditioner and a guttural belch from the coffeepot. "The first officer's only been on board a few weeks," he finally said. "Captain Carvalho doesn't think he has a strong personality."

I could see where this was going. "He doesn't need a strong personality," I said. "He just needs to take the ship out."

Gustavo cleared his throat and said, "I'll go put this back." He went out with the file.

Jim said, "Captain, you know I'd go if I could do any good, but I don't know anything about ships." He gave a painful smile. "If it was a paper mill . . ."

I said, "You mean Captain Carvalho wants me to take the ship out?"

"He thinks it would be best."

I almost spat. "You know what? If it weren't for the bonus situation, I might have considered it."

"What bonus situation?"

I said, "When I hired on, Captain Tiwali promised me a thousand dollars a month as a cash bonus. In twenty-six months I've gotten exactly ten thousand dollars."

I wasn't surprised that Jim didn't know. In the two years I'd been with the company, I'd seen him in the Miami office just twice. Cartones del Sud was actually just a shipping company for the paper goods Jim bought and sold. He spent most of his time running paper mills and box factories in Central and South America.

"I'm sorry. I didn't know anything about that." He gave me a calculating look. "Suppose we make it right? Would you take the ship out?"

I hesitated at first. Then I finally said, "All right, I'll do it. But it's not for the company and it's not for the bonuses. I earned those bonuses whether I take the ship out or not. But I'll do it to keep those assholes from stealing our ship."

He reached across the desk and patted my hand. "Thanks, Captain."

Gustavo came back in. "It's nine-fifteen," he said. "We should go over the pilot's signal." He sat down and spun his chair around to the small built-in counter where he kept his coffeepot. He poured coffee into three small china cups, each delicately printed with a fouled, rose-colored anchor. He placed Jim's and mine on the corners of the desk and put a small bowl of paper-wrapped sugar cubes between them.

"The pilot office overlooks the channel," he began, unwrapping two cubes at once. "The duty pilot watches the channel and the relief pilot sleeps in the back. If the duty pilot has to take a ship in or out, he wakes up the relief pilot and the relief pilot watches the channel." He dumped the cubes in his cup, folded the empty wrappers into very small squares, and put them in the ashtray. Like me, Jim took his coffee unsweetened. I sipped at the thick, bitter liquid.

"Adolfo comes on at midnight," Gustavo went on. "He and the other pilot usually chat a bit before the other pilot goes to bed."

Jim asked, "So the coast guard and navy don't know whether a ship has a pilot on board or not?"

"That's right," Gustavo said. He tossed the empty box of cigarettes in the trash can and pulled another out of a drawer. "Of course, the ship should display all normal lights."

"Of course."

He chuckled. "At the moment, I do not think the navy has any ships that can put to sea. But we must be careful of the *guardacostas*. They have a base right at the mouth of the harbor, with an armed launch."

"I noticed," I said. "And it looks ready to go. There were a couple of men on board yesterday."

He glanced at me curiously. I hadn't told him I'd been doing surveillance. He went on, "So we must be careful that another ship does not call for a pilot before the *Patric M* gets out. Adolfo says there's nothing scheduled until eight A.M., but sometimes a ship will arrive early and call for a pilot on short notice."

I glanced at my watch. Nine-twenty. "So the call will come after midnight?"

"Only a few minutes after. When Adolfo is alone, he will call the ship on VHF, channel sixty-seven. The signal is, '*Neto, Neto, las chicas te esperan al Café Americano*. The girls are waiting for you at the Café Americano.'"

I repeated the Spanish version. "All right. But how do we get into the port? No way we can make the ten o'clock shift change."

Gustavo grimaced. "Yes, that's too bad. Try the stevedore gate. Perhaps they will not ask for a pass." He glanced at a blackboard on the wall behind us. "The *Principe Felipe*, loading cement at dock four. If the guard stops you, tell him you're off the *Principe Felipe*."

Jim asked me, "Is the *Patric M* ready for sea?"

"More or less. I've been talking to the chief engineer about it. He says the air-compressor housing is cracked, and the backup air compressor doesn't work. They fixed it with JB Weld, but it's still leaking."

"With what?" Jim asked.

"JB Weld. Underwater epoxy. It's a water-cooled compressor." I turned to Gustavo. "Maybe you'd better let me take a walkie-talkie to the hotel, so the chief can talk to the second engineer about it. We need to let the crew know that everything's been moved up to tonight."

Gustavo came back with a heavy iCom walkie-talkie in a scarred leather case. "It's charged. You can leave it with Jim."

"Where's your hotel?" I asked Jim.

"I haven't gotten one yet."

"Then check into the Miramar. It's almost empty. We just have to arrive separately, and stay away from each other. That way I can leave my bag with you."

"Leave your bag?"

Gustavo explained, "He can't take a bag into the port. He'll have to sneak in. I was hoping they could go in with the stevedores at the ten o'clock shift change, but it's too late now. If they go in by themselves, the guards will almost certainly ask for their passes."

Jim looked at me. "Then what will you do?"

"I might have to go over the port wall. Whether the chief can go with me, I don't know."

"What do you mean?"

Gustavo chuckled. "He's a fat little man, like me." He slapped his stomach. It made a solid sound, like a ham hitting a countertop.

"Hmm," Jim said. "So you might have to take it out with just the second engineer. I guess we'd better ask the chief engineer about him, too."

I took a leather purse out of my back pocket. "Here's the rest of the money I brought down. Mr. Gonsalves gave it to me at the Miami airport." Mr. Gonsalves was the company's chief financial officer, an elderly gent whose hands trembled like aspen leaves. I glanced at the paper slip I'd stuck in the purse. "Eighty-three thousand left. I brought down one hundred and forty thousand. Forty went to pay off the judge. Eight thousand went to the Policía Judicial to spring the captain and chief engineer. Here's an accounting of the rest."

"That's fine," he said.

I took out ten hundreds and slid the purse to him. "These are for the guard on board. I promised him two thousand U.S. dollars to go on a long vacation. I'll give him a thousand when I get to the ship, and Gustavo's man will give him the rest when the ship reaches international waters."

"Do they know each other?"

I put the bills in my wallet. "I gave Gustavo half of a torn five-bolivar note. I'll give the guard the other half. He matches halves with Gustavo's man and gets his money. Just like the old-time charter parties." A charter party is a contract to carry cargo.

"Very clever," Jim said. "'Charter party' comes from 'torn contract,' doesn't it?"

"From *carta partida*. Torn letter. They used to write the same contract twice on one page, top and bottom, then they tore the page in half. The captain got the top half and the receiver got the bottom. When the ship reached port, the receiver gave his half to the captain. If the edges matched, he got his cargo." I stood up. "It was Gustavo's idea."

"Actually," Gustavo said, as he drained his coffee cup, "it was the Romans' idea. Ready to go?"

I waited a few minutes before hailing a taxi, so Jim could get to the hotel first.

The lobby was deserted except for the night receptionist—a sallow young man with a Zapata mustache—and the guard. The café was closed off with a black velvet rope. The guard was sitting in the lobby, in one of the low, leather-upholstered chairs, reading a dog-eared magazine.

The first thing I did on reaching my room was call home, but I got the answering machine. I left a message for my wife saying I would call again, but if I didn't get a chance for a few days, not to worry. Then I realized that if I weren't going to call every day, I should have thought up a reason. I was about to call back, but there was a knock on the door, and after that I never got another chance.

Jim came in. He'd taken his bags to his room. I pointed to my suitcase. "Everything's in there. I travel light."

We took my suitcase in his room, then went down to the fourth floor. The hallway was deserted. I knocked on the door, two-three-one, and the chief engineer let us in. Captain Menenzes was sitting on his bed with his forearms on his knees, his rayon shirt sticking to his shoulders in spite of the air-conditioning.

"Chief," I said, without preamble, "what about the air compressor? Is it working?"

"The housing, what you call the jacket, is cracked. Water leaks out. We cannot run it for very long before it overheats."

"But it can get up enough air pressure to start the main engine?"

"Yes, yes, the rings and valves are good. We can run it for ten, fifteen minutes, then we have to shut it down to cool off." He put his cigarette to his mouth with a flat hand, like a World War II spy.

I unslung the walkie-talkie and asked the chief, "If I call the ship, can you talk to the second engineer in Hindi?"

"Of course."

We had a code for calling the ship, "Vessel off Punta Baja." Nobody knows where a radio signal is coming from, and ships call each other in English—the common language of the sea—all the time. So I called in English and the ship's watch officer responded with the fake name we'd agreed on. I handed the radio to the chief engineer and he asked the officer in Hindi to bring up the second engineer.

A few minutes later the second engineer came on. He had a high, singsong voice and a breathless delivery. The chief spoke to him for a minute or so.

"He says they have thirty bar in the receivers," the chief reported. "The main engine needs thirty bar to start." Thirty bar—the European way of measuring air pressure—is thirty times atmospheric pressure, or about 450 psi.

"How's the engine been starting?" I asked. "First try?"

He shook his head shortly. "No. Perhaps the third or fourth."

"How many tries out of thirty bar?"

"Three or four. Sometimes we have to wait to get air up before we can try again."

Jim rolled his eyes. I said, "It'll have to do. Let's go before it gets too late." I told the chief, "Tell the second that you and I are coming on board just before midnight. The guard's been taken care of. Tell them to do nothing unusual that can be seen from the dock. No navigation lights, no radar."

The chief translated and listened. After getting the first officer's confirmation of the instructions, he signed off and handed me the walkie-talkie. "I'm ready to go," he said.

Jim asked him, "Want me to take care of your bag? We can send it to the next port."

"Very well," the chief said. "What is the next port?"

"Aruba," Jim said.

The three of us went to the door. Jim glanced at Captain Menenzes and said, "I'll be back later. You'll be getting a visit from the police in the morning, so we have to make sure you're ready."

The captain nodded without looking up, his long brown face in shadow. The three of us went out and down the corridor. Jim shook hands with that two-handed clasp of his and wished us luck. The chief and I took the stairs to the ground floor and followed a narrow service alley to the laundry room.

An old black woman was folding sheets at a long counter. She stared in fright when I pushed the door open but managed an apprehensive smile when she saw we were heading for the outside door and not for her.

The air was still hot. We threaded our way through the parked cars and went around the corner of the building to the street. An unmuffled motorcycle roared by with a thin young man hunched over the handlebars, an enormously fat girl on the back holding a tiny baby.

The hotel's entrance was only a dozen yards away. The doorman was standing under the portico. I held the chief back with my hand until the doorman turned and disappeared, then we stepped smartly around the corner and hustled away. The sidewalk here was deserted, but behind the row of shuttered buildings lay half-seen streets teeming with people. We could hear music, faint shouts, and an occasional car horn.

After we'd put a couple of blocks between us and the hotel, I stepped into the road and hailed a taxi.

"The port," I told the driver. "The stevedore gate."

He looked back briefly, a middle-aged man with a grizzled mustache. We didn't look like stevedores, but he didn't comment. He put the car in gear and pulled away.

We didn't talk on the way. I looked out my window and thought about my children, Karla and Alex, six and three years old. If we got caught—if the pilot was a double agent, if we couldn't get the engine started, if any of a dozen things went wrong—Karla and Alex would be adults—strangers— by the time I got out of a Venezuelan prison. I glanced at Namrah, but he was looking stolidly ahead. I took a long, deep breath and forced myself to concentrate on the task at hand.

Traffic was light. As we turned left onto the *malecón*—the waterfront— we saw some couples and groups of seamen strolling along the sidewalk, and sitting at the open-air tables in the bars and restaurants. The port appeared on the right, fronted by a cinder-block wall ten feet high and topped with barbed wire. A railroad track ran along the wall and turned into the port just beyond the stevedore gate. I tapped the driver on the shoulder and he let us out.

"Are we going to try it here?" the chief asked quietly.

"We'll have to." I nodded toward the floodlit main gate. "They'll check our passes at the main gate for sure."

The guard shack at the stevedore gate was a small cinder-block hut inside the wall, painted institutional blue. The flickering light of a black-and-white television lit the interior, and I thought for a moment we might be able to walk right past. But then a short man with a holstered automatic stepped out, his face shadowed by the low brim of his cap. "*Pase,*" he said, holding out his hand.

I deliberately slurred my words. "No passes," I said in Spanish. "We forgot them on board. We're from the *Principe Filipe*, dock four."

The guard shook his head. "*No pase, no entre aqui.*" He jerked his thumb. "Go to the main gate."

I thanked him and we went back out. Once under an overhanging balcony across the street, we looked toward the main gate. A solitary guard stood by the striped traffic barrier, his white leggings and gun belt gleaming.

"I don't think we'd better try the main gate," I said. "Let's take a look at the wall."

The chief grunted skeptically but followed me eastward. The sidewalk ended and we had to take to the street. After a dozen blocks we reached the end of the port's property. Here the wall left the street and ran a dozen yards back to a private warehouse, where it was crudely cemented to the warehouse's side wall.

"I can't get over that wall," the chief said. "Can you?"

"Maybe," I said. "Chief, I think you'd better go back to the hotel. The second engineer will have to take the ship out."

He winced, his glossy goatee shining like a beetle's back.

"What's the matter?" I asked. "Can't he do it?"

"He's new," the chief said cautiously. "I do not know him well. I hope he has been learning the ship in the last few days."

"I hope so, too. If he has any trouble starting the main engine, we'll be screwed." I pressed some bolivars into his hand. "Go back to the hotel. Go through the laundry room so the guard won't see you."

"Very well," he said. "I feel badly about going back, though."

"There's no help for it. Listen, I'll see you in Aruba." We shook hands and he started up the street; a streetlight on the next block threw his elongated shadow far back along the pavement.

I decided the wall was too well lit to try to climb, so I walked back to the railroad gate, a wide gap blocked by two swinging gates made of galvanized pipe and chain link, padlocked together. I stood in an alley and watched. The guard at the main gate was looking in my direction, his face a dark spot under his helmet. He'd see me if I tried to cross the road.

Suddenly a car came up from the direction of town and passed me, heading for the port entrance. The guard couldn't see anything behind its headlights, I realized. With no time to think, I dashed across the street and slid into the dusty ditch. In another moment I was over the nearest rail and crawling toward the gate, pinned like a bug by the port's pitiless blue floodlights. The sharp rocks between the railroad ties dug into my chest and stomach. Any car coming from town would see me clearly.

A second later I had my head up against the bottom pipe of the gate. I had counted on being able to push it up a bit, but I couldn't lift either side. I was going to have to squeeze under. Luckily, the gate was halfway between two ties. I clawed at the rocks furiously, ignoring the pain in my fingers, and managed to dig a shallow depression. I shoved my head through, the rough pipe tearing at my ear, just as a truck came out of the port. But I was half concealed from that direction, and it went past.

Unable to breathe with the pipe pressed deep in my back, I gave a desperate heave and got my chest through. I sucked in some air and pulled the rest of me through.

I had to get out of the lights quickly. I didn't know what was on this side of the wall or who could be looking. I rolled over into the shadow of a low concrete embankment on the left. To the right, unimproved ground stretched off toward the end warehouse and the port's eastern wall. The better cover was on this side, hidden by the embankment.

The track continued in a gentle curve toward the water. I could see the quay and the dark bay beyond, and a thin sparkle of lights on the far bank. It was too painful to keep going on my hands and knees, so I crept forward in a low crouch until I came to a small cantina full of laughing stevedores tanking up on java before they started their shift. The north wind brought the smell of fresh coffee. I remembered I hadn't eaten supper.

I had to drop back onto my hands and knees to get past the cantina. It was nothing but a small, dirty trailer with a counter on one side and a hinged flap that could be lowered when it closed, but the tables in front came to within a few yards of the tracks. The wind here was cut off by the warehouses and the embankment, and my shirt stuck to my back as I slipped past. The smell of coffee got stronger, the stevedores' laughs louder, then I was past, hidden by the shadow of the next warehouse.

The *Patric M* appeared on the left, looming over the quay, her white bowlines spreading down like skeletal fingers. I could hear her harbor generator in the forecastle, and some of her house lights were lit. The wheelhouse was dark.

The *Patric M* was a standard ocean freighter, built to carry the maximum amount of cargo for her size and draft, with a high forecastle forward, cargo hatches amidships, and a small accommodations house perched on the stern. Lights shone from her foremast and along the house, but otherwise she was dark.

The guard was leaning on the bulwark just forward of the house, looking out over the dock; I could see the orange glow of a cigarette under his helmet. He had a shotgun slung over his back. I made sure I had my passport and wallet, then ran up the gangway into the ship's deck lights.

The guard frowned when he saw me. "Everything okay for tomorrow, *señor?*"

I led him to the shadow of the mast house. "We have to do it tonight. Tomorrow night's no good. You have to get off right now. I have your money."

"What is the problem?"

"No problem, but we have to do it tonight." I slipped a fold of bills into his hand. "Here's a thousand dollars. Go to the Fisherman's Wharf at one-thirty. You will see a white Jeep parked in front with a red ball on the antenna. Understand?"

"Yes. A red ball."

I handed him the torn half of the five-bolivar note. "The driver will have the other half. Give this to him and he'll give you the rest of your money."

He gave me a long look. *"Bien, señor,"* he finally said. "I will do it. But remember . . . I know about the agent. If I do not get my money . . ."

"The man will be there," I said quickly. *"No te preocupues."*

He counted the bills, looked up and down the deserted quay, and ran down the gangway, his shotgun bouncing on his shoulder. I watched to make sure he left the port—the concrete wall ended at the quay, with a tangle of barbed wire jutting out over the water—but after he disappeared behind the warehouse to the east, I didn't see him again. It didn't surprise me that there was a hole in the wall somewhere. Most ports have one.

A tall, gangling youth, as black as night, appeared at my elbow. "Captain Max?"

"Yeah. Where's the first officer?"

"He's waiting on the bridge. We saw you come on board. Is the guard gone?"

"He's gone. Are you on deck watch?"

"Yessir." He held up his walkie-talkie.

"Good. Stay here. Call the bridge if anyone comes."

The door to the house was open. I ran past the bright, empty rooms—the officers' and crew's messes, a large television lounge, the ballast control room—and up to the bridge. It was dark, but the engine console was lit. Two shadowy figures stood near the forward windows. As my eyes adjusted, I recognized the first officer, tall and bony, and one of the able-bodied seamen, a heavyset young man with jug ears.

"Captain Max," the first officer said, "is everything okay?"

"Yeah. Ready to cast off?"

"Yessir."

"Axes forward and aft?"

"Yessir."

I glanced at the engine console. The air receivers were showing thirty-three bar. "Oil is up?" I asked.

"Yessir."

"Does this ship have a bow thruster?"

"Yessir."

Some ships—happily, the *Patric M* was one of them—have an underwater tunnel running across the bow with a reversing propeller in it, to help the rudder control the ship's direction. A bow thruster can make the difference between navigating a channel safely and careening into a dock or another ship.

"You tested it?"

"Yessir."

"Good." I glanced toward the VHF on the after bulkhead. "Any radio traffic?"

"No sir."

"All right. The signal will be, 'Neto, Neto, the girls are waiting for you at the Café Americano.' It'll be in Spanish. Listen for 'Neto' and 'Café Americano.'" I checked my watch: 12:04. "Who's the quartermaster?" I asked. The quartermaster is the man at the wheel.

"I am, sir," the AB said. He stepped up to the wheel and grasped its spokes.

"Tested the steering?"

"Yessir." He grinned, his white teeth gleaming in the console's light.

"All right," I said. "Nothing to do but wait."

We didn't have to wait long. The pilot going off duty must have been sleepy that night. About three minutes later the VHF barked to life. A gravelly voice rumbled, *"Neto, Neto, las putas te esperan al Café Americano."*

I winced. The signal was supposed to be "The girls are waiting," not "The whores are waiting," but there was nothing I could do about that. I grabbed the microphone and gave three clicks to acknowledge receipt. Nobody on board spoke native Spanish, so it was better that our voices stayed off the air.

"Cut all lines," I told the first officer. I heard the solid whacks of the axes from fore and aft. "Start the bow thruster."

Deep in the bottom of the ship, below the forecastle, the bow thruster engine started with a rattle. Blue-gray smoke, whitish under the lights, burst from its exhaust pipe by the foremast and drifted forward over the bows.

"Rudder thirty degrees starboard," I told the quartermaster. To the first officer I said, "Bow thruster one-half to port, main engine dead slow ahead." The main engine popped a few times and fell silent. The pressure dropped to thirty-two bar.

The first officer shook his head, waited a second, and pressed the start button again. The engine hissed and popped and again fell silent. Thirty-one bar. "Jesus," I said, "we've only got one more try."

The first officer didn't say a word. He pressed the button again; this time the engine huffed slowly, painfully, only to roll to silence. Thirty bar.

"Hard to port on the thruster," I said. "We've got to get out in the channel."

The first officer thumbed the joystick over and the bow started a slow swing to port. The stern hit the dock with a soft splintering sound.

"Can we start with thirty bar?" I asked the first officer.

He shook his head, only his eyes showing the movement. "I think not, Captain. Maybe we should wait for one more bar."

"How long will that take?"

"Five, maybe ten minutes."

The wind was rising from the northwest, and the press of it on the empty ship's forecastle was slowing our turn. A ship adrift in the narrow channel would soon attract attention. I was a little surprised at the sudden thumping in my chest. If we were caught stealing the ship out, I knew a Venezuelan prison term could well be a life sentence.

"Thirty-one bar," the first officer called a few moments later.

"Try again."

I went out on the starboard wing. The engine rolled and thumped and coughed on a deeper note. A single black ball of smoke flew out of the stack. Then the engine stopped. The thruster brought the ship broadside to the wind and the turn rate slowed. The stern hit the dock again, harder, with a screech that reverberated back from the warehouse as the steel hull scraped against an exposed bolt head.

"Jesus Christ," I muttered to myself, "that'll do it."

"Thirty bar," the first officer called tonelessly, and he pushed the starter button. The engine popped again, two coughs, another empty pop, two more deep coughs, then silence. I heard a wail of tortured steel as the hull found another exposed bolt head. The ship lurched heavily.

"No good," the first officer called. "We're at twenty-nine bar. We'd better tie up and wait for air pressure."

"You mean tie up and wait for jail. Are you giving the thruster all it's got?"

"Full over, Captain, but the wind's keeping us against the dock. The ship's too light."

Now we were bumping along between the warehouses. The cantina came into view, but the stevedores were gone and the flap was down over the side. Slowly the bow rounded to windward. It was getting harder to breathe past the lump in my throat.

I ran through the wheelhouse to the port wing. "What's the bar?" I called on the way.

"Thirty."

"Try again." Now I could see the lights of the navy base. A couple of fishing boats were dragging their nets in front of us, half a kilometer away. We were beam-on to the wind and getting blown sideways. Another few minutes of this and we would go up on the rocks, a dark line of dragon's teeth only two ship-lengths away. There, stuck fast and probably holed, the ship could only grind on the boulders while we waited for the harbor police.

I leaned my head through the wheelhouse door. The first officer was still waiting for more air pressure. "Goddamn it," I said. "Give it a shot. Keep trying until it starts or we're out of air. There's no time to wait."

He didn't answer, but a second later the ship shook with the engine's laboring. Black smoke rolled from the stack. Thump-thump-pop-thump-pop-thump-thump-thump . . .

At last the engine rattled to life. The starboard rudder kicked the stern off the dock. I called for 15 degrees of port rudder and half ahead. The steering gear whined in the bowels of the ship. I ran back through the wheelhouse and looked aft. Our stern was five meters off the dock, now ten. "Hard a-port," I called.

"Hard a-port," the quartermaster repeated. If he was as relieved as I was, his voice didn't show it. We were already closing with the nearest fishing boats. The bow swung into the eye of the wind.

"Thruster amidships," I ordered. The donkey engine fell to idle. Even from the port side I could tell we were clear of the quay, but dangerously close to the rocks, maybe a ship-length away. "Half ahead," I called.

The ship gained speed, the hull shaking. The wind cooled the sweat on my brow. The navy base was now dead ahead. To port, the dark bulk of the *Principe Filipe* was silhouetted against the bone-white port lights. We drew past her and into the darkness of the bay.

The first officer's teeth shone in a broad grin. "That was bloody close," he said. "She started at twenty-nine bar."

"We're not out of port yet," I replied. To the bosun, "Midship your helm."

"Midships."

"Secure the thruster," I ordered the first officer.

The donkey engine died with a rattle, leaving only the sounds of the main engine and generator.

Suddenly I realized that I hadn't ordered our running lights turned on. There was nothing more suspicious than a ship under way without lights. "Christ," I said, "turn the lights on, First. All normal steaming lights. Hurry."

He went to the electrical panel on the rear bulkhead and flipped some switches. Red and green lights glowed beyond the wings of the bridge. By then we were doing two to three knots.

"Stay in the center of the channel," I told the quartermaster. "Port five. Now steady as you go."

"Steady as you go." He caught the bow expertly and held it. The commercial port fell behind and we steamed slowly past the navy base, the frigates' spidery superstructures and long gun barrels casting ghostly shadows out into the channel. A few figures could be seen moving about on the quay, but none paid any attention to us.

The pilot office came up to starboard. The duty office was on the third floor, overlooking the channel. A head appeared in the window, silhouetted against the yellow light. The silhouette raised a hand and disappeared.

A few minutes later we drew abreast of the old Spanish fort to starboard and the small coast guard base to port. The patrol boat was still at the dock, a fitted tarpaulin over the machine gun on the bow, rocking in the low onshore swell. Lights burned in the windows of the stucco building behind it, but I saw no movement.

Still the *Patric M* glided on, past the fort, past the coast guard station, out into the channel. To the west, hotel and restaurant lights curved around the bay. The squat bulk of the bosun, preceded by the orange glow of his cigarette, appeared from the after companionway and stepped up to the steering console. He said something in Hindi to the AB, who handed over the wheel and went below.

The channel led to the north-northwest, marked by three red lights and one green. "Steady as she goes," I told the bosun. "Keep her between the buoys."

"Steady as she goes." He glanced at the rudder-angle indicator and spun the wheel. The bow lifted to the first ocean swell. I don't think any of us was breathing.

"Full speed ahead," I said. "Steer for the sea buoy." Then, to the first officer, "Secure all lights."

"Yessir. Running lights, too?"

"Yes. Turn everything off, including the running lights." Now that we were out of the port channel, I didn't want anyone to see us until we were in international waters. I glanced at the radar. Nothing was moving in the port. The two long, cigar-shaped frigates lay like sleeping sharks in the rectangular cage of the navy base. I looked back through the chart-room windows. The lights of the coast guard base were already indistinguishable in the necklace of lights along the shore.

At last we reached the sea buoy, the last buoy before open water. The wind was a steady force 4 out of the east, and the buoy rolled silently in the swells.

The first officer had already laid out the shortest course to international water. "Steer zero-fifteen, Quartermaster," he said, stepping out of the chart room. He joined me at the radar. "Looks okay, Captain?"

"So far, so good." I went out on the port wing. A quarter moon, as sharp as a flensing knife, floated above Punta Baja, the thin promontory of land to the east. The ship was completely blacked out now, her bow rising to the quartering swells, leaving an incandescent green wake in her trail. The headlights of a car on the *malecón* flashed briefly, far away, and turned off. The first officer appeared beside me.

"Three miles to international water," he announced.

"You can go over to Iron Mike. Nothing on radar?"

"No, sir. All quiet." He went in the wheelhouse and set the autopilot, then came back out. "Those bastards will be pretty damn surprised tomorrow morning, eh, Captain?"

I made a motion with my hand, letting a bird go free. "Yeah, in one hour they went from snatching a three-million-dollar ship to having nothing but a hole in the air."

"We're safe now, right? Even if they came out now, they couldn't catch us before we got to international water."

I grunted. "Don't forget about the rule of hot pursuit. If they came out now, they could claim they had us in sight while we were still in national waters. As long as they kept us in continuous visual contact, they'd have the right to chase us into international waters and intercept us."

"We'll be there in a few minutes."

"Then that ends it. They have to start the pursuit while we're still in national waters."

He scanned the shoreline with the binoculars, then handed them to me. "Nothing. I wonder what they will do about this."

"Who? The Venezuelan government?" I made a quick scan and put the binocs back on the repeater.

"Perhaps we get in trouble in our next port?"

"Don't worry about that. The owners'll have it all fixed up."

A few minutes later, the bosun called from the chart room, "Satellite pass okay, Captain. Satnav says we're in international water."

"Thanks, Bosun." I looked at my watch. Five after one. I clapped the first officer on the shoulder. "Well, that's it, First. We did it. Log that we cleared the sea buoy at 1215 hours."

"What about pilot-off time?"

"The same."

"Turn on all normal lights?"

"Yes, all normal steaming lights."

"What course?"

"Head for Orangestad, Aruba."

As it turned out, we didn't sail for Aruba after all. When I called Captain Shrinivas in Miami, he ordered us to lay a course for San Juan, Puerto Rico, and maintain full sea speed. "Well," I told the first officer, "I guess we lay a course for San Juan. God knows why." I picked up the intercom handset and called the engine room.

The second engineer answered, his voice faint against the roar of the generator and the thumping of the main engine. "Engine room!"

"Second," I yelled, "please get me bunker figures for tomorrow morning by 0800 hours. Can you do that?" In the days of steamships, coal was kept in huge compartments called bunkers, so fuel came to be called bunkers. The term survived the transition to oil-burning ships.

"I have all bunkers now," he yelled back. "I'll send an oiler up."

"No, you come up."

"Okay," he yelled into the intercom, "I'll come up."

I looked at the first officer. "First, who's got the keys to the bonded-stores locker?"

"I do, Captain. Do you need something?"

"Whisky," I said. "What do you give the pilots?" It's been a tradition since windjammer days that the master of a cargo ship gives the pilot a bottle of whisky for guiding his ship in or out of port. Every ship has a few cases of "pilot whisky" in the bonded-stores locker.

"Johnnie Walker. Do you want a bottle?"

"Yeah. We're going to drink a toast."

He flashed a brilliant grin and went down the aft companionway. He was back up in a few minutes with a bottle of Johnnie Walker, the Filipino cook right behind him with a tray of glasses full of ice, each neatly wrapped in a napkin. I hadn't met the cook before. He was an interesting character in the half-light of the bridge, gnomelike, bald as Beata Rock, with a round brown face full of moles and thick tufts of white hair growing out of his ears.

The second engineer appeared at the after companionway, sweaty in an old boiler suit with the sleeves cut off, his ear protectors stuck on his neck like a mechanical appendage. He handed me a slip of paper. I put it in my pocket and handed him a glass. Then I poured each man a splash of whisky—I made the cook join in as well—and we raised our glasses in toast.

"Confusion to the Venezuelans!" I proclaimed. "Long live the ancient and honorable freedom of the seas!"

We drank the toast. Then the crew started their sea watches. As the master of the ship, I didn't stand watch, so I poured myself another finger of whisky and went out on the starboard wing. The long ocean swells winked and shimmered under the rising moon. All that remained of Venezuela now was a faint glow on the southern horizon, getting darker. Soon, I thought, I would be heading home.

But that turned out to be wishful thinking. The next morning, I had the second officer call the main office to report in.

He talked to Captain Shrinivas for a few minutes in Hindi, his face growing longer by the second. As he put the microphone down he said, "Captain, we have a big problem. Venezuela has reported us to Interpol as a stolen ship. It's on the telly in the U.S. We can't go into port."

"What? We have to go to port somewhere. We can't sail around like the Flying Dutchman."

"He wants to know if you know some place where we can hide."

"Hide? For how long?"

"Long enough to change the name, I suppose."

I shut the call down and went to the chart room. I'd been faced with this situation once before, on a Haitian-owned ship that needed a new identity. The owner had told us to take the ship to the Bay of Flowers, a tiny cove west of Les Cayes, while he proceeded to sell her to himself.

That was four years ago, though, and I didn't know what the village was like now.

*　*　*

I plotted a course to the Baie des Fleurs, worked up our ETA, and called Captain Shrinivas. Through the second officer, I gave him the coordinates of our destination and Ronald Joanuel's telephone number. Ronald had been my Haitian associate in my previous experience in changing a ship's identity in Haiti. "Tell him to send Ronald at least three thousand dollars by Western Union. We're going to need it as soon as we arrive. Tell him to have Ronald come to the Bay of Flowers. Ronald knows where it is."

They talked some more in Hindi, then the second officer said, "Captain Shrinivas wants to know if you know someone who can change the registration, 'under special circumstances.'"

I grinned sourly. "'Special circumstances' is right. Yeah, tell him to call Pablo Fraca at Pan-Ocean Ship Registry. They're in the phone book. Pablo'll take care of him."

Pablo Fraca was a Mexican who'd lived in Honduras for many years, and had married a *catracha*—a Honduran woman—with ties to the Honduran navy. The navy runs the Honduran flag state, and Pablo could get things done with ship registration, like giving a ship a "stateless registration" without a Deletion Certificate.

In recent years, the International Maritime Organization, the association of seafaring nations that governs ship registration, has attempted to prevent ship theft by requiring all flag states to withhold a vessel's registration unless the owner can produce a piece of paper from the vessel's previous flag state, called a Deletion Certificate, that shows that the ship was properly registered. However, many countries, like Honduras, still have a law on their books allowing a ship to be registered without paperwork, called a "stateless registration."

Pablo lives in Hong Kong now because he got caught issuing "FedEx certs"—certificates couriered to vessels he'd never seen, much less surveyed. But I knew of a great story about his earlier days in Miami. Pablo, being a proud descendant of conquistadores, had breastplates and crossed swords and other medieval paraphernalia mounted on the walls of his office. One day he got in an argument with Johnny Knowles, a notorious Miami River pirate, and in a fury he snatched down a sword and started swinging. Johnny grabbed the other sword to defend himself, and suddenly they're swordfighting around the office.

Pablo's pretty young wife, Juana, was working next door. Hearing the commotion, she ran in and stopped the fight before either man got hurt. Johnny told the story up and down the river, and the more he told it, the funnier it got. Wherever Pablo went, men would make crude swordfighting gestures and exclaim, *"En garde!"* and *"Touché!"*

Maybe he and Juana really moved to Hong Kong to get away from the embarrassment.

"I don't like this, Captain," the second officer said. "Can we really stay long enough to change the ship's names?"

"Well," I said, "to paraphrase Aldous Huxley, 'if the earth has any ends, the Bay of Flowers is surely one of them.' There's no patrol boat in Les Cayes. The police would have to come by land. At worst, we'd have to buy them off."

He lit a cigarette. "I didn't sign on to this ship to get arrested, Captain. We took the ship out of Venezuela without a clearance—that was bad enough. Now we're all thieves, maybe pirates."

"Look," I said, "what's done is done. The best thing now is to get the ship into hiding, turn her into a new ship, and deliver her to her new crew. You could be home in two to three weeks."

"Jolly good," he said stiffly. "If we fail, we go to jail. If we succeed, we're out of a job."

He grunted and went down the aft companionway. I took the bunker report out of my pocket. We had 128 tons on board. At five tons a day, that gave us twenty-five days' steaming. We could go to Africa on that.

During our morning call the next day, steaming past Curaçao under a bright summer sun, Captain Shrinivas told us that the ship's new name would be *Marylin*. "That's not too bad," I told the first officer. "I once had to change a ship's name to the *Benjamin & Christopher*. Only a sadist would do that to a crew."

He laughed politely. I was getting to know him a little. His name was Ajay Dayal, a tall, restless man of about thirty-five, from Mumbai. His father had been a ship captain until his death of a stroke, at sea; all of his brothers were seamen as well. Ajay had a master's ticket, but with all the Poles and Russians coming onto the market in those days, he was happy just to have a first officer's berth. Eastern Europeans were considerably cheaper than Indians, and probably the only reason Cartones del Sud was still using Indian crews was because all the operations men, apart from me, were Indian.

"And what will be the new build name? *Marylin* is the ship's new name, but we must change the build name as well, mustn't we?"

He was right. Every ship gets its first name, its "build name," welded onto the bows and stern in foot-high, raised steel letters. Since a new owner usually changes the ship's name, every ship could have a dozen ex-names, but it has only one build name. Anybody looking past the latest name painted on the hull can see the original name in raised letters.

"It doesn't matter what we call the build name," I said. "Something easy, of course."

"If you can give me something now, I can get one of the oilers to start cutting the letters out. We'll need three sets."

I went into the chart room and glanced at the stability book. The build name had been *Faroah VII*. I doodled on a piece of paper and handed it to him. "Okay, the new build name is *Lapo VI*. You cut off the last *A* and *H* and the second *I* in the Roman numeral. You make the *F* an *L* and the *R* a *P*. Easy as pie."

He nodded. "Easy enough."

I finally called home that afternoon. What I told my wife was a simplification of our real situation—that I'd had to take command of a ship when the master got sick. I felt pretty silly when she revealed that Captain Carvalho had called her and told her the whole story. She started asking questions, and I had to head her off pretty abruptly . . . everything is recorded on the High Seas Operator frequencies. Anyway, she hadn't been overly worried—I'd been incommunicado longer, under dicier circumstances. The kids, she said, were fine.

It was a hazy day, with the sea and sky an unbroken veil of blue; the lifting of the stern in the long following seas gave the ship a languid, easy motion. With the first officer and an AB on watch, there wasn't much for me to do for the time being.

CHAPTER THREE

THE BAY OF FLOWERS

I WAS AN unlikely pirate, or sea captain, for that matter. I had grown up a child of books. My parents were displaced Protestants from north Louisiana stuck on the southern, Catholic coast, my father a professor at Nicholls State University in Thibodaux and my mother a grammar-school teacher. They'd grown up as sharecroppers in the Great Depression and had spent their childhood in hard work, study, and sacrifice. They saw no reason for mine to be any different. So in place of social interaction— playing sports, having sleepovers, going on school outings—I had only books as companions.

My parents were not adventurers, but they loved adventure books, especially books of nautical adventure. In the years between the world wars, there was a genre of boys' adventure books set on tramp freighters, the protagonist having run away to sea, or been shanghaied, or captured by pirates. I read every one I could get my hands on.

My parents didn't own a television, but we had a library larger than those of some towns, and they never censored what I read. By the time I reached my early teens, I'd read thousands of books, and I was beginning to find life on the bayou pale by comparison.

There could not have been a greater disconnect than that between my literary life and my everyday life. Small and thin, the youngest child in my grade, I was an easy target for bullies. And with a preternaturally sharp tongue, I was easily capable of provoking them. In the pages of the books I read, I could outwit pirates, escape buccaneers, and drink rum companionably with my shipmates in seedy waterfront bars from Havana to Pernambuco. To a lonely fifteen-year-old, the disconnect between my interior life and my real life became almost intolerable.

It came to an ugly head in the last days of my sophomore year. In a fight with several of the bullies who tormented me, I broke the arm of one and inflicted permanent eye damage on another—an admittedly excessive reaction to years of being picked on. School officials and local authorities convinced my parents that I would be better off in a military school.

So in the fall of 1964 I was packed off to Castle Heights Military Academy in Lebanon, Tennessee. It was there that I found my first taste of freedom. I learned how to fly planes, how to play drums, and how to fight. One of the school's teachers, Captain Gary Mullins, was a hard-nosed ex-Marine who taught math and science during school hours and, for those of us who could stand the pain, jujitsu and self-defense in the afternoon. After a few weeks of instruction, I found that nobody at Castle Heights bullied me again; the few who've tried it since are probably still wishing they hadn't. Captain Mullins taught us that only a sucker fights fair; it was a lesson I took to heart.

My friends at Castle Heights were iconoclasts who knew how to beat the system. One, Donnie Carson from Atlanta, bought a Volkswagen Beetle for a hundred dollars and hid it in the deep brush behind the school's golf course. For my entire senior year we used that car for clandestine dates with local girls and AWOL trips to Nashville.

I was offered a couple of scholarships to college, including a debate scholarship to Marquette, but my parents wanted me under their close supervision and brought me home to Louisiana. I put in two years at Nicholls before transferring to the University of New Orleans in 1968. I had a canary-yellow Mustang and an apartment in the French Quarter, so life was good.

In those days, most male college students in south Louisiana worked in the oilfield during holidays and summers, and I was no exception. Then, after college, I did a short stint as a drummer for a mediocre Austin-based blues band called the Jelly Rolls.

The band had been touring the Chitlin Circuit, a routine of frat parties and beer halls plied by southern bands since time immemorial, when our singer quit with girlfriend problems. We had just started a one-week stint at a college bar in Tallahassee, Florida, when he gave us ten minutes' notice and left for home. The band decided to break up; I had barely enough money to reach my parents' house. I immediately took a job as a deckhand on a supply boat, the *Magcobar Mercury,* to get back on my feet.

The *Magcobar Mercury,* owned by the Magcobar Mud Company, was a three-hundred-foot boat that delivered liquid mud to offshore rigs. Oilfield mud, weighted with ground-up rock, is used to keep oil from spurting up during drilling.

I worked for a couple of years as deckhand, and then a mate, on the *Magcobar Mercury,* before I got a captain's license. But when Magcobar's engineering department learned that I had a college degree, I was shanghaied into going to mud school and working as a mud engineer. Oilfield mud is a tricky substance, and drilling rigs need specialists, called mud engineers, to maintain the fluid's properties. For seven years I ran mud systems on offshore and Latin American oil rigs. Between oilfield hitches, I continued flying lessons and earned commercial and flight instructor licenses. I took on every kind of flying job I could get, from towing banners to dusting crops. At one time I even flew dead bodies around for a mortuary service. I'd dreamed of flying since I was five years old, and it didn't matter to me what kind of plane I was in as long as I was at the controls.

Eventually I drifted into cropdusting full time. By the time I tired of that in the mid-1980s, I turned back to my other love, the sea. And now, here I was, at the age of forty-two, stuck captaining a Flying Dutchman freighter through the Caribbean, looking for a place to disappear.

For an hour the mountains of Haiti's rugged southern coast rose from the hard blue sea. At 1500 hours I called the first officer and asked him to come to the bridge. The wind had fallen off to a whisper, so we rolled along in an oily, sweaty doldrum. He stepped through the starboard wing door buttoning his uniform shirt, sleep creasing his saturnine face. "Yes, Captain?"

"We'll be slowing down in a few minutes," I said. "Baie des Fleurs is about three miles ahead, right off the starboard bow." I pointed to a low, treeless headland that jutted out into the ocean. There was no offshore reef here, only deep blue water. "Just west of that point."

He glanced at the chart. "Are you sure there are no policemen there?" he asked.

"Nothing but a little fishing village. But the people are very friendly."

"How close is the nearest road?"

"About a day's walk. From there it's a two-hour ride to Les Cayes, and the nearest police station."

He opened a Balkan Sobranie box, took out the last cigarette, and threw it in the trash can. "I cannot believe there's a place where a ship can stay for a week and the police not know."

"Hell, the Haitian police can't even control Port-au-Prince, much less the Bay of Flowers. Signal the chief and call up the quartermaster."

The entrance to the Bay of Flowers was marked on the east by a scraggly coral islet about thirty feet wide and a hundred feet long, covered with pelicans, and on the west by a low seaside cliff that shallowed inland to a wide, sandy beach backed by coconut groves. The islet wasn't marked on the chart, but the bald hill behind it was labeled Pointe Mouton.

Off our port bow, a dozen dugouts were pulled up on the butter-yellow sand in front of a scattering of thatched huts among the coconut palms. I remembered the village as being larger, but it had been four years since I'd been there, and I didn't remember it clearly. Now the long swells were coming off our starboard stern quarter, giving the old ship a heavy, corkscrewing motion. The water was still blue and deep. It was a little unsettling, heaving like this so close to a rocky shore.

"Dead slow ahead," I called. The second officer pulled the throttle lever back and the main engine's thumping slowed. Now we had the coral islet four points off our starboard bow. Someone had stuck a sapling into the end of the reef with a faded red gallon jug on it.

We eased past the jug and into the bay. It was long and narrow, with the hills on the right rising from Pointe Mouton to a spine of barren gray mountains. A broad, creamy beach ran inland from the village on the left to the Ange River, dead ahead, and disappeared into the dense vegetation at its narrow mouth.

Now the sea was only a thin slice of blue behind us. I rang for "stop engine" and the main engine ceased its rumble for the first time since we'd gotten under way—four days earlier. The anchor chain clattered in its hawsepipe.

The villagers were running their dugouts down the beach before the anchor was set. Children who'd been left behind dashed along the water's edge, waving their arms. Their shrill cries reached us faintly on the land breeze.

I joined the first officer on the port wing. "Listen, First, we've got to keep the villagers happy here. I want 'em too drunk to walk."

His eyebrows shot up.

I pointed toward the rocky eastern shore. "There's a police station twenty miles in that direction. The only way to get there is to walk ten miles to the nearest road and catch a ride. I don't want anybody in this village sober enough to make the journey."

He grinned. "Will they drink scotch?"

I snorted. "They wouldn't drink it if we gave it to them. No, I'll send somebody ashore to get some *clairin*."

"What?"

"*Clairin*. Haitian moonshine. Costs about a dollar a gallon. It's what they're used to drinking." I went to the intercom and rang for the officers' mess.

"Cookie," I told our Filipino chef, "I need a good inventory of the food on board. Can you come up to my saloon?"

He arrived out of breath, sweat glistening on his bald head. I scanned his meat inventory—it was, fortunately, enormous. "Two hundred kilos of chicken? Forty kilos of bacon? A hundred and eighty kilos of ground beef? Cookie, does the ship normally carry this much frozen meat?"

He spread his speckled hands. "We always take on meat in Venezuela. I think because of the price."

"I see. Cookie, I want to keep a rolling party going on the afterdeck."

He cocked his head. "A rolling party?"

"For the Haitians. I want them happy and drunk. I want to feed 'em on board every afternoon. Can we manage that? How much rice do we have?"

"Six fifty-kilo sacks, plenty of rice, Captain." He hesitated. "But who will control these people? My mess boy . . . he's just a boy, you know."

"I'll have a watch posted. You have any problem at all, you call me and I'll take care of it."

By then, the villagers were coming up the ship's side, led by a long, lean young man with matted dreadlocks. I leaned out of the window and shouted down, *"Mon ami! Longue temps, vraiment?"*

He looked up, recognized me, and gave a wide grin. *"Aie, Capitaine, vous a retourné! Les bons temps viennent maintenant."* The good times are here again. I went down to meet them. They were mostly men, with a few thin, bare-chested women among them. Their naked feet danced on the hot metal of the deck.

"My friend," I asked the young man, "what is your name? I've forgotten."

"Michel Mauvin." He seized my hand and pumped it.

I looked past him. "My friends," I called in my schoolboy French, "I have come back to visit the beautiful Bay of Flowers. I have told my crew what a wonderful place this is."

They clapped and hopped.

I pointed to the sun, then to where it would be about six o'clock. "This evening we will have a party. I need to send one of my men to buy *clairin*. Is that possible?"

They laughed at the thought that it might be impossible to buy *clairin*. Michel promised to take one of my crewmen to the nearest *clairinaire*. The bosun brought back one of the cadets, a chubby young man with very black skin. "This is Sataporn Chatree," the bosun said. "Very smart young man."

Sataporn shuffled his feet and grinned. "Change into shore clothes," I told him, "and go with this man to get some rum. Here's ten dollars. Get a couple of gallon jugs from Cookie to put it in."

"Very well, sir," he said in a soft British accent.

The first officer arrived from the forecastle with a big wrench in his hand. The brake on the port anchor winch was missing its handle, and the crew had to use a wrench to tighten it.

"Everything okay, First?" I asked.

"All okay, Captain. We have four shackles out." A shackle of chain is about ninety feet.

"We won't see any waves in here," I promised. "Four'll do fine."

It was hot and close in my saloon. I threw open the forward windows, breathing in the cool, flower-scented air, and turned on the wall fans. "Have a seat, First," I said, indicating one of the leather chairs bolted to the floor.

I slid open the bookcase doors and pulled out one of the cloth-bound folders: "Table of Plans and Diagrams."

The folder held about a dozen pages of typed lists: winch plans, hold plans, tank-top plans, general arrangement plans, hatch cover specifications, wiring diagrams, plumbing diagrams, emergency-lighting diagrams, sludge tank diagrams, and many, many others, all categorized by where they were to be found. Most were in my cabin, in the ship's office on the main deck, or in the chief engineer's cabin. "We're going to have to gather all the plans and diagrams on the ship, First, everything on this list. White out the build name on every document and write in the fake build name. You might as well get the second officer, or one of the cadets, to start collecting them."

He looked at me carefully. "But, Captain, anybody can scrape off the white-out and see the real build name underneath."

"Right—that's why it's not as simple as that. After we get the new name written in, all of them will have to be taken to a blueprint place for copying. Then the originals will be destroyed or sent to the home office."

His eyes got wider. "And how will we do that in this place?"

"My friend Ronald is coming this afternoon. He'll take 'em to Port-au-Prince and copy 'em there."

He took the folder and started taking the deck plans out of the bookcase. I went up to the wheelhouse. The water between the ship and village gleamed like a silver river. I looked forward. Two ABs were already lowering a stage over the port side of the forecastle.

Since I'd come on board without luggage, I'd borrowed a few boiler suits—coveralls—from the crew to wear. I changed into my shore clothes and went down to the afterdeck to get one of the Haitians to paddle me to the beach. A young woman in a threadbare T-shirt was squeezing mangoes into a bucket, a gallon of *clairin* sitting on the table ready to make punch. An AB named Mohammed was on party watch, wearing a plastic hard hat and reading a well-thumbed Indian movie magazine. He nodded to me.

One of the Haitians lounging on the fantail took me ashore. The village was half deserted, with most of the inhabitants still on the ship. A few naked children scattered from the path ahead of me.

When I got to the edge of the village, I saw a heavyset man in a city shirt and long pants being transported in a crude wheelbarrow, a small backpack between his legs, his black patent-leather shoes dangling over the front ledge. A wiry, white-haired old man pushed the wheelbarrow over the rocks at a good clip.

"Captain!" the man in the wheelbarrow called. Then I recognized him. It was Ronald.

We hugged. I looked at the wheelbarrow and laughed.

"Well, what could I do?" he said in a huff. "It's a long way from the river." He picked up his bag and gave some gourdes—the Haitian currency— to the old man, who stuck them in his tattered shorts, spun the wheelbarrow around with an expert flip, and trotted smartly back down the path.

Ronald shouldered his pack and we walked through the village. With his newfound bulk and prosperity, he looked like a Port-au-Prince chicken merchant. "Did the office send you some money?" I asked.

"Yes. Three thousand dollars." He patted his pocket. "So, what are you doing here, Captain? Some problem with your ship?"

"We're hiding out." I told him about stealing the ship from Venezuela.

He shook his head. "Very dangerous, Captain. The people around here will talk, and sooner or later the police in Les Cayes will hear about it."

"I just need three or four days," I said earnestly. "Just enough time to change the names and get all the documents changed."

We came out of the brush with the ship right in front of us, dominating the narrow cove. "*Mon Dieu*, Captain," Ronald said, "but this ship is huge. Look how easily it can be seen from the sea."

"I know, I know," I growled, "but I couldn't think of anywhere else to go. Even Miragoane is no good for this."

"The people will talk," he said glumly. He looked around, saw a small boy staring at us, and sent him off to get a boatman.

"Don't worry, *mon vieux*," I said. "I'm controlling the village."

"Controlling the village? How?"

By then, we could hear the music playing on board. A dozen canoes were tied to the pilot ladder, some tied to one another, and a trail of blue barbecue smoke was already drifting off toward the ocean. I pointed to it. "With booze and barbecue."

* * *

The music from the fantail got louder as we reached the Jacob's ladder, a rope ladder with wooden rungs that the crew had hung over the port side. A woman shrieked with laughter as Ronald and I reached the deck.

"Come on and have some punch," I told him. "This stuff'll curl your toenails."

I left Ronald with a glass of punch and went forward to check on the work. The bosun was on a stage—a plank supported by ropes where men can sit to work on the hull—smoking a cigarette and fitting a new disk to his grinder. He grinned at me. I leaned far over to look at the hull. The second *A,* the *H,* and the second *I* on the build name, *Faroah VII,* had already been ground off. All the welder had to do now was turn the *F* into an *L* and the *R* into a *P.*

"How long to finish?" I asked. "Maybe tomorrow?"

He shook his head. "At least two more days, Cap."

"Keep up the good work, then."

I went back to the party. *"Capitaine,"* one of the Haitian woman called, waving her plastic cup in time to the music, *"veux-tu danser?"* She was about twenty-five or thirty, bony as a king crab, wearing a long, ragged T-shirt that stretched to her knees. She wriggled her knifelike hips under the shirt. The other Haitians hooted and urged me to dance, but I made my apologies and escaped to the master's saloon.

A shout and a shriek sounded some hours later. I pulled myself up and looked at my watch: 2 A.M.

I went to the forward window and looked down. Nattaphon, the second engineer, was standing with two Haitian women by the pilot ladder. He was shirtless, his black back gleaming in the deck lights. I recognized the women—they'd come on board when we anchored and hadn't left. One was young and pretty and the other young and ugly.

The ugly one went down the pilot ladder, still cursing and shouting. The pretty one kissed the second engineer before descending. A minute later a canoe emerged from the shadow of the ship, both women paddling. I opened my window and called down, "What's going on, Second?"

He looked up. "Oh, so sorry, Captain. Very sorry for the disturbance."

He made a little bow. "I'm not really sure, you know. Don't speak the language."

"How many Haitians still on board?"

"Five or six, I think."

"Who's on watch?"

"I am."

"Okay. Keep an eye on 'em. And Nattaphon, don't piss 'em off."

"Excuse me, sir?"

"Don't get them angry. I don't want any trouble, understand?"

"Of course, Captain."

He went aft. The air was cool and damp, with a steady wind out of the northeast. I went to bed, but after a while I got up, put my clothes on, and went downstairs. The officers' cabins were quiet. When I got to the lower deck, where the other ranks lived, I heard music and laughter behind the doors. A girl's voice, speaking Creole. A crewman's voice, in English, "I no understand, see? No speakee French." Then the girl laughing.

At another door I heard the cadet's voice. He had his door on the hook—held open six inches for ventilation—and there was a soft light in the room. A girl's voice, in Creole. The candlelight flickered.

I rapped on the door. The girl's voice cut off in mid-laugh. I heard a scramble, then the hook lifted and the cadet's round black face appeared. He struggled to pull the open front of his shirt together.

"Captain?" He came to attention with a quick glance toward his bunk.

"Do you have a candle lit here, Mr. Chatree?" I asked, pushing into the cabin. A chubby young Haitian girl with small, high breasts was sitting on his bunk in a pair of ragged running shorts. Her skin was highlighted orange by the candle flame.

I turned on the cabin's overhead light and blew the candle out. "Mr. Chatree," I said, "candles are a fire hazard and cannot be used on a ship except in emergency. Is this an emergency?"

"No, sir."

I went out and turned around. "And Mr. Chatree, make sure you stay with your girlfriend whenever she's on the ship. I don't want anyone from shore walking around unattended."

"Yes, Captain."

I went out and walked along the hallway. Now the cabins were quiet. They knew the captain was on the prowl.

"They are talking in the other villages," Ronald told me the next morning, after breakfast. We were drinking coffee on the afterdeck, enjoying the cool morning breeze. "About the ship with the black men with white-man faces."

"White-man faces?"

He drew his hand down his own round black face. "Not white color. Shaped like a white man's face."

"Well," I said, "just get to Port-au-Prince and get those plans copied. You'll be back tomorrow?"

"Late in the afternoon," he said, "if the roads are open. No roadblocks, I mean."

He left a few minutes later, accompanied by a village boy, a gangling youth with huge hands and feet, whose job it was to carry the box of plans. There were three streams between the Bay of Flowers and Les Cayes that, during the rainy season, had to be crossed on hand-drawn ferries. Since that time, bridges have been built at Port Salut and Port-à-Piment, but even today the road ends at Les Anglais—just west of the Bay of Flowers—and the thirty miles from there to the tip of the peninsula can only be crossed by foot.

By noon of the third day, the new build names were welded on the bows and Sompoch, the welder, had already rigged his stage over the stern, but I was getting nervous. I told Sompoch to leave the build home port of Oslo on the stern. Maybe somebody would get ambitious someday and grind it off. Besides, lots of ships are homeported Oslo.

Sompoch estimated that he would have the new build name welded on the stern by the following afternoon. After that, with the stencils already assembled, painting on the new name would only take a few minutes. I ate lunch in my saloon, a delicious plate of rice and shredded beef, creole style, with beans and corn and other vegetables I didn't recognize. I'd given Cookie a hundred dollars for local produce, with interesting results.

I called the Cartones del Sud office after lunch and gave Salil, the second officer, the microphone. "Tell them we'll be finished tomorrow," I said. "And find out where we're going."

He and Captain Shrinivas talked in Hindi a few minutes, then he gave me the microphone back and I shut the call down. "We're going to Puerto Limon, Costa Rica," he told me. "He says everything is arranged."

I nodded. "That's fine. We've got a good agent there, a guy named Mario O'Gar." I went in the chart room and plotted the course. At ten knots, Puerto Limon was only three days away. I stuck the dividers in their hole and went in the wheelhouse, where the second officer was smoking a cigarette. "Now," I said, "if we can just get out of paradise."

I was snoozing on the saloon settee when Cookie stuck his round head around the door. "Some Haitian here, Captain, making problem. He wants to see you."

"Bring him up and mix us a couple of drinks. And bring some cookies."

"Yessir," he said with a deadpan face. "Anything for the Haitians."

I gave him a sharp look, but he was already going down the companionway.

The Haitian was one of the villagers who rarely came to the ship, a muscular fisherman about forty, his bald head scarred and dented like a tugboat prow. He spoke no English, but I soon came to understand that he was there about his daughter. She had been on board for two days and her *ami* had not paid her anything.

The mess boy arrived with *clairin* punch and cookies. I got on the intercom and asked the Cookie which one of the crew had been keeping a girl in his cabin.

"Oh, Captain," Cookie said, "there are more than one. But the first officer said it was okay."

"Yeah, but now I got an angry father here. From his description, it sounds like the cadet, Mr. Chatree. Can you send him up?"

While we waited, the man drank his punch and described how much he liked his daughter's boyfriend. He was glad the ship had come to their little bay for repairs; he regretted any misunderstandings. I said the crew were very happy to be there. Perhaps, I said, the Indian cadet was too young to know the ways of the world, as we men did.

The cadet arrived, sweaty and out of breath. "Mr. Chatree," I said sternly, "I think this is the father of your girlfriend."

He glanced at the man nervously, nodded quickly, and said to me, "Yessir?"

"What is your girlfriend's name?"

"Marie Jeanne."

"What have you paid Marie Jeanne so far?"

"Paid? But, Captain, Marie Jeanne and I . . . she's not like that. She hasn't asked me for any money."

"How much French do you speak?"

"None, sir."

"And how much English does she speak?"

He looked down. "Not much. Actually, none."

I sighed and tapped my fingers on the desk. "Do you have any money?"

He shook his head. "I don't get paid, sir. I'm only a cadet. My parents sometimes send me money, but I, I have none now."

I turned to the father. "Mr. Chatree loves your daughter, *monsieur*. He has asked me to give you one thousand gourdes to show you how much he cares for her."

The old man shook his head firmly. "Two thousand gourdes. She is a very young girl, very beautiful."

Now it was my turn to shake my head. "She is very small. Perhaps she will only have very small children and he will be ashamed of them. But she is worth one thousand, five hundred gourdes." I went to my desk and removed a pile of filthy Haitian bills. I counted out the amount and took it to the coffee table. He thumbed through it, then gave me a big smile and put the money in his ragged shorts.

"*Capitaine*," he said, "I am so happy that my daughter has met this young man. He must come to our house tonight. My wife will make him a conch soup with *lian bandé*, that will make him strong down there. And you must come too."

To the cadet I said, "Mr. Chatree, see your father-in-law off the ship, and don't do anything to make him angry. Do you understand me?"

The boy nodded unhappily and followed the fisherman downstairs, already bowed under the burdens of matrimony.

By 1400 hours the next day, the fake build name had been welded on the stern and the ABs had the stage rigged to paint on *Marylin*. All we needed now were the ship's documents and plans, and as the afternoon wore on, I became increasingly anxious to get the ship out of there. I stood at the wheelhouse's forward windows and watched the fishermen on the beach mending their nets, and the women scouring pots at the water's edge. "Come on, Ronald," I muttered to myself, "come on."

A gust of wind eddied through the port door, and the ship surged uneasily. I glanced toward the south. Black clouds had formed an unbroken line across the horizon.

I turned on the Navtex receiver and studied the tape as it scrolled out of the machine. A fast-moving low-pressure area was racing north from Panama behind a violent storm front, with force 8 winds up to fifty miles per hour and seas up to twenty-five feet. The center of the low would pass to the east during the night. I hoped we could wait until the front had passed to set sail. I didn't want to subject the ship's ancient hull to that kind of pounding.

By 1600 hours Ronald still hadn't arrived. I was starting to pace. The country had been convulsed by strikes and roadblocks for days—we'd followed the story on BBC radio—and, according to one report, more than two dozen people had been killed in street battles in Port-au-Prince.

The storm clouds were closing in on the coast with ragged blue-black tails, and the torpid seas that had been lapping at the reef turned gray and confused as the rising wind whipped at them.

The wind turned the ship at an angle to the river's flow, swinging the stern toward the beach, making the rigging hum. I watched the rain getting closer.

Suddenly I heard a shout from the beach. I went through the wheelhouse to the port wing and saw Ronald sitting in a canoe, the box at his feet, waving his arms and shouting. The boatman paddled furiously through the windswept waves toward the pilot ladder.

The sun had disappeared behind the roiling clouds, but the deck still burned under my feet. The canoe glided up to the pilot ladder. One of the ABs, Harmandeep Jokur, already had a rope over the side to take the box.

"Careful with that," I told him. "What's the problem?" I called down.

"The police are coming!" Ronald yelled. As he reached the deck, he said breathlessly, "The police are almost here. Somebody must have reported the ship."

"Come on," I said, and rushed aft. There were half a dozen Haitians on the afterdeck, drinking punch. "Ronald, tell them they have to get off."

He spoke to them in Creole. This crowd hadn't been sober in three days, and they were slow getting up. I ran into the crew's mess and rang for the bridge. The first officer answered. "Get us ready to go, First," I said. "The cops are coming. Tell the chief to get oil up."

I ran back outside. The Haitians were climbing over the side, protesting and waving their arms, with Ronald and the AB crowding them on. I scanned the beach. Nothing but a few villagers going about their tasks, and children splashing in the shallows.

"How far away are they?" I asked Ronald.

"I came across the river first. They were waiting for the next ferry. I asked them where they were going, and they said they were going to a ship hiding at the Bay of Flowers."

"Did they know the name?"

"I don't think so. They said they were going to arrest the captain and take him to Les Cayes."

"So how long? Five minutes? Ten minutes?"

"Maybe ten minutes."

"Do they have rifles?"

"No, Captain. Only pistols."

"Okay, you've got to get off. I'll call you soon and we'll settle up." We hugged and he hurried out. I ran up to the bridge and asked the first officer, "Steering okay?"

"Yessir."

"How many bar?"

"Thirty-three."

I called the engine room. The third engineer answered.

"Oil up?" I asked.

"Oil is up, Captain."

I dropped the phone and told the first officer, "Up anchor. Quick."

He called the bosun, standing with a party forward, on the VHF, and the chain started rattling. The last canoe reached the beach, Ronald's bulk hunched into it. No cops yet. The bell on the forecastle rang. "Anchor up," the first officer reported.

"Hard a-port," I told him, "dead slow ahead. Half to port on the thruster."

The donkey engine rumbled to life. Already swinging under the pressure of the rising wind, the bow's rotation gained speed as the thruster's propeller dug in. The main engine started on the second try, and within a couple of minutes we had our bow pointed toward the open sea.

"Captain!" the second cried, pointing. Four men in blue uniforms stood on the beach talking to a gaggle of villagers. There was a lot of arm waving and gesticulating, but no movement toward the canoes. In any event we were quickly gaining speed, and already out of effective pistol range.

"Half ahead," I ordered. The engine's thumping quickened and the open windows rattled in their casings. When I looked back again, I could still see the uniforms, but barely. None of the canoes had put in the water. A few minutes later, we cleared the reef and I had the quartermaster turn the bow to the southwest, directly into the heaving swells.

We ran into the storm front an hour later, taking the boiling seas directly on the ship's blunt bow. The empty ship reared and plunged like a rodeo bull, shuddering in the troughs and corkscrewing wildly on the crests. The sky turned black, and blinding rain hammered against the wheelhouse windows.

The bosun took the wheel, an unlit cigar clenched in his teeth as he fought to keep the bow into the wind and seas. The first officer and I hung on as the ship rolled heavily from side to side, sending every loose object on the bridge flying. Pens and navigation instruments clattered across the floor of the chart room behind us.

With no cargo to stabilize her, the ship veered heavily under the force of wind and waves. The bosun racked the wheel from stop to stop trying to keep her head-on to the seas, but she still fell off every time a rogue wave slammed against one side of the bow or the other, turning her nearly beam-on. With the weight of the ballast water far down in the double-bottom tanks, she had a fast, wicked roll, whipping back through the vertical with breathtaking speed.

An hour later the front had fled northward. Patches of rain still swept over the ship, but the sound of the wind in the rigging had fallen off to a low keening. I told the first and second officers that I would take the rest of the afternoon watch, and sent them below to rest. Finally, when the seas had subsided to the point that the autopilot could handle them, I switched it on and the bosun sank back against the after bulkhead in relief, flexing his fingers after a solid hour of fighting the wheel.

"So, Captain," he said, a grin splitting his chubby black face, "the Flying Dutchman disappears again, eh?"

"Poof," I said, showing him how. "Like a fist when you open your hand."

We arrived at the Puerto Limon sea buoy at 0745 hours on July 11. As I'd predicted, Mr. Gonsalves sent the crew only what they were owed. There were still two weeks left in the month, so in essence they did get two weeks' severance pay, but nothing for the risk they'd run, or the extra work. I flew to Miami and took a taxi to the Cartones del Sud office.

Since my job was to load and unload cargo in faraway ports, I didn't spend much time at the office. I was close to some of the women who worked there, though, and occasionally when I happened to be in the office at quitting time we'd go to a local bar and knock back a few.

Today they were at their desks, chatting in Spanish, checking their makeup, and tapping desultorily at their keyboards. Several of them came up to me as I put my bag down inside the door.

"Captain, we're so glad you're safe," Carmen, a tall Hispanic in spike heels, said. I reached up to give her a buss on the cheek.

"Me too," I said. "Everything okay here on the home front?"

It was, they chorused. Captain Shrinivas's door opened and his lopsided face stuck out. He beckoned to me and disappeared back inside. "Gotta go," I told the girls. "Y'all better get back to work or there'll be no bonuses this month."

They winced. So they'd been getting the boner, too, I realized. I put on a big smile and went to Captain Shrinivas's door. His office was a windowless box in the center of the building. The *Patric M*'s original plans and diagrams were stacked in one corner, thigh-high. He'd already reseated himself behind his mahogany desk and was fiddling with a faxed sheet of paper.

Captain Shrinivas's business card prominently reported his license as "Extra Master," but since my license was "Master, Unlimited Tonnage Any Oceans," I didn't see how his could be much better. It was like olive oil being "extra virgin."

"So, all went well in Puerto Limon?" he asked.

"Sure. No problem. Still only one air compressor, though, and it's not working very well."

"Yes, we're having a new one installed now."

I lifted my eyebrows delicately. "We?"

He gave his smile another careful centimeter. "The new owner, I should say." He gave me that guileless look Indians get when tea is over and they're ready to talk business. "I understand you told Mr. Maher that you're unhappy with your wages?"

"Not my wages. It's my bonuses. When Captain Tiwali hired me, he said I would get two thousand five hundred dollars per month in salary and one thousand a month in cash bonuses. I accepted the job on that basis. I've been with the company twenty-six months and I've gotten exactly ten thousand dollars in bonuses. I'm owed sixteen thousand dollars."

"Well, Captain," he said, "I wasn't with the company when you were hired, and Captain Tiwali is no longer with us. But bonuses are only paid when there are profits, and unfortunately we have not been making a profit recently."

"That doesn't keep Mr. Maher from driving a hundred-thousand-dollar Mercedes." I stood up. "Jim Maher promised me that the company would make up my missing bonuses if I took the ship out. I took the ship out. So I expect to be paid."

Captain Shrinivas frowned. "Did Jim say that?"

I realized I would get nowhere with him. But I was damned if I would ever work for him again. I stood up. "Don't worry about it. That's between Jim and me."

"Fine. Was there something else?"

"Nope, that's it. Nice seeing you."

I closed the door and went out. The girls were at their desks, making themselves look busy. It was interesting to watch people coming out of Captain Shrinivas's office. Secretaries came out sniffling. Businessmen came out grim-faced, standing for a moment to compose themselves. I marched over to Dolores's desk.

"Dolores, my dear," I said in Spanish, "when are we going to leave those worthless spouses of ours and run off to a little *bohio* in the country?" Dolores was a sweetheart, a real beauty, who'd fled Nicaragua with her husband when the Sandinistas took over. He was a tall, dignified man who had been a lawyer in Managua, and now scraped by with a small import-export business near the Miami airport.

The girls giggled. Dolores gave me a stern look. "You are quite *escandaloso,* Captain." She cocked a painted eyebrow. "Besides, it is not necessary to leave our worthless spouses just for a *bohio* weekend."

The girls hooted. I laughed and headed toward the door. On the way out, I stopped to visit Mr. Gonsalves, the company's financial officer.

"Mr. Gonsalves?" I stepped into his glass-fronted office. "Have you heard from Mr. Maher? He was supposed to authorize payment of my back bonuses."

"Oh, Captain Max," he said, rising painfully and giving me a frail handshake, "I did get a note from Captain Shrinivas." He fumbled around on his littered desk and picked up an envelope with a note clipped to it. "'One thousand dollars to Capt. Max for services rendered.' Is that it?"

"No, I'm owed sixteen thousand. You should have a note from Jim Maher."

He shook his head sadly. "I have not heard from Mr. Maher in some time." He opened a leather-bound appointment book and wrote himself a laborious note. "I will ask him when he calls in next."

"You do that," I said shortly. I plucked the envelope from his fingers. "Meanwhile, I'll take what you got." His eyes opened wide at my effrontery. I showed him the ten hundred-dollar bills. "On account," I said, and walked out, once and for all.

* * *

We were living in a stucco ranch house on an acre of pasture land in Davie, Florida. I parked behind my wife's car and went in. The kids were home from day care. They came running and I hoisted them up like sacks of rice.

My wife was cooking supper. We managed a kiss with my hands full of children and hers full of breading. "I got a bonus," I said. "A grand. That's what I get for a month away from home." Alex scrambled off toward the television. I laid Karla on the floor and tickled her neck with my mustache.

"What about the other bonuses?" my wife asked.

I stood up and tucked my shirt in. "Mr. Gonsalves will have to check with Mr. Maher. Basically, he blew me off."

"The boner again," she said lightly.

"I want to move back to Louisiana," I said. "I've had it with Cartones del Sud. And with South Florida in general."

"Okay. Thank God we kept the house in Louisiana. Hand me that potholder, please. We have to give Mike a month's notice."

I tossed it to her. "That's all right. We have to give a month's notice on this place anyway. I'll call 'em both tomorrow." I stole a small chicken finger—a pinkie—from the warming dish. "I don't know what I'll do for work, though. The oilfield's dead."

She stirred some more butter into the mashed potatoes and took the rolls out of the oven. "You'll find something. You always do."

CHAPTER FOUR

FORTY-SEVEN CROP DUSTERS

BACK IN LOUISIANA, I dropped by my old flight school, Pelican Aviation in Slidell, and let myself get talked into doing some instruction. Business was slow—the single men who'd supported three flight schools at the airport in the late 1970s had all but disappeared with the oil-drilling slump—but a friend and former colleague, Carlos Esposito, was now chief flight instructor at the remaining school. He had a part-time instructor who flew a fish-spotting plane, and needed another part-timer to take up the slack.

I wasn't happy about part-time flight instructing, since it paid less than a hundred dollars a day. I was even thinking about going back to crop-dusting. However, some years earlier my wife had urged me strongly—and successfully—to quit dusting, and I knew she wouldn't like me going back to it. So, for lack of something better, I started teaching flying.

One day, a few weeks later, when I arrived at the school for a lesson, a big, moon-faced boy was waiting in the lobby. "Mr. Hardberger," he called out, "remember me?"

I peered at him. "Jimmy Boyer?"

"Yessir, it's Jimbo." He bustled over to shake my hand. "My dad says I can start taking flying lessons. They told me you'd be my instructor. I couldn't believe it. I thought you were off in Guatemala or something."

"I was, but I'm back. What are you doing these days?"

"Working for my dad. I always wanted to fly, and Dad says he'll pay for lessons."

I'd taught him world history at Pope John Paul II High School in Slidell during the 1984–85 school year. He was still heavyset, but his face had gained definition and he'd grown a wispy little mustache.

"What about your old gang?" I asked. "Any of 'em still around? Eddie Dardienne?"

"Eddie's going to law school at Tulane. He graduates this year."

"What about, what's her name, Lisa Pennington? The one with the thick glasses."

"Don't know. I think she married a Yankee and moved up north."

"Too bad. And Michael Bono?"

"Law school. He's rooming with Eddie."

My flight student arrived, a serious man about my age who had made a small fortune in construction and was now pursuing, without much aptitude, a private pilot's license. I made an appointment with Jimmy for his first lesson on the following day, and took my student out to the plane.

I hadn't thought much about the year I'd taught at Pope John Paul II. After my last student of the day I drove over to the east side of town to see what the school looked like now. There was a new auditorium behind the main building, and a much larger parking lot, but otherwise it was unchanged.

In the same way I found most of my jobs, I'd fallen into teaching at Pope John Paul II through necessity and circumstance. I'd worked as a mud engineer on an oil rig in Guatemala for a couple of years, and when my wife got pregnant in the late summer of 1984, she sat me down the next time I got home—I was working twenty-eight days on and twenty-eight days off—and said that I had to find a job that would keep me home until the baby was born.

I called around to the high schools in the area to see if any had a last-minute vacancy. It was already a couple of days into the school year, but Pope John Paul II needed an English-and-history teacher, and I was hired over the phone. I went down that afternoon, signed a contract, and started teaching the next day.

I had always enjoyed teaching English—I'd taught in high schools in Louisiana and Mississippi many years earlier—but my world history class that year was a real pleasure. I had some brilliant students, seniors clearly destined for great things, and our tour through mankind's checkered past was memorable. The students and other teachers liked me, and the administration left me alone, so we all had a good time. In fact, the principal wanted me to sign a contract for the following year, but by spring I was ready to move on. My old mud-engineering boss had been calling to find when I would be ready to go back to Guatemala. I'd told him I'd go as soon as the baby was born.

The company had been having trouble finding men for the job because nobody wanted to go to northern Guatemala in the middle of the civil war. In fact, during my work there in 1982 and 1983, I'd had to pretend to my wife that everything was peaceful so she'd let me go back. But El Naranjo, where we were drilling, was in the center of the fighting, and a few times rebels had directed automatic weapons fire at the rig, although none of the foreign workers had been hit.

My daughter, with the willfulness she would later display in spades, refused to be born on time. My hitch was to begin on May 30. May 29 arrived and she hadn't. My mother-in-law arrived from north Mississippi to help, and my wife went on long, brisk walks to hurry things along, but still Karla clung to the last real security anyone ever knows. My wife started getting frantic.

But at 0200 hours on May 30, my wife's contractions began, and we tore off for Lakeview Hospital in New Orleans. With a genetic affinity for water, Karla threatened to emerge into the world on the Lake Pontchartrain Causeway—the world's longest bridge—but she prudently held off until 0400 hours, by which time we were in the hospital's maternity ward and I was properly suited up.

Somebody, maybe my mother-in-law, took a Polaroid photo of Karla only minutes after she was born, lying under a heat lamp with a knit cap on her head, loudly protesting the injustice of it all. My flight to Guatemala was to leave at seven o'clock. I ripped off my mask and gown, kissed my wife, snatched up the photograph, and rushed downstairs to catch a taxi to the airport.

I nearly wore out that photo during the next twenty-eight days. It was especially hard because the rig had no contact with the outside world except by company radio. I knew nothing of Karla and my wife until my hitch was up. I stared at that photograph for hours at a time.

*   *   *

In the fall of that year, after repeated attacks on the rig and the truck caravans bringing supplies from Guatemala City, Texaco decided to abandon the El Naranjo project. When my last hitch was over, in September 1985, I returned to Louisiana to look for work. But by then, oil had dropped to eighteen dollars a barrel and Louisiana was in a deep recession. With a new baby to feed, and with my wife's work as a court reporter curtailed by caring for Karla, I searched about for a local job, but without success. Then I got a call from Lafayette Cropdusters in Breaux Bridge, my old outfit.

Bill Boudreaux, the owner, had decided to start a cropdusting school at the end of the season, and he needed a cropduster pilot with an instructor's license. My wife opposed it, as Breaux Bridge was three hours away, but any job was better than no job. So I packed my kit, got in my little Datsun pickup, and drove to Cajun country.

I taught cropdusting through the winter, then we closed the school when the dusting season started, and I stayed on as chief pilot. It was a wet summer, and business was good, but by the fall of 1986 I realized it was time to quit dusting for good.

On the day I decided to quit, I'd been spraying 2,4-D, a really virulent herbicide with a distinctive smell. Like many small outfits, Lafayette Cropdusters made its pilots mix their own chemicals. I was as careful as time and equipment allowed, but there was no way of keeping all the chemical off my skin.

After I got off work that day, I took a long shower and went out to sit on my porch. I was living in a little rented house in the middle of a sugarcane field. The sun was almost down, but it was still hot, and as I sat there I started to sweat. Then I smelled 2,4-D. I raised my arm and smelled my sweat. It smelled like 2,4-D.

Not long before that, a retired crop duster from the area had died at the age of about fifty, and when he was autopsied, the doctor found that his internal organs were swollen to twice their normal size. Or at least that was the word among the local crop dusters. This, coupled with the 2,4-D incident and my wife's unhappiness with this line of work, made me decide to seek my fortune in some other way. This was when I went into ocean freighters.

At the end of the season, I piled my kit into my trusty pickup and drove to Miami. In those days, the Miami River was full of small freighters plying the Haitian trade. I already had a U.S. captain's license that I'd earned in the Louisiana offshore oilfields, and the day after I arrived I got a job as master of a tiny, four-hundred-ton freighter named *Jolie Marie*. After that came the *Naruda*.

After a couple of years running old freighters, and with my wife pregnant with our second child, I returned to Louisiana to eke out a living as a marine surveyor. But I soon got tired of that. When the new owner of a derelict ship, the *Erika*, begged me to take over as captain, I returned to the Haiti trade. A couple of years later Captain Tiwali hired me as a port captain for Cartones del Sud, and two years after that I quit the company and returned to Louisiana.

In late September 1990, I was thinking of calling Bill Boudreaux to see if he needed an instructor for the winter cropdusting school when I got a call from an old buddy, Eddie Cashman. I'd met Eddie while he was dusting crops in Rayne, Louisiana, and we'd stayed in touch over the years. In the late 1980s Eddie had taken a job at High Plains Ag Service in Yuma, Colorado, and soon afterward he married the boss's daughter and bought the business.

"Mad Max!" Eddie said. "You still in Miami, what, running ships or something?"

"Naw, I'm back home teaching flying. What's up with you? Still killing bugs?"

"Yeah. Real dry summer, though. Didn't hardly make no money. But I got something cookin' that I need help on. And I mean fast, good buddy. I got fifty cropdusters in Germany and a buyer in Venezuela, but I got no idea how to get 'em there. I figured you're in shipping, maybe you can get it done."

"That's no problem. Just fly 'em over. Pipe the hoppers for fuel, fly 'em to Africa, and hop across the pond to Brazil."

I heard a spitting sound, and remembered that Eddie chewed tobacco. "Cain't do it," he complained. "We got kind of a time problem."

"What do you mean?"

"Well," he said cautiously, "they was owned by the East German government, and now the West German government is looking for them."

"How'd you get 'em?"

"That's another thing. I ain't exactly got 'em yet. I'm buying 'em from a guy in West Germany named Heinrich Moller. He bought 'em from some pilots in East Germany. Reunification comes in two weeks. We gotta get 'em out before then."

"Or what?"

"Or the West German government gets 'em. If we get 'em out now, I can get them for twenty grand. I got a guy in Venezuela that'll buy them for forty. That's where you come in."

"I guess it would be a little tough to find fifty pilots willing to fly 'em to Venezuela."

"Heinrich says he's got some of the old cropduster pilots that used to fly them for the government, but nothin' like fifty. Maybe ten or fifteen."

"So what can I do for you?"

"You know all about ships. You can figure out some way of putting them on a ship, cain't you?"

I rubbed my chin. "I don't know. I guess they can't be taken across the border to West Germany. Maybe they could go to Poland and get on a ship at Gdansk."

"You cain't put crop duster planes in the bottom of a ship, can you? They'll git all smashed up."

"No, no, they'd have to go in containers."

"Jesus," he cried, "we ain't got the time to build fifty boxes."

"No," I said, "shipping containers. Well, I can do it," I said, with more confidence than I felt, "but it'll be expensive."

"How expensive?"

I gave him a figure. He whistled. "Man, you're a pricey bastard. When can you get to Germany?"

"Tomorrow."

He gave me Heinrich Moller's telephone number and promised to wire my expense money that morning. By then it was late afternoon in Germany, but I caught Mr. Moller at his office. He had a dry, scratchy voice like a quill on parchment.

"Mr. Cashman just called me," he said. "What do you think, Captain?"

"Well, they'll probably have to go in shipping containers. I assume they can't go across the West German border?"

"Oh, no, no. In fact, I'm afraid the Westies already know about them. They can't go looking for them until Reunification, but I hear there've been some questions in Berlin."

"Can they go out through Poland?"

"The Poles would never permit that."

"What kind of planes are they?"

"Zlin Bumblebees. Six hundred horsepower."

"About the size of an Ag-Cat, then. We ought to be able to get 'em in FEUs."

"What's that?"

"There're two sizes of ocean shipping containers. The larger one, forty feet long, is called an FEU. I guess I'd better get over there as soon as possible. Can I fly into East Germany?"

"No, there's no commercial service to the East yet. Can you fly to Frankfurt? My pilot can pick you up there and fly you to the planes."

"Okay, I'll make the arrangements and call you back."

"Thanks, Captain. Cheerio, then."

I called a lady freight forwarder in Miami I'd done business with before, a tough-talking woman of about fifty who seemed to know freight forwarders in just about every port in the world. Freight forwarders are specialists in arranging ocean transport from anywhere to anywhere. I wouldn't want to be one, since they never get out of the office.

"Captain Max!" Helen barked. "How's it hanging?"

"I'm okay. Listen, I've got fifty cropdusting planes in East Germany. They gotta get out before Reunification, in two weeks. They can't be flown out, so they gotta go by ship. Probably fifty containers."

She lit a cigarette and blew smoke into the mouthpiece. "How about Hamburg? I got a guy in Hamburg."

"They can't go out through West Germany. I think the best thing is to send them out through some port in East Germany."

"All right, handsome, let me check on it. I'll call you back."

I used the time to call my travel agent.

When Helen called back, she said, "My friend in Hamburg has a guy in Rostock, in East Germany. There's a company called Baltlines that ships out of there twice a week. You sure these planes are legal?"

"I'm not sure they can be manifested," I said cautiously.

"They gotta be manifested."

"I mean, manifested as airplanes."

She coughed. "Well, the name of the man in Rostock is Lothar von Gruber." She gave me the number. "So, when you coming to Miami? You still married?"

"Yes," I said, "still married."

"You take care of that problem, you come see me."

"Helen," I said, "you're a scary woman, you know that?"

"You're telling me. I scare myself every time I look in the mirror."

Next I called Mr. von Gruber. "I have some cargo that needs to go from East Germany to Venezuela," I said carefully. "I'll need to send about fifty FEUs. I understand Baltlines ships out of Rostock."

"*Ja,*" he said. "Two time a week zey go. But fifty containers, hmm, must get zem from Hamburg. Ve can do it. Must come by truck, I zink."

"What about the manifests?" I said. "Will the containers get inspected by customs in Rostock?"

He suddenly got suspicious. "What zis cargo, henh?"

"I can't really say right now," I said. "Let's just say it's government property."

"Hah! You a *Schwarzhändler,* zen?"

"Excuse me?"

"Zis black market goods, zen?"

"No, no," I protested, "these goods were legally purchased from the East German government."

"There is no Ostdeutschland now. Okay, Mr. Max, you come zee me in Rostock, ve zee. I no promize nothing, you know, but ve zee vat can be done."

I landed in Frankfurt early in the afternoon the next day. It was bitterly cold, with a sharp wind sweeping across the tarmac. A beefy young man named Hugo, wearing a houndstooth suit like Sherlock Holmes's, met me at the terminal and led me to a neat little Cessna 320 with a sporty green-and-white paint job. I got in the right seat and we took off for Magdeburg.

The radio traffic between Hugo and the controllers was in German, but there didn't seem to be any special formalities about crossing the border. As we flew over the cleared strip of land that had separated the two countries, Hugo nudged me and pointed down. A line of tall, forbidding watchtowers, spaced every few hundred yards, cast spindly shadows across the bare ground.

"The mines are still there," Hugo said in his heavily accented English. "The watchtowers are empty, but if you try to walk across that land, kaboom!"

I started getting a bad feeling. I was used to operating in half-baked Third World dictatorships like Colombia and Venezuela, but this was a different matter. But I'd said I would sneak the planes out of East Germany, so I had to do it.

A half hour later, Hugo cut power and eased the nose down. He circled a farmhouse set near a thick forest. As we flew over it, I could see a long flat strip of land near the house, oriented east and west, that ended just short of the treeline. In the field next to the strip were three long lines of humps that looked like ammunition bunkers, brown and green against the dun-colored earth around them.

Hugo pulled the engines to idle and pushed the props' pitch controls forward. The wind was out of the west, so we had the setting sun in our eyes as we lined up on final approach. But a shallow hill to the west finally blocked the sun, and we touched down in shadow.

Hugo stood on the brakes, holding the nosewheel off the ground until the last moment. We finally came to a stop a few yards short of the trees.

A small group of men were waiting for us, several of them in gray coveralls. One, a tall, white-haired man with a bony face reddened by wind and cold, wore a trench coat with an astrakhan collar. He shook Hugo's hand and spoke to him briefly in German, then turned to me and gave a slight Prussian bow. "I am Heinrich Moller. You are Captain Max?"

"Yessir."

"It is our pleasure to meet you. Mr. Cashman has spoken highly of you."

The other men crowded around with curious looks. From their identical gray coveralls, they were clearly mechanics—a couple of them had grease-smears on the backs of their hands.

I looked around. What I had thought were ammunition bunkers were actually airplanes covered with camouflage tarpaulins. I waved a hand at them. "These are the planes?"

Heinrich nodded. "Yes, fifty Zlin Bumblebees. You are familiar with them?"

I shook my head. "Never even heard of 'em."

Hugo opened a box of cigarettes and passed them around. While the men went through their ritual of lighting one another's cigarettes and pulling the first grateful puffs into their lungs, I looked over the field of planes. One had its camouflage tarp pulled back, showing yellow wings and a squat, humpbacked fuselage painted in the East German colors of red and black. I saw with some surprise that they were two-seaters.

"Two seats?" I asked Heinrich. "That's odd."

He smiled faintly. "A special order by the East German government, along with the bigger engines, so no pilot could fly alone. It's only a hundred kilometers to the border. Without a Stasi man in the back seat, I suspect very few planes would have come back."

"I see."

"We will go to the apartment," he said. He led me to a big Mercedes sedan parked among the battered Ladas and Trabants in the narrow driveway.

It took us half an hour to reach downtown Magdeburg, driving along rutted country lanes and then along a short stretch of narrow highway lined with trees. Here and there the carcass of a Trabant or Wartburg lay on the side of the road, its headlights and other fittings stolen or salvaged. Most of the cars on the road were ambulatory wrecks, puttering along and trailing clouds of smoke, but occasionally new Mercedes or Audi cars dashed by, flashing their lights.

We left the dreary outskirts of Magdeburg and made our way through the narrow streets to a large stone building that occupied a whole city block. A light snow was falling. We parked on the street and walked toward the building's front door. The air had an acrid smell, like grave-earth.

"Strange weather," Heinrich said as we got out. "Never have we snow in September." He gave the lowering sky an apprehensive look as we hurried to the vestibule of the building. He unlocked the door from a ring of medieval-looking keys and we stepped into a bath of hot air. He chuckled. "The government keeps us warm here," he said. "Even if it does mean dying from lung cancer from the brown-coal smoke."

"Brown coal?"

"A low grade of coal, very cheap. Every cellar is full of it."

The vestibule opened on a short hallway leading to a wide, wooden stairway that turned back on itself at a narrow landing. We went up to the third floor. Heinrich opened the last door on the right with another of his huge jailers' keys.

We walked into a large, sparsely furnished apartment with antique furniture scattered over the cracked parquet floor. A heavy table stood against the far wall, with a half-empty whisky bottle on it.

A stone building stood directly across the street, with boards covering the ground-floor windows. Some of the second-floor windows were broken out and unboarded.

Heinrich came over and stood next to me. "The Stasi building," he said. "Nobody will buy it. I'm waiting for the price to go down." He waved a hand. "I bought this building for very little. It used to be an apartment building for Stasi officers. Even now, I have trouble finding people to move in. I have offered rent for almost nothing, just to have it occupied." He shook out a cigarette and stuck it in his mouth. "But with Reunification coming, they will forget. In a few months, I'll be able to double or even triple the rent."

That night, at dinner, we had the restaurant to ourselves. There was no menu. Apparently, diners were expected all to eat the same thing. The waiter, a consumptive old man with a threadbare sweater, brought us a thin barley soup. "Mr. Moller," I said, sipping at the scalding broth, "I need to go to Rostock. There's a man there who can arrange for the planes to go through the port, but he says we have to talk about it in person. I think he's afraid of the phones being tapped."

Heinrich shook his head. "That's silly. There is no one to tap the phones anymore. Stasi is kaput. But it will take the people some time to forget old habits. Okay, Hugo will fly us up there tomorrow. But we must hurry. You say the planes will have to be put in containers?"

"Yes. Do you have enough mechanics to do that?"

"We have dozens of mechanics. All the mechanics that worked on the planes for the East German government. And they're dying for work. But I'm afraid the containers will be stopped on the road and searched."

"Even if they're sealed?"

He smiled faintly. "The Bereitschaftspolizei—the highway patrol—still control the roads. You don't think we're the only ones trying to get East German assets out of the country, do you? Seals will mean nothing."

"What about customs in Rostock?"

He shrugged. "That I don't know. Your man in Rostock will have to make the necessary arrangements."

"Can we fly them to Rostock?"

"Perhaps. We must ask the pilots tomorrow."

The next morning, the snow was six inches deep. A faint north wind was stirring, blowing the leaves off the elm trees that lined the streets. A dozen cars were parked at the farmhouse when we arrived, mostly the same battered lot of Ladas and Trabants. Some of the airplanes had their tarps off, with men crawling around them. Halfway down the middle line of planes, black smoke, turning to blue, burst from the one of the airplanes and blew away toward the field. The plane's wings shook. I could see a man's head, buried in a heavy Russian-style fur cap, behind the cockpit's Plexiglas.

Heinrich handed cigarettes around and the men lit up. I stuck my head into the cockpit of one of the planes. It smelled like all cockpits do, of leather and oil and ancient sweat. Although the gauges were in some odd places on the dash, they were mostly recognizable. The stick was a massive aluminum pipe rising from the floorboard, and the money handle—the knob that opens and closes the spray valve—was on the right side, which meant that you had to fly the stick with your left hand.

I stamped my feet and said to Heinrich, "One more important thing. We're going to need some place to land near Rostock where we can disassemble the planes. I doubt that the freight forwarder in Rostock will know anything about that."

"Let me ask the pilots," he said. "I know some of them were working near Rostock."

After some discussion between Heinrich and one of the pilots, Heinrich said to me, "Werner here used to fly out of a field near Rostock. He says it's a good field, plenty long, very near the coast. He'll take the lead plane in each flight."

"Maybe he'd better come with us to check it out," I said. "I'd hate for the pilots to get there and find it's been plowed up."

"Good idea," Heinrich said. The four of us went out to the 320. Heinrich and Werner got in the back. The cockpit was freezing. It was hard to believe it was only September. Back in Louisiana, people were still running their air conditioners.

The plane soared up into a cold blue sky. We leveled off at nine hundred feet and Hugo talked to a controller somewhere. The flat countryside sped by under our wings, small towns dotting the landscape. Half an hour later we landed at Rostock-Laage Airport and took a taxi to the city of Rostock.

The forwarder's office was a run-down building on the ancient waterfront. Hugo and Werner continued on to check out the strip, about ten miles to the west. Mr. von Gruber was a young man in a thick roll-neck sweater. Flecks of cigarette ash spotted his broad stomach. I could hardly see him above the piled-up files and folders on his desk.

He and Heinrich talked in German for a while. Heinrich translated. "Mr. von Gruber says the customs officials can be, er, taken care of. It will take about five thousand marks for each container. He says there are about twenty long containers—what did you call them, FEUs?—here in Rostock, and he can get the rest brought by truck from Hamburg. Do you think we can put one plane in each container?"

"Yes, I think so. Of course, the wings and props will have to come off. We can leave the tailplanes on. They'll fit."

Mr. von Gruber made some calls and finally said that everything could be arranged. He could start getting the containers delivered to the strip as soon as the pilots got back and told him where it was. He and Heinrich discussed money, then we retired to a workers' café near the port for a pitcher of warm beer.

Werner and Hugo returned around eleven to report that the strip was still good for landing. Heinrich promised to call Mr. von Gruber when the first flight left the farmhouse the next morning. Mr. von Gruber promised that enough containers would be at the strip so the mechanics could start stuffing the planes into them as soon as they landed.

We reached the farmhouse around 2 P.M. There were a couple of dozen men in the huge living room, standing around drinking beer and eating. The mechanics were mostly about my age, in their forties, but the pilots were much younger.

I took a plate and a glass of warm beer and sat by the fire.

"Captain Max," Heinrich called, from across the room, "can you fly one of the planes? We only have eleven pilots."

"Sure," I said. "Cropdusters is cropdusters. But I don't know the route. I'd hate to get lost."

He laughed. "None of the pilots know the route. The Ossie government never let them fly beyond their own cropdusting area. But don't worry . . . you'll be flying together. All you have to do is follow the plane ahead of you."

I shrugged. "I guess I can do it, then."

"Do you want to take one up now?" Heinrich asked me. "Willi here will go with you."

Willi was a slight man about thirty, with a sunken chest and gray face. We put on our coats and went out. He took me to the plane at the end of the first line. I climbed in and he got in the backseat. I hauled the door up and studied the instrument panel.

The throttle was a quadrant on the left. I eased it forward a hair and pushed the stick forward to unlock the tail wheel. The engine was running rough, and it took some power to get the wheels free from their muddy slots. More power and a heavy foot on the right pedal got the plane moving and turning. I trundled down to the very end of the strip.

I rolled forward, pulled the stick back to lock the tail wheel, and shoved the throttle all the way to the stop. The engine roared to a crescendo. The airframe shook. I took my toes off the brakes and, in anticipation of P-factor, pushed the right pedal halfway to the floor.

That was a big mistake. I hadn't noticed that the propeller rotated in the opposite direction from American engines' propellers, and not only did the plane veer to the right when it began rolling, I had exacerbated the P-factor by pushing the wrong pedal. The plane leaped toward the tailfeathers of the plane at the end of the line. With gritted teeth and hair standing on end, I jammed on the brakes and got us stopped a foot short. I didn't dare turn around to look at my passenger.

I horsed the plane back onto the strip and put the throttle to the firewall. With an empty hopper and only half a tank of fuel, the plane shot into the air. I turned north, away from the city and toward the black swath of forest, staying under seven hundred feet.

There was no wind at all. I dropped the left wing and circled back toward the farmhouse in a wide arc. It was an odd feeling, an equal mixture of exhilaration and apprehension, to be skimming over East Germany in an unregistered plane without a flight plan. A few minutes later I picked out the two dark lines my wheels had left on the strip. Since there was still no wind, I cut power and made a straight-in approach from the opposite direction, pulling full flaps as we crossed the tree line, making a perfect three-point landing in the center of the strip.

Back in the farmhouse, I told Heinrich, "No problem. Flies like a dream." I looked at Hugo. "Are you going to fly one of the dusters?"

"No, I have to fly the mechanics up to the strip and bring you chaps back."

"In the 320? That'll take a few trips."

"No, in an AN-2."

"A what?"

"A big biplane, made in Russia. It's the one I fly for a skydiving club in Hannover. Holds a pilot and twelve passengers. Very easy to fly, like a cropduster. In fact, they use them for dusting in Russia."

Hugo spread out an air chart on the table and tapped our location, about twelve miles north of Magdeburg, near the town of Colbitz.

"Who knows about these planes?" I asked.

"Only the pilots and mechanics. These planes were based at small strips all over East Germany. When the government fell, the pilots in the Agricultural Pilots' Union got together and brought them here."

I nodded and plucked another meat roll from the tray. Hugo took out a gold-plated mechanical pencil and drew a jagged line from the farm to the Baltic coast. "You'll have to stay away from the cities. Somebody might notice planes flying low overhead. Even over the open countryside, you need to fly under two hundred meters to avoid Westie radar. But no matter what, you must keep the plane ahead of you in sight."

"With those colors," I said, "that shouldn't be hard."

He chuckled. "Yes, they are easy to see."

"Can the West Germans—the Westies—do anything if they see us?"

Hugo shook his head and finished his beer. "I don't know," he said. "Legally, the Westie Luftwaffe doesn't have the right to overfly East Germany yet."

"When is Reunification?"

"October third."

I started. "That's next week! I thought we had a couple of weeks."

He shrugged. "That's why we've got to get them out quick. They're still East German assets now, but after Reunification all East German government property will belong to the West."

"What about the East German air force? Would they scramble?"

Heinrich shook his head. "There's no East German air force left." He made a spitting sound. "The pilots were all Russkies anyway. They didn't trust East Germans in their precious fighters."

"So we have fifty airplanes?"

"The mechanics say only forty-eight are flyable. The other two we'll disassemble and put in the barn."

"I hope I can keep visual contact with the plane ahead of me," I said dubiously. "I can see me putting down somewhere in East Germany and trying to hitchhike back."

"Don't worry," he said. "One of the mechanics speaks a little English. He'll go with you, and if you have to put down he'll get you back."

"Okay, then," I said. "Flight charts in all the planes?"

"There's a copy of this chart in every airplane. Each pilot will need to bring his back."

We drank some more beer, then trooped out to the planes. Some of the mechanics had started tearing down the two planes that wouldn't be going, and the others swarmed around the planes that were going to fly. I walked around for a casual inspection.

Each plane had a cardboard box in the backseat. I opened the one in the plane I was going to fly and found that it contained a stack of logbooks, blue ones for flight logs and brown ones for maintenance and repair. They went back to the plane's first hour of flight. Somebody had said about the East Germans, "They're East Germans, but they're still Germans." It was clear that their Teutonic traits included meticulous record keeping.

The rest of the afternoon was spent in getting the planes ready. Every engine was started. Planes that needed fuel got it from those with a surplus. Tires that had gone soft were reinflated. The two planes that couldn't be flown were rolled into the barn. We worked until dark.

The next morning we arrived at the strip just as the sun was appearing above the tops of the beech trees. I climbed up into my plane and buckled my harness. The leather seat was freezing, even through my pants and insulated underwear. The wind was blowing at a steady Force 4 out of the northeast. Since we would be below electronic-navigation range, the lead plane would have to navigate by ground reference and dead reckoning. I hoped he remembered to hold his heading to the east to compensate for wind.

The plane rocked as my companion hauled himself on board. The first plane took off, trailing icy slush. The next plane lumbered onto the strip and took off. The third was already in position. I did my mag check and pulled carburetor heat. Everything stayed in the green. The third plane started its run, blowing billows of snow back over the driveway. I waited until it had cleared the ground, then moved into position. This time I remembered to hold hard left rudder, and the plane tracked straight down the runway.

The air was as smooth as a millpond. As I rose over the tree line I could see the third plane ahead of me, a red-and-black dot, lit by the rising sun, and the second plane ahead of it. I lowered the nose, eased back to twenty-two inches of manifold pressure, and squared the prop. Icy air buffeted my face. I could see daylight through gaps in the cockpit's Plexiglas, and the door shook in its frame. An hour of this, I thought, and I'll be frozen stiff.

We dashed over some forests, then a few fields, sere and brown, then across a narrow farm road. It had been a while since I had done any cropdusting, and the low-level flying was exhilarating. I forgot about being cold and concentrated on keeping the third airplane in sight. When I raised my scan to the horizon, I could see the second plane and, occasionally, the first plane, their bright red fuselages racing across the dull brown landscape.

A few minutes later, we crossed the broad flat stripe of the Berlin auto-bahn. The forests fell behind and we streaked over broad, irregular fields with strange round lakes in them. A quick glance at the chart showed that we were passing the town of Pritzwalk, the spires and roofs of the town scrolling by off my right wingtip.

Now we were about forty-five miles from the Baltic coast, and the horizon was becoming indistinct, with a brownish tint to the sky. Another autobahn. I was surprised at how populated the country was. I had thought we would be flying over open countryside, but, even avoiding the towns, we'd flown mostly over developed land. We crossed several railroad tracks. The autobahn and tracks led to Hamburg. The Baltic coast would appear in a few minutes.

We crossed a strip of trees, a swamp, then a huge area of fields. Our airstrip was on the northern edge of these fields. The third plane did a hard right, his yellow wings flashing as the sun caught them, and I eased the stick over to follow him. Then I saw the airstrip, a narrow band of smooth, level ground cut at an angle to the field's furrows. Along the edge of the field were rows of what looked like long, rectangular houses, but as I turned to follow the plane ahead I saw that they were shipping containers with BALTLINES painted on the sides. The first plane had already landed and was turning off.

For a moment, I caught a glimpse of the Baltic Sea above a thin strip of trees, a pale blue basin of water under the weak sun. The fence flashed under my wings, then the rough ground, then the end of the strip. I was too hot and too high.

I thought about going around, but decided that with heavy braking I could stop in time. My wheels touched and the plane bounded back into the air. I held the stick back. The end of the airstrip, with a black line of trees beyond it, rushed toward me. Rigid with fear, my frozen face racked in a grimace, I hauled the stick back to the stop and prayed that the plane would stall and take the ground.

Slam! We hit with all three wheels, hard, but the plane stayed planted. I jockeyed the pedals furiously. The strip wasn't even as wide as the plane's wings, and the wingtips flashed over the stubble of the summer's crops. The end of the runway was coming up fast, the trees filling my windshield, and the first of the shipping containers flashed past my right wingtip. Now I was committed. If I tried to add power and go around I would end up in the trees.

In the end I had to stand on the brakes, but we were slow enough by then that the wheels didn't start skidding. The plane shuddered to a stop about sixty feet short of the tree line, with barely enough room for the wingtip to clear it when I turned off.

The fifth plane had already landed. It must have been right on my tail. As I lowered the door, the sixth plane touched down in a neat three-pointer and crossed in front of me, pulling off with plenty of room to spare. I unbuckled my harness and climbed out. My knees were weak and I had to hold them stiff to keep from falling down.

My passenger climbed out and unsnapped his collar. "Fery close, eh?" he said. "I fink ve hit tree."

"Yes," I said, "and I would have gotten there first."

His face broke into a sudden grin. "But ve did not," he said cheerfully. "Zat is all zat matter, eh?"

I looked around. The other pilots were gathered near the nearest container, and now I could see a line of cars and trucks parked under the trees that bordered the small country lane leading to the strip. Among them were the mechanics I'd seen at the farm, in the same gray coveralls. A few men in civilian topcoats and fur hats stood among them. Heinrich was there in his trench coat, his craggy face peaked with cold. I shook hands around.

Heinrich asked me, "Any problems?"

I shook my head. "All I had to do was keep the plane ahead of me in sight. The only hard part was landing."

Heinrich translated and everybody laughed. "Yes," Heinrich said, "we didn't think you would be able to stop. You did a good job." By then the other pilots had joined us, stamping their feet on the hard ground to get circulation back. I was starting to feel my toes again, stinging. I clapped my hands together and looked around. "I guess there is nowhere to get warm," I said.

Heinrich shook his head regretfully. "Unfortunately, no. But you can get in my car and I will turn the heater on."

I shook my head. "No, I'll be all right. So what next?"

"As soon as the AN-2 gets here, the mechanics will start breaking the planes down. Then you'll fly back to Magdeburg."

Within minutes we heard a heavy drone from the southeast, at first just a vibration in the air, growing to a low throbbing. The plane appeared, approaching as slowly as a blimp, a bright blue biplane moving against the hazy blue sky.

"Here she is," Heinrich said with satisfaction. "Hugo left Magdeburg at the same time the last Bumblebee took off. I knew he would be right behind you chaps."

The huge biplane wheeled slowly onto final, the radial engine backfiring as Hugo cut power, and sank toward the end of the strip like a prehistoric beast gliding in for the kill. It lumbered to a stop well short of the end of the runway.

Up close, the plane was not in particularly good condition. The fabric was ragged on the control surfaces, and paint was peeling off the fuselage. Even the legend, painted in rolling script on the sides, "Fallschirmverein Hannover," was faded and worn through in places. A small cartoon of a stick figure under a square Para-Commander parachute hovered uncertainly beside the legend.

An airstair door on the other side of the fuselage unlatched, and the mechanics climbed down, followed by Hugo. He bustled up looking at his watch. "We must hurry so the next flight can take off by two o'clock. We do not want to get back to the farmhouse after dark."

I said, "Let's go."

I climbed up the frail metal steps into the biplane's cavernous interior and took a seat on the right-side bench. The other pilots had already strapped themselves in. Hugo followed me and pulled up the door by its cables.

Parachute static lines ran along the top of the fuselage on both sides, and a red lamp, unlit, was mounted above the airstair door. Otherwise the passenger compartment was unadorned, with the unpainted fabric skin stretched against the aluminum tubing of the airframe.

A heavy grinding sounded as the starter began to turn the giant four-bladed propeller. A couple of cylinders caught, then a couple more, then the rest joined in with a thunderous roar. We jolted over the rough ground to the end of the strip, then slowly, slowly, the giant biplane rose into the air. An hour and a half later we landed at the farmhouse.

The blond *mädchen* at the farmhouse served us coffee and American-style sandwiches with thick slices of coarse sausage in heavy brown bread. We wolfed them down, took several cups of coffee each, then bade the girl *auf Wiedersehen* and went out to the planes.

This time I was flying the second-to-last plane in the line. The ground was soggy, but I got off quickly. When I reached cruising altitude, I could see a long line of planes stretched out in front of me, a half dozen still in sight. The air got bumpy after the forests fell behind and we reached the first of the vast fields that would stretch to the Baltic Sea.

We were following almost exactly the same track we had earlier. Nothing moved on the still earth. Even the country roads we crossed seemed deserted. The air was clearer than it'd been in the morning, and I could generally keep two or three of the planes ahead in sight.

The airstrip was a beehive of activity, the air full of shouted commands and the clanking of tools. Half of the planes were already in the process of being dismantled. Only eight remained, four with their wings off. The containers were being pulled out as soon as they were stuffed.

The AN-2 landed a few minutes later, and we bundled on board. It was almost dark when we landed back at the farmhouse, and after quick hand-shakes all the way around, we got in the waiting cars and drove off to the apartment for the night. Heinrich was silent and preoccupied.

A few drifts of snow were still banked between the buildings, covered with a thin film of dirt. "Brown coal," Heinrich said shortly, as we hurried toward the apartment's door. "In January and February, the snow here is black with it."

I woke in the morning with a fierce headache and a burning, parched throat. When I spat, my phlegm was brown and thick. No wonder East Germans had the highest rate of lung cancer in the world.

It was colder on the next trip north, and my fingers and toes were numb by the time we reached the coast. A half-dozen planes were still there, their wings off, a bustle of activity around each one. The AN-2 had already landed, and we got back to the farmhouse shortly after noon.

On the last flight, the plane on my right had a hard time getting the engine started, and I was fuming with impatience by the time the mechanics managed to get it ready. By then all the other planes were well along. I hoped desperately that the pilot could find our destination without having planes ahead to follow.

By this time, the strip was a rutted, sloshy morass of chewed grass and mud, and I couldn't get the plane airborne until we'd used up most of it. However, once in the air the radial's six hundred horsepower pulled us over the trees without difficulty, and I turned north behind the other plane.

My cheeks, nose, fingers, and toes were stiff and numb by the time we landed. One of the planes hadn't made it. The plane behind him had seen him go down, trailing blue smoke; he'd put down in a field, but was uninjured. The activity at the strip was at a fever pitch, with even more mechanics at work. A dozen wings were lined up on the ground, leading edges down, and teams of mechanics were carrying them into the containers.

A few minutes later, an automobile horn honked from the lane, and we turned to see Heinrich's Mercedes bumping over the rough grass toward us.

He spoke rapidly in German, and the other pilots started hurrying toward the parked cars. "Come," Heinrich said to me, "we must hurry. Something has gone wrong. The AN-2 landed at Rostock-Laage for fuel, and the police have detained Hugo there. He called my office in Frankfurt. Thank God I checked in. My secretary says he may be under arrest."

"Under arrest for what?"

"We don't know. Come, we must go." He took my elbow to urge me along. "Don't worry," he said, in answer to my unspoken question, "this is not the East Germany of old. There are police, but no Stasi. They cannot torture us for information. Unless they can find these planes before we get them shipped out, there will be no evidence. And no one will talk, that is certain."

"Where are we going now?"

"I'm taking you to Berlin, then I'll drive up to Mecklenburg to see what can be done about Hugo. You can take the train to Frankfurt."

We got in the car and sped through the lengthening shadows of the beech trees lining the road. I asked, "Do you think the authorities will be looking for us?"

He shrugged. "I don't think so. It's very chaotic here now. No one knows who is in charge. Legally, the West German police cannot act in the East until Reunification, and the East German police have mostly deserted their posts. We won't have any trouble."

And he was right—we didn't.

After what seemed like an eternity, the Frankfurt train pulled into the station, hissing and rumbling, with the yellow lights of the coaches shining cheerfully out over the gloomy platform.

There were no formalities as we crossed into West Berlin. The streets were bright and thronging with nightclubbers and shoppers; plate-glass windows displayed diners at crystal-appointed tables in the upscale restaurants. The contrast between Western capitalism and East Bloc communism was stark and revealing.

After the conductor punched my ticket on to Frankfurt, I fell into a shallow, restless sleep with my head cradled against the back of the bench. We arrived at the Frankfurt main station shortly after midnight. I had to wait almost nine hours for my flight home. Once in the air, I fell into an exhausted sleep that lasted all the way across the Atlantic.

Eddie called sometime later to say there was a problem with the payment for the planes. I knew he was selling them to a Venezuelan, so I wasn't surprised. "It's something about the wire transfer," he said. "I'm starting to get pissed off. I'm supposed to send Heinrich his money this afternoon."

"Where are they?"

"The planes? In some place called LaGura. They arrived yesterday."

"La Guaira? That's a port near Caracas. The containers are still in bond, I hope?"

"What does that mean?"

"In customs bond. They can't leave the port until you release them. You haven't done that, I hope."

"I sent something to the shipping company this morning that said the containers could be taken out of the port."

"That's taking them out of bond. Christ, you'd better call the forwarder and tell him to hold everything until you've been paid."

"But the money's already been sent. My bank got the Swift Code."

"Better call your freight forwarder. That money should've arrived seconds after the Swift Code was issued. If they get those planes out before you get paid . . ."

"I see what you're saying. I'll call you back." Twenty minutes later he called again. "I'm fucked. The planes are out of the port, the money was never sent. The Swift Code was a fake. The guy that sent it has disappeared."

Eddie hired me to go down to Venezuela to try to find the planes, but by that time they were long gone. It had been a scam from the beginning. The consignment address was a closed-down warehouse. A guy in a store-bought uniform had been posted there to tell the truck drivers where to drop the containers.

I called Eddie and told him, "The warehouse owner—if he's ever found—will say, 'I don't know what you're talking about. That place has been closed for years.'"

Eddie spat in his tobacco can and didn't say anything.

"I'm curious," I went on. "Why'd you and Heinrich send those planes to Venezuela without getting a deposit? Half up front, something like that?"

"I made Miguel—the buyer—put the purchase price in escrow."

"In the same bank that sent the fake Swift Code?"

"Yeah."

There wasn't much that could be said after that. It was a neat scam. All it took was a man inside the bank to send a fake fax confirming the escrow amount and a telex to Eddie's bank with a Swift Code that didn't exist.

The last time I talked to Eddie was about ten years ago. He was still killing bugs in Yuma.

CHAPTER FIVE

ADRIFT ON THE *PERCIVAL J*

ONE DAY, I got a call from a man in Miami who had bought a small freighter in Seattle. He wanted to get into Caribbean shipping but knew nothing about ships. I agreed to go to Seattle to put the ship into service.

The ship's broker, a big, square woman named Annie Lindgren, met me at Sea-Tac Airport and drove me to the vessel, docked at a commercial marina in the suburb of Ballard, on the north shore of Salmon Bay. After spending a couple of days taking inventory and surveying the ship's general condition, I called some crewing agents to source the crew. One of the agents was a Nicaraguan woman in Miami named Naomi Gonzales, who sent me a strapping Trinidadian named Ramesh Chawla, a dark-skinned, pleasant-faced young man with a shock of wild hair and a heavy black beard that started under his lower eyelids and continued down into his shirt.

Ramesh came on as an able-bodied seaman, or AB, but he actually had had no experience on freighters. He had worked on his father's fishing boat and as a deckhand on tugboats in the Trinidad oilfields, and had gotten a green card to work in the United States, but he had only been in Miami for a couple of months, looking for work, when Naomi sent him to Seattle.

Ramesh was a brilliant young man, able to do complicated mathematical equations in his head. He was also stable, responsible, and even-tempered, and I came to rely on him to get things done on board when I was away. He could have been a doctor or a university professor, or anything he put his mind to, but his ambition in life was to become a ship captain.

After getting the *Cathy Jean*—named for my client's wife—out of Seattle, I returned to marine surveying in New Orleans. But by the fall of that year I was getting restless again. I was getting hungry for action. It finally came in November, in the form of a call from a man with a thick Caribbean English accent.

"Dis de mon dat steal ship from de port?" he demanded.

"Excuse me?"

"Dis is Max Hardberger, no true? De man what took the *Patric M* out of Venezuela?"

"This is Max Hardberger," I admitted. "How can I help you?"

"My name is Jack Jukes. I got a friend name Otto Volmer. He tol' me you was de mon w'at done dat."

"Ah, yes," I said, "how's Otto doing?" Otto was a chief engineer; he used to be a good one until rum addled his brain. I first saw him one day while I was lounging on the fantail of my ship in the Miami River, and he was standing on the afterdeck of a small ship that'd just come across from Germany. We had waved to each other, and later I went across to say hello. We'd become good friends, in the way it sometimes happens. He never went back to Germany, and it was sad to watch him descend, over the months and years, into alcoholism and disrepute.

At this time he was occasionally working on Haitian freighters—the only ones he could get jobs on—and he sometimes called me to talk over old times. He was a small man about sixty, with pipestem arms and a big, swollen belly.

"Not too bad," Jack answered. "He was in Nassau last week, you know, working on one of dem banana boats. He tol' me all about how you took dat ship out. I read about dat in de magazine, but I didn't know who did it."

"If you see Otto again," I said, "tell him hello for me."

"I will do dat," Jack promised, "but tell me dis . . . I got a freighter, four t'ousand ton, dat the shipya'd in Trinidad want to steal from me. Can you get de ship out for me?"

"Which shipyard? Hamidad?"

"Yas, mon, dat de ya'd. You know it?"

"Yessir. That's a bad yard for stealing ships. Let me guess . . . They told you one price, and when they finished they wanted twice as much."

"Twice?" he exclaimed. "T'ree time, mon! Dey quote me t'ree hunnert t'ousand dollar, and when I went to get de ship, dey want one million dollar. One million U.S. dollar!"

"I'm not surprised. You didn't have your own superintendent there?"

"No, mon, I trus' dem. De repair was easy . . . jus' de tank top and some shell plating."

This was the oldest scam in the Caribbean. I'm sure buccaneers of the Spanish Main used to quote pirate captains one price for scraping and painting their hulls, then outpirate the pirates when they presented the final bill.

"That yard still run by Indians?" I asked.

"Yas," he said, and gave a rueful chuckle. "An' wild Indian at dat."

I had meant East Indians, of course. Most large businesses in Trinidad are run by East Indians whose families immigrated many generations ago. The East Indians of Trinidad, like East Indians throughout the Caribbean, are known for sharp practices, but the management of the Hamidad Shipyard was especially notorious. Many an unwary shipowner has sent his ship to that yard, failing to send a good superintendent to watch over the work, only to find on return that he has donated his ship to the yard.

"How long since the work ended?" I asked.

"T'ree month now. I jes' recover from my heart attack."

"You mean, when you found out what the bill was going to be?"

"Yas, mon. Dat de trut'. When I year w'at dey gonna cha'ge me, I fall down on the floor of the office wit' a heart attack. I had to come home by ambulance flight."

"Is that the truth? I thought you were kidding."

"No, mon, dat the God trut'. I an old man, you know. Sixty-five year old. When de mon tell me I mus' pay one million dollar to get my ship back, I feel a pain like a knife in my heart. De nex' t'ing I know, I in the hospital wit' tube in my arm. De dactor say I lucky to be alive."

"Have you talked to Hamidad since then?"

"Yas, I call dem, try to settle de bill. I offer dem five hunnert t'ousand, all I hab, but de mon, dat Captain Rami, he say no. He say I mus' pay de whole one million. Den I get a letter from a lawyer in Port-o'-Spain sayin' dey gonna sell my ship for de debt. I didn't know what to do. I don't hab one million U.S. dollar."

I thought about it. The Hamidad Shipyard was located on the southern side of the northern peninsula that stretches westward from Port-of-Spain. I had been there once before, trying to buy a ship for a client. Undoubtedly, that ship had fallen victim to the same scheme, except in that case my client was unconcerned about the previous owner's loss and just wanted a bargain. The ship had not been in good shape, though, and I had recommended against buying her.

"All right," I said, "I'll go down and take a look. It'll take at least four days—one day to get down, two days to check out the situation, and one day to come back. If you pay my expenses and four days' day rate, I'll see what can be done."

"Dat wonderful, mon," Jack said fervently. "Otto said dat you're de mon to get dat ship out. I'll send de money raght now."

"There's one other thing. If I get the ship out, you'll still owe the amount you agreed on. If you don't pay it, the yard can have the ship arrested in any port where it can be found."

"I do it, Cap, I promise. Jus' get de ship out so dem bastids can't hol' it hostage."

I gave him the amount to wire me and we hung up. I was on the kitchen phone, and my wife had come in behind me. She looked at me curiously. "What was that all about?"

"A little job," I said. "A guy with a ship in trouble in Trinidad. If he sends the money tomorrow, I'll probably leave Tuesday."

"You seem awfully happy to be leaving home."

"No, darling, I'm not happy to be leaving home, but I'm happy to have work."

She raised her eyebrows. "You've been getting marine surveying work."

I grimaced. "Draft surveys. Off-hire surveys. Watching iron ore get unloaded. That's not real work. Real work is saving ships."

"You just want to get away from home," she said. I opened my mouth, but I couldn't get an answer out in time. By then she had gone to her office and shut the door.

I went to my office and got out a nautical chart of the lower Caribbean. There were islands south of the Hamidad dock, but the chart's scale wasn't large enough to tell much else. I could remember the shipyard vaguely, and getting a crew on board the ship undetected, much less starting a generator and the main engine, was going to be a challenge.

I didn't realize it at the time, but the phone call I had received was the beginning of my career as a professional ship extractor. I'd already sneaked three ships out of port without clearances—two as captain and one as port captain. But this was my first time to do it for a client.

Caribbean shipping is a small world, and word was getting around.

I had a hard time getting through Trinidadian customs. I'd told the immigration woman that I was there to inspect a ship, and she immediately demanded to see my seaman's visa and work permit. However, after two hours of interrogation by a succession of surly officials, I finally got my passport stamped and left the terminal for a downtown hotel.

The next morning I took a taxi to Chagaramas. The road runs along a rocky, precipitous coastline, and when you come around a sharp bend in the road, halfway up a steep mountainside, you suddenly see a line of boatyards spread out below you, as if in miniature. Before we reached the boatyards we passed a small, resort-type hotel on the right, set behind a wide, grassy lawn dotted with primitive statues of nude women carved from limestone boulders. I told the driver to pull in.

The tourist season hadn't started yet, and the hotel had a room available—actually, a bungalow, as the hotel consisted of an open-air reception area and bar, with a scattering of pastel-colored bungalows stretching back to a raw limestone cliff. I put my bag in my bungalow and went back to the taxi, telling the driver that I wanted to see what was west of there.

We followed the road past the boatyards and around the tip of a steep, rocky point covered with scrub brush. The Hamidad Shipyard appeared on the left. I let the driver take me halfway up the next point, where the road climbed a grade to go over a hump, and told him I wanted to get out.

He craned his head to stare at me. "W'at you want to get out year for?" he demanded. "Dere not'ing year, mon."

"I know," I said. "I just want to look out over the ocean for a while."

He shrugged. "Okay, den. Dat will be twenty dollar U.S."

I paid him and got out. He drove off trailing blue smoke. I waited until there was no traffic on the road, then scrambled up the hillside. The bramble bushes and steep slope made climbing difficult, but I soon found a relatively comfortable seat on a flat-topped rock.

I sat there until early evening. The sun was hot, and burned pleasantly on my forehead and arms. The steady trade wind out of the northeast blew over the mountains behind me and cooled the sweet tropical air. Small lizards—fat, gray, horned little dragons about four inches long—scurried over the rocky soil at my feet, cocked insolent eyes up at me, and darted away.

I could see workers at the yard, small figures in coveralls moving slowly around on the deck of a ship being readied to go into the floating drydock. However, when work stopped at 5 P.M. and the workers streamed into the narrow parking lot between the office building and the road, they still hadn't gotten the ship into the dock. I hoped her owner had a superintendent there.

My client's ship was the last one in a row of three ships tied alongside the quay, at the eastern end of the yard's property. I could tell it was the *Percival J,* Jack's ship, because he had faxed me a copy of the general-arrangement plan, and she was the only ship at the dock with union-purchase derricks.

I dusted off the seat of my pants and made my way down the hill to the road. There was a bus stop across from the yard, and while I was sitting on the bench, a taxi came up from the direction of Port-of-Spain and let out a watchman in a faded gray uniform. He wasn't carrying a pistol.

I got in the taxi and told the driver to take me to the Gasparillo Hotel.

That night, I went back to my lookout spot. The yard's quay stretched out before me, well lit, but the ships alongside the quay were dark and cast giant black shadows out over the still water. The moon had not yet risen, but in the starlight I could see the dark humps of the two offshore islands, Gaspar Grande and its little sister to the north, Gasparillo.

A couple of hours passed, and I never saw a guard patrolling. The moon was rising over the rocky hills, silvering the placid sea and dimming the anchor lights of yachts riding at their moorings.

Shortly after one o'clock I gave up and picked my way carefully down the hill. The moon, now high overhead, showed me the way. I would have taken a taxi, but none came along, so I trudged the two miles back to the hotel. The hotel's bar was closed, with a bamboo cover let down over the counter.

Nine o'clock the next morning found me getting out of a taxi in front of the shipyard's front gate. I told the guard I was going to see the manager, and he waved me past without formality. The first floor of the main building was open, a cluttered warehouse filled with machine tools and ship parts. Two men near the roll-up quayside door were measuring, in an unhurried way, a length of steel pipe. A small dirty sign said OFFICE, with an arrow pointing up a narrow flight of steel steps.

The receptionist was a slim black woman of middle age, with straight orange hair and a lot of faux gold jewelry. I told her I wanted to see the manager. A few minutes later a short, dark Indian man, about fifty, wearing a wrinkled business suit, came out of the door behind her.

His name was Captain Rami, and yes, he told me, the yard was interested in selling the *Percival J*. He guided me back to a cluttered office overlooking the quay and gestured toward a metal folding chair. I gave him my card and told him I was a marine surveyor sent by a prospective purchaser. I worried for a few moments that he might have heard about the *Patric M* extraction and recognize my name—there'd been an article in *Florida Shipper Magazine* about the incident—but he didn't. He put my card on his desk.

"How did you hear about the ship?" he asked. "We haven't put her on the market yet."

"I heard about it on the Miami River. A guy named Bob Colton told me." I really did know a ship trader named Bob Colton, but he was in England at the moment, and, I hoped, unreachable.

"Interesting," Captain Rami said. "Actually, the ship won't be available until the auction on the twenty-ninth."

"Okay, I'll tell my client, and maybe he'll send me back to bid on her." I stood up.

The Indian raised a small hand with thick, stubby fingers. His skin was black, but his palm was as pink as a baboon's bottom. "It will be better to buy the ship directly from us." He lowered his voice. "The yard has a claim of one million dollars against her. No one will bid that."

"For a four-thousand tonner built in '71? No, it's not worth that."

"But you should take a look at her. She's a good ship. I can give you our drydocking report. She should be able to get her class certificates with no trouble."

"Can I look at her now?"

"Surely. I'll send one of our chaps with you." He pressed a button on the phone and asked someone named Lal to come up to his office.

"Is your client ready to buy?" he asked, while we waited.

"Yes, certainly. I've already inspected a couple of ships for him, but the prices weren't right."

"What's his budget?"

"It depends on the ship. If the—what's her name, the *Percival*?—if the ship's in good shape, she should be worth half a million. My client can pay that."

Up went the hand again, showing a soiled shirt cuff. "Oh, no, we would have to get more than that."

"Well, let me take a look. Will you be here for another hour or so?"

"Of course. Please stop by after your inspection and we'll talk."

Lal arrived, a skinny Indian boy of about twenty. Captain Rami told him to escort me around the *Percival J*.

The *Percival J* was at the end of the quay, with a battered old shore gangway leading up to her main deck. The ship was empty of cargo and unballasted, so the deck was high above our heads.

The deck was littered with bits of rope and pieces of steel left over from cutouts. The ship heaved restlessly against her ropes in the low backswell. I led the Indian boy aft to an accommodations door. It opened with a screech of steel hinges. There was no power on board, but he had a flashlight.

I made a cursory inspection of the accommodations, but I was most interested in the engine room. We went downstairs, below the lower deck and into the machinery space, Lal's flashlight making darting, grotesque shadows of the pipes and railings.

The main engine looked complete, and the engine room seemed orderly and well fitted. I walked around the engine's casing, checking for parts or pieces that might have been removed by the yard. Sometimes people will take the air-start lever off to keep an engine from being started. It's not totally effective, as a jury lever can be welded up from flat bar, but it can cause a delay.

These Indians were cleverer than that. The lever was there, but when I followed the air-start tube to where the valve should have been, I found that the entire valve, including its housing, had been removed from the casing. The end of the tube dangled free and a piece of red rag had been stuck in the hole in the casing.

That was a problem. You can't make an air-start valve out of flat bar. If I couldn't find the valve on board, Jack would have to get a replacement from a parts broker, and it would almost certainly have to come from Europe.

I didn't say anything to Lal, but I looked carefully around the engine room and never found the valve. It had either been hidden well or taken off the ship. I went down to the lowest level, where the great base of the engine stood, its man-sized doors giving access to the connecting rods and oil sump. I found the engine's data plate, a large brass plate with the manufacturer's name, Wartsila, cast into it. I copied the serial number on a scrap of paper.

The main engine's day tank was only about half full. That was ominous, since ordinarily the engineer would top up the day tank every day. I thought about sounding the fuel tanks, but a buyer wouldn't normally do that.

After a perfunctory look around the rest of the ship, glancing through the open hatches into the holds, I nodded to Lal and we went down the gangway. Back at the office, I found Captain Rami on the phone, arguing with someone over money. I waited outside until he hung up and motioned me in.

"Not so bad," I said. "My client might be interested."

"What do you think he'll pay?"

"I don't know. Maybe five."

He shook his head. "That's not enough. Why, that ship's worth eight hundred thousand if she's worth a penny."

"Is that what you're asking?"

"We don't own her yet," he said quickly. "We shouldn't be negotiating until we own her, of course." He got up and closed the door, then sat back down and picked up my card. "So you're an independent surveyor?"

"That's right."

"How well do you know your client?"

I lifted my eyebrows. Even for a pirate that was bold. He covered by saying, "I mean, do you know if he's really got the money to buy this ship?"

I played him like a suspicious bass. "I don't know him at all. I've inspected some ships for him, that's all." I was getting hungry and looking forward to an early lunch; I hoped the pitch would be coming soon.

It did. He put my card down. "You could make a lot of money off this sale, you know."

I cocked my head.

"Let's say your survey finds that the ship is worth seven . . . eight hundred thousand. There could be fifty thousand in it for you."

"I couldn't have Luther—my client—find out. That would be very bad for me."

He shook his head. "That would be bad for both of us. But there's no reason why he should. It would be strictly between you and me. Nobody here at the yard would know."

"How could I be sure of getting paid?"

"We can hide you here. As soon as your buyer arrives and pays for the ship, we will take out your share and give it to you. Mr., em, Luther will never know you're here."

"That could work," I said.

He pushed his chair back to show that our meeting was at an end. "Very well, then. The auction is next Friday. Call me Thursday afternoon. Are you flying out today?"

"Yes," I said. "I have a flight this evening."

We stood up and he shook my hand. "I'm sure you won't be saying anything to anyone about our little arrangement, then," he said.

I blinked innocently. "I have no idea what you're talking about."

We gave each other conspiratorial smirks, and I left.

* * *

Back in my hotel room, I called Jack and told him what I had found. When I told him about Captain Rami's plan to bid the shipyard's claim at the upcoming auction, he groaned. "Jesus Christ and all de saint! Captain Max, can you get de ship out before den?"

"I can try," I said. I told him about the missing air-start valve. "You'll have to order one right away."

"I have a parts broker in Hamburg. He answer his phone at all hour. I will call him now."

"Do that. I'll call you back in twenty minutes."

I went down to the bar and bought a beer to take back to the bungalow. The wind was still steady out of the northeast, a good sign. When I called Jack again, he said that his broker was going to call Wartsila's Hamburg office as soon as it opened.

"It'll still be tricky," I warned him. "That shipyard is very quiet at night, so we can't start the engine alongside. Even if we get the air-start valve fitted without making any noise, we'll still have to start a generator before we can start the main engine. You know how loud generators are. Unless the night watchman is passed-out drunk, he'll come running."

"What about a tugboat? Can't you hire a tugboat to come and pull her out?"

I thought for a minute. "It would have to be a good-sized tugboat. Maybe two thousand horsepower. And you know tugboats are loud as hell. Remember, we've got to make it twelve miles to international water. And there's a coast guard station only a couple of miles away."

"Yes," he said sadly, "I know war dat is. You mus' pass it to get to the ya'd."

"I have an idea," I said. "Do you have a crew ready to take over the ship?"

"Yas, mon! I got de crew from the ship raddy to go, for true. Dey're a good bonch of Jamaicans. Mos' of dem war on de ship already."

"And the chief engineer? Was he the old chief engineer?"

"Yas, mon. An' a damn' good chief, too."

"All right, I think something can be done. We'll have to send them to Venezuela. It's too hard getting a crew into Trinidad, and I know a man with a tugboat in Puerto la Cruz."

"W'at you planning to do, Cap?"

"We're going to have to cut the dock lines and let her drift to international waters. That's the only thing I can think of."

He whistled. "You t'ink dat work?"

"Yeah, it'll work if the wind holds out of the northeast. It's pretty steady this time of year."

"Okay, den, Cap, I'll get dat sta't valve coming."

We hung up and I called Naomi Gonzales to ask if she knew where Ramesh Chawla was. She said she had gotten him a job on a small Haitian freighter that had been held up in Miami. She offered to take a ride down to the river to see if he was still on board. I gave her the hotel's number and asked her to have him call me as soon as possible.

Then I called an agent friend in Puerto la Cruz, about a hundred miles from Chaguaramas on the Venezuelan coast. During my days as a port captain for Cartones del Sud, I had discharged a load of wastepaper in La Cruz, and the agent and I had gotten to be friends. He was an expatriate Belgian named Jan Merck, a big man with thick ears and a blond crew-cut.

Jan was an avid beer drinker, and every day after my ship finished discharging, he would give me a ride to my hotel, where we would toss back a few in the hotel bar and swap sea stories. He'd spent his youth as an oiler, then engineer, on German-owned ships, and although he hadn't been to sea in some twenty years, he remembered those days with great fondness.

"So," he said, after his secretary had gotten him on the line, "Captain Max, are you keeping your pants on these days?"

I grimaced. He wasn't the only one who wouldn't let me forget that incident in the La Cruz hotel when I lost my pants. The girls at Cartones del Sud still laughed about it whenever they saw me.

I had gone to sleep one night in my fifth-floor room on the Puerto la Cruz *malecón*, with my blue jeans lying on the floor next to the bed. It had been a hard day, and I guess I was sleeping heavily.

The next morning I woke up, got ready to go to work, and couldn't find my pants. That had never happened to me before. I could clearly remember taking the elevator up from the hotel bar after our drinking session, and I certainly had my pants on then.

Then I noticed that the window was open. I stuck my head out and saw a narrow ledge about three feet below the sill, not more than eight inches wide, running along the wall of the building. The ledge was tarred, and footsteps showed clearly on the ledge between my window and the next.

So I went down and told the manager, a nervous little man with a pompadour and hands that fluttered like birds. He called the police, and two men came to the hotel on motorcycles. I led them to my room and one of them looked out the window and at the ledge. Then they went to the next room and knocked on the door, with the manager and me behind them.

The two young men in the room had been sleeping. One of them opened the door a crack, saw the policeman, and tried to shut it. The policeman shoved it open. They were both young Venezuelans, but I don't remember much else about them. The policemen searched their clothes and found three U.S. hundred-dollar bills in the tip of a shoe.

There was a brief interrogation, accompanied by some heavy, short punches to the men's necks delivered by a forearm—the policemen were obviously experienced in not leaving marks—and further searching revealed a small sack of *basuco* in their bags. *Basuco* is a garbage drug made from leftover coca leaf after the cocaine's been extracted. It's illegal in Venezuela, and the discovery prompted more beatings. The hotel manager and I went out to the hallway to wait.

Eventually a squad car was called and the two men were brought out, dazed and bruised, in handcuffs. As the policemen were leading them down the hall I called, "What about my money?"

The policeman who had discovered the three hundred-dollar bills pulled them out of his pocket and held them up. *"Evidencia,"* he proclaimed proudly, and put them back in his pocket. He followed his colleagues and the prisoners to the elevator. I never did get the money back, of course.

I told Jan, "No, no, I've managed to hang on to my pants ever since." Then I told him what I was planning to do.

"No problem, Captain," Jan said. "I can give you the name of a ship I have here that is laid up, so the crew can tell the immigration man at the Caracas airport that they are coming to it."

"Do you still have that little tugboat? It doesn't have to tow the ship. It just has to meet the ship with the crew on board, and transfer fuel if there's not enough on board."

"Well," he said slowly, "I still have the *Dos Hermanas,* but I can't send her into Trinidadian waters for this. I don't want to lose her, and I don't want the crew to go to jail."

"How about meeting in international water? There's what, thirty or forty miles between Venezuela and Trinidad in the Gulf of Paria. She can stand by in international water."

"Yes, I suppose," he said slowly, then, briskly, "Yes, we can do it. But it'll be expensive."

We soon came to an agreement, and I promised to have the ship's owner call him to arrange payment. "So let me get this straight," he said. "You're really planning to cut the dock lines yourself and let the ship drift to international waters?"

"That's right. Me and a Trinidadian boy I know. A good kid."

"Better not get caught, *amigo.* I hear prison in Trinidad is very bad. You'd be better off in a Venezuelan *jusgado.*"

I didn't believe that, although I was sure a Trinidadian prison wouldn't be Club Fed. "There's no other way to do it," I said. "It's too quiet there to start a generator, and you've got to start a generator to start the main engine."

"Well, it's your decision. I hope you're getting a lot of money."

But of course I wasn't getting a lot of money—just my regular day rate times four days. "It's the fucking principle of the thing, Jan. Those Hamidad fuckers have been getting away with this for too long. I'm gonna teach 'em a lesson."

He grunted. "I hope you don't learn one yourself. Okay, I'll wait for that guy's call."

We hung up and I called Jack again. "De crew ready, Cap'n," he said. "War you say I mus' send dem?"

"Puerto la Cruz, Venezuela. I've got a buddy there with a tugboat. You need to call him now to make arrangements." And I gave him the number.

After that, I lay down on the bed and drifted in and out of sleep for a while. I wasn't sure that the ship would clear the offshore islands under the press of the wind, even if it held steady from the northeast, but I couldn't think of anything else to do to get the ship out of port. And I'd learned long before that if you can't do the impossible, you have to try the improbable. I knew one thing: I wasn't going to let that snake-oil salesman Captain Rami steal Mr. Jukes's ship without a fight.

Finally, in midafternoon, I got up and walked down the street to a little chicken shack. Sitting next to half a dozen local boys—dreadlocked Rastas in ragged clothes—I had a plate of jerk chicken—spicy shredded chicken meat and beans on rice—washed down by a cold Polar.

After lunch, I walked back to the hotel. The sun was sinking in the west. A tattered Trinidad-and-Tobago flag on a pole in front of the yacht club jerked and snapped in the wind.

The hotel's receptionist called to me as I passed her counter. "Telephone call for you," she said in her musical Caribbean accent, waving a piece of paper.

Ramesh had called. I called him back from the room phone. "Hello, Captain," he said. "It's good to hear from you. I hope you have a good job for me. I'm sick of dese Haitian freighters."

"I've got a job for you right now, in Trinidad. How quick can you get here?"

"In Trinidad? I can be on de flight tomorrow marnin', get in 'bout noon."

"Good. I'll call the client and get him to make arrangements for a PTA ticket. Just go to the American Airlines counter and it'll be there for you."

"What kind of ship is dis?"

"Well, it's not a regular hitch." I described the situation briefly. "There'll be good money in it, though. I'll see that you get at least a thousand, and if we get the ship out, I'll get the client to give you another thousand as a bonus."

"I can use de money, for true. But after dat, you don't have a job on a ship for me?"

"No, I'm sorry, but I've been out of the business for a while, doing marine surveying. I'll call around and see what's up, though."

"Yas, mon, I'm ready to move op to big ship now. I'm sick of dese lee Haitian boats."

"One other thing. Do you know anybody on the island—in the

Chaguaramas area—who can rent us a small boat? We will need to get on board the ship from the water, since the yard is fenced off."

"Of course, Captain. You know my fadder is a fisherman. We can use his boat."

"Would he be willing to drive it for us? He'll get paid well for doing it, and there won't be much danger for him."

"Sure he will do it, Captain. I will call him now to tell him dat I'm coming home."

"Be sure to tell him not to say anything about this. We can't afford to have Hamidad Shipyard find out what we're up to."

We hung up and I called Jack again. I gave him Ramesh's name and he promised to make arrangements for the flight. He had already made arrangements for the Jamaican crew to arrive in Caracas the next day. They would reach Puerto la Cruz that afternoon. We set the rendezvous for 0600 hours on Sunday morning. I gave him a rough estimate of the money I would need on my end, and he agreed to wire it by Western Union.

I took a taxi to the nearest Western Union office, in a shopping mall near the Port of Spain waterfront, and got back to Chaguaramas at dusk. After supper in the restaurant, I waited in the bungalow until nine o'clock, before going on another reconnaissance of the Hamidad Shipyard. Still no sign of the watchman.

The next morning, Jack called to say that Wartsila had shipped the air-start valve to New York via Lufthansa, then on to Caracas via American. I called Jan and gave him the waybill number, and he promised to have a man pick it up at the Maiquetia airport on arrival.

Jan and I agreed that his tugboat would meet the ship about thirteen miles off the Trinidad coast, to the southwest, with the understanding that the tug's crew would be watching for the ship over a distance of several miles to either side. We agreed on flashlight signals between the vessels, in order to keep radio silence.

Jan called again in the afternoon. Jack's crew had arrived at the Caracas airport and were on their way to Puerto la Cruz. The tugboat had been bunkered with an extra fifteen tons of diesel to pump to the ship if necessary.

At 4 P.M., Ramesh showed up at my hotel door, wearing a Miami

Dolphins T-shirt and a pair of running shorts, his feet in flip-flops. He had gotten a haircut since the last time I saw him, but his thick black beard sprouted as heavily as ever, descending from his eyes down into his T-shirt. Ramesh was the hairiest man I've ever known. He even shaved the backs of his hands, "to keep from looking like a gorilla," he once told me.

"Come on," I said, "let's go down to the bar for a beer."

"Is it a good idea to be seen togedder?"

"Sure. Nobody here has any reason to suspect what we're up to, and after it's all over it won't matter."

"But you told me you already talked to somebody at de shipya'd about it. Don't dey know your name dere?"

"Yeah, I gave Captain Rami my name, and I'm sure he'll figure out that I had something to do with it, but I have a flight leaving Port-of-Spain for Santo Domingo on Sunday morning. I'll be long gone before they can put two and two together."

"I hope you're right," he said.

A sunburned couple sat at one of the tables in the bar, a youngish man and woman, obviously Americans, probably down to charter a boat. Ramesh and I sat at the bar with cold Polars.

"So," I asked, "what's the news on the *Cathy Jean*? She been in Miami recently?"

"Man," he said, "dat ship always have problem. Dat crazy American owner, he always fight wit' everybody. He fight wit' de crew, he fight wit' de charterer, he fight wit' de customs and immigration, he fight wit' de agent, he fight wit' everybody. I t'ink dat de most hated man on the Miami River."

"So what ship are you on now?"

"No boat now. I got off de *Dieu Mon Berger* a mont' ago because de owner no pay. I been living wit' my sister in Plantation ever since. It was lucky Miss Naomi was able to find me. I'm ready to go to work, I tell you."

I took a sip. "So where's your dad's boat? Will he be bringing it up tomorrow?"

"It already year. He brought it op today. It's at a dock n'ar de coast guard station."

"Is that where we'll go on board?"

"Yassir, we can do dat anytime."

"Where's your family live?"

"Dey live in Tunapuna, on de odder side of Port of Spain. I wanted to get here as soon as I could, so I haven't been home yet. I go soon." He downed his drink and we went to the bungalow to get his bag. After he left, I took a shower and started a Ross MacDonald novel. I'd read it a couple of times before, but it's one of those books that get better with every reading.

Ramesh arrived at the hotel at about ten the next morning, in his sister's old Nissan Sunny, and we drove to a small, decrepit concrete pier a few hundred yards from the Chaguaramas coast guard station. It was hidden from the station by a rocky outcropping covered with thick scrub brush. There were several fishing boats bobbing in the backswell along the pier, held off the naked concrete by rubber tires strung on a frayed and kinked steel cable.

Ramesh's father was a wrinkled, energetic old man, covered with gray fur like a mountain goat, a smaller incarnation of his son, wearing a threadbare boiler suit cut off at the knees, his hairy calves as muscular as a hod-carrier's. The old man bounded up from the boat's deck as we approached and pumped my hand. "Call me Mamo," he cried. "My's name's Mamul-shahid, but everybody calls me Mamo."

Mamo's boat was a high-prowed dory about thirty feet long, with a small house aft and a welded exhaust pipe sprouting from the roof. The boat was as old as its owner, the gunwales splintered from many hard contacts with docks. The deck forward was low behind high bulwarks, piled with bundles of brown nets bordered by orange floats. Mamo led Ramesh and me aft along the narrow side deck to the house's only door, in the rear.

There was just enough room in the house for the steering station and a small table with benches on each side. A counter against the port bulkhead held a washbasin and a propane-fueled camp stove with a battered tin coffee percolator on it. Mamo lit the stove and, although I protested I'd had my coffee for the morning, he insisted on brewing up. "Aie," he said, "you a seaman, no true? For a seaman, always time for coffee." Ramesh winked at me.

Over our heavy china cups of coffee, Mamo spread out a torn and water-stained chart of the Gulf of Paria. "Here de shipya'd," he said, thumping the chart with a horny forefinger. "And raght bastards dey are. Your friend is not the first 'un to come crossways wit' dem, I guarantee. Many ship I see dere, mont' and mont' after de work is done, dat mus' hab been seized by dem pirate, an' de gober'ment won't do a t'ing 'cause dat rascal dat call hisself Captain Rami, he pay plenty money to de gober'ment to let him be. Men like dat Captain Rami make me shame of our people."

I drew my finger along a course downwind from the yard. "Ramesh told you what we plan to do? We're going to cut the dock lines at night and let the ship drift out to sea. There's a tugboat coming from Venezuela with a crew. Also, I don't know how much fuel is on board, so the tug'll bring a few tons so the ship can get to Curaçao to refuel."

He glanced out the starboard window, a grimy old ship's porthole, and rubbed his whiskery chin. "Don't know, Cap," he muttered. "If de wind stay lak dis, prolly okay. But dese island"—he tapped Gaspar Grande and Gasparillo islands—"dere a reef between dese island. If de wind come more from de nort', de ship maybe hit dat reef."

"Does the reef go west of Gasparillo? The chart shows twelve fathoms here."

"Yas, dat deep water, deeper dan twel' faddom. Hit prolly okay, 'cause de current run from eas' to wes', prolly carry de ship wes' of Gasparillo." He clapped me on the shoulder. "Dat the correck t'ing, mon. You fock dem pirate op good, eh?"

I gave him a confident grin and took another sip of the bitter coffee. "Yas, mon," I said.

I wasn't as confident as I sounded, but my long experience in leading men into dicey situations had taught me to keep my qualms to myself.

Mamo started the boat's engine and we pulled away from the pier, headed west. The exhaust was loud. I shuddered at the thought of bringing that heavy rumble into the quiet water fronting the shipyard.

I studied the coast guard station with Mamo's battered binoculars as we passed, about two hundred yards offshore. There were two boats at the station's concrete pier, one a small, outboard-powered launch, unarmed, and the other a large patrol boat, about a hundred feet long, with a machine gun on the bow. Both of the boats looked in good repair and ready for sea.

We cruised past the yacht club and boatyards, rounded the next point, and reached the Hamidad yard. I had Mamo slow to an idle. A shrill whistle sounded from the shore, cutting through the engine's low, loping rumble. It was noon. The workers in sight, clad in gray coveralls, started moving toward the roll-up door in the main building. Cars started out of the parking lot, heading toward Port of Spain. So the shipyard operated only half a day on Saturday.

I turned the glasses toward the western tip of Gaspar Grande island, directly south of the yard. The wind was still out of the northeast, and if it kept its bearing I was pretty sure it would carry the *Percival J* clear of the island. The water here was blue and deep.

I had Mamo turn the boat toward the southwest, following the route I was hoping the ship would take. As the boat idled along, I watched carefully for any difference between its heading and the course made good, but the current was slack and the boat seemed to track fairly straight. We puttered past Gasparillo, a steep, uninhabited islet covered with scrub brush, and then past the western tip of Gaspar Grande, a much larger island with a scattering of brightly painted houses on its slopes.

Once past Gaspar Grande, I stepped into the house and checked the chart. International law says that a country's national waters extend twelve miles from the nearest territory, and any islands owned by a country are part of its territory, so we had to be at least twelve miles from Gaspar Grande. I marked the point on the chart and used a chipped, yellowed set of parallel rules to take off its latitude and longitude.

Back at the dock, I gave Mamo two hundred dollars so he could buy a truck muffler and stick it on the end of his exhaust stack. Ramesh still had his sister's car, but it was already one-thirty by the time we had the boat secured to the dock, and they had to hurry to the parts store before it closed at two. I gave Ramesh another two hundred dollars to buy a handheld VHF walkie-talkie and a couple of machetes, and took a taxi to the hotel.

Jan was out of his office, but he had a phone in his car, and his answering service put me through. He said the tug was on its way with the crew and air-start valve on board, and the captain had instructions to check in every six hours by SSB radio. I gave him the coordinates for the rendezvous. "If the ship doesn't show up," I said, "just tell the tug to steam back to Puerto la Cruz and I'll call you in the morning. I can call the tug by VHF if necessary."

"It's too far for the tug to come back here," he said. "I already told the captain that if the ship doesn't make the rendezvous, go to Guiria—that's on the other side of the gulf from Chaguaramas—and wait there for further instructions."

"Excellent."

I called home, but the answering machine picked up. I left a message for my wife that all was well and that I hoped to be home in two days.

By late afternoon, a low overcast had covered the sky, rushing across the humped spine of the peninsula and out over the turbulent Gulf of Paria. Better and better, I thought. If the overcast held, even the faint light of the quarter-moon would be obscured; it would take radar to find the ship once it slipped away from the lights of shore.

I found that I couldn't wait in the bungalow any longer. I took a walk to my perch west of the Hamidad yard and surveilled the quay once more. All was quiet. Still no sign of the watchman.

When dark finally fell, I pulled on a pair of blue jeans and a dark long-sleeved shirt and packed my bags for a quick exit. I wrapped my passport and visa in plastic before buttoning them into my shirt pocket. Waiting for the agreed-upon time, I watched a Trinidad news broadcast about over-crowding and torture in the Port of Spain maximum-security prison. That, I figured, would be where I would end up if the ship went aground and Mamo couldn't get me out to the tugboat: stuffed in a filthy, packed cell, and perhaps dying from untreated torture wounds. It was a dispiriting thought. Although I had planned to call home before I set out, I decided to wait until I was in a better mood.

That mood never arrived; when Ramesh knocked on my door at 10 P.M., I left without calling. The receptionist, a black girl in a crew-cut who looked like Grace Jones, was talking on the phone and gave us only the briefest of glances.

The night was black, the wind still out of the northeast, blowing harder than ever. We got in the Sunny and drove eastward. The coast guard base was lit like a prison. Half a dozen cars sat in the parking lot.

Ramesh preceded me along the pier, his bulky shoulders backlit from the shore. The boat was rocking at the end of the pier, its faded white paint luminescent against the black sea. As I stepped over the bulwark, I saw the truck muffler that Mamo and Ramesh had fastened to the end of the exhaust pipe. It didn't look very secure—I hoped the first blast of throttle didn't shoot it straight into the air—but there wasn't much we could do about that now.

A dim yellow light burned in the cabin, stretching into a parallelogram across the back deck as Ramesh opened the door. The light came from a small, naked bulb hanging by a twisted coat hanger from the ceiling. Mamo sat behind the wheel with his feet up on the planked dashboard, his hairy feet looking like a rabbit's in the faint light. He spun the chair and put them down as we came in.

"All right, gemmen," he said, "le's go, den."

"How's that muffler work, Captain Mamo?" I asked. "You think it'll stay on?"

"Yas, mon, we tes' it good. All de way to half-power. I t'ink no problem."

"Quiet it down any?"

"Dat t'ing quiet lak a whore in church, I tell you. Maybe I weld it on good later . . . I lak de soun' of it. I can year mesef t'ink now."

He started the engine. It was measurably quieter, with a low rumble instead of a hard diesel rap. Ramesh went on deck to throw off the lines, and Mamo backed the boat away from the pier. He turned off the interior light, and as my eyes adjusted to the dark, I could see the lights along the road dwindling as we gained the cloak of darkness. He spun the wheel to port and engaged the forward gear. The boat heeled as the rudder slewed her around.

I unwrapped the VHF Ramesh had bought and put in the six AA batteries he'd had the foresight to buy. It gave a satisfying hiss when I turned it on. I clipped it to my belt and went on deck.

It was too dark even to see the big island of Gaspar Grande. The boat rose and fell in the short chop off the shore, unseen waves lapping at the starboard bow. The coast guard station drew abreast and fell behind. To seaward, the lights of a couple of anchored ships flickered in the blackness.

I made my way forward along the port deck. The engine was running at about half throttle, making a low, throaty roar. I stood on the bow next to Ramesh and watched as the yacht club appeared from behind the point, floodlights on its glass-fronted face. Ramesh turned to smile at me, his face lit green and red from the running lights.

"Looks like the wind will hold," I yelled into his ear. He looked up at the clouds rushing past and nodded.

Now the boatyards came into view. Lights stabbed out over the water from cars rounding the point on the other side, then flickered and disappeared as they descended to the coast road. I looked into the cabin. The only light was the compass binnacle's red glow, lighting Mamo's bearded face from below.

I thought of my children. What would it be like growing up with a father in a foreign prison? Nobody'd know I'd been acting on the side of right. Hell, I was doing this for a man I'd never met. Then I thought about Mr. Jukes having a heart attack in the office where that buccaneer Captain Rami had offered me a kickback. That made me mad. I put thoughts of my family away and turned my face to the west, where the lights of the Hamidad yard were just appearing.

Mamo cut power as we drew abreast of the *Percival J,* and the engine note fell to a dull rumble. The black bulk of Gaspar Grande stood off the port bow, and as we closed with it tiny house lights appeared on the slopes. Still at half speed, the boat's motion sharpened when we turned into the wind, the bow pitching in the short chop off the shore.

Ramesh handed me a machete in a canvas sheath. I slipped it on my belt. "Got yours?" I asked.

"Yes, Cap, raght year."

We eased past Gaspar Grande. The wind still whistled through the boat's rigging, but the chop fell off as we neared the shore. Now the three ships lined up at the yard's quay were clearly silhouetted against the lights, with the *Percival J* directly ahead. Mamo pulled power to a dead idle.

I scanned the quay, but there was no movement. Most of it was hidden by the ships' hulls, and as we came closer, the visible pieces of the quay became foreshortened, and then disappeared, so that the ships formed an unbroken obstruction to our being seen.

I went to the back and opened the door. "Take her up to the dock in front of the ship," I said. "Ramesh and I will get off the bow."

"Dat a wery high dock, Cap," Mamo said. "You t'ink you can do it?"

I studied the quay with the binoculars. "Yeah, I think so. Go straight in."

By then, we were within fifty yards of the *Percival J*, and hidden from the lights by its bulk. Ramesh had changed into a black sweatshirt and black running pants, with his machete strapped to his belt, but he was still wearing his flip-flops. I'd seen him wearing them on the deck of the *Cathy Jean* in a Seattle winter, so I wasn't surprised. We went out and around to the bow.

The quay's breastlog—the heavy timber that ran along the edge of the dock and protected it from ships' hulls—was silhouetted against the floodlights. The ship's headlines stretched out above us. The engine's note rose in pitch as Mamo took it out of gear. The bow bumped the quay, and before it could rebound I was up on the bow and across, grasping the quay's breastlog with both hands. I handed myself sideways to give Ramesh room, and a second later he was beside me.

The engine's note deepened as the boat went into reverse, and within seconds the noise had all but disappeared in the wind. We were far enough from the *Percival J* that I could see the length of the yard's building, dazzling white in the floodlights. There was no sound but the whirring of the wind past the ship's dock lines.

I crouched down and put my mouth to Ramesh's ear. "We're going to have to drop the gangway after we get on board. If we don't, it'll hit the ship's side when we pull away, and wake the guard."

"We'll need ropes."

"You look aft, I'll look forward. Ready? Let's go."

We pulled ourselves up on the quay, scrambled to our feet, and ran to the gangway. The wheeled lower end had pulled close to the breastlog as the wind held the ship off the quay. Ramesh reached it first, and I followed him up, slipping on the crossbars.

We reached the main deck and crouched down behind the bulwark, both of us looking toward the building. Nothing moved. Ramesh found a coil of heaving line and we tied its ends to the gangway. "Try to hold it out," I whispered. "Otherwise it'll scrape going down."

"Wait a sec," he said, and scurried aft. He was back in a moment with one of the ship's fire hoses. We wrapped the hose around the end of the gangway. If we'd tried it the way I'd planned, it would've screeched like a banshee going down the hull, with the empty hold acting as an echo chamber. It wasn't the first time Ramesh showed his swift mind.

We lowered the gangway, with the hose making only a soft rubbing sound. We threw the ropes down to the dock and, without discussion, rushed to the ends of the ship, Ramesh aft and I forward. I scrambled up to the raised forecastle deck, where the heavy hawsers went from their bitts through the Panama chocks—rounded, cast-steel holes in the bulwarks—and out to the shore bollards. The wind on the ship's side was keeping the lines under tension, and they were stretched taut. Three whacks on the spring line, a rope going aft to a shore bollard near the ship's middle, and it fell in the water with a splash.

Another splash from astern. Ramesh had cut the stern spring line. I chopped through the breast line that went out at a right angle. It fell to the dock with a thud.

I should have told Ramesh to wait until all the bowlines were cut before cutting the stern breast line, but I'd forgotten. I slashed at the headline going forward, the last bowline, and it shot off into the dark with a whir like a bumblebee. The bow started turning. I ran aft.

Ramesh had cut the tail line and was standing over the stern breast line as I ran up. "Wait," I hissed, "wait!"

"Le's wait 'til de bow is out," he whispered. "Dat way de ship will drif' straight." I nodded and clapped him on the shoulder.

The stern closed with the dock as the bow swung out, the stern breast line acting as a fulcrum. Then the stern went aground, and as the bow tried to keep swinging, the stern breast line groaned and trembled under the strain.

I fumbled at my machete, trying to get it out. Before I could do it, though, the hawser snapped. The ragged end shot back through the Panama chock, knocked over a ventilator trunk, and slammed into an empty fifty-five-gallon drum, bending it double. Ramesh's mouth worked, but no sound came out. The three-inch-diameter hawser had whipped right between Ramesh and me, and we weren't more than two feet apart. I had a sudden vision of blood and brains and glittering glass.

Only a month earlier I'd gone on a tugboat in the Mississippi River where a man had been decapitated by a breaking hawser of the same size.

The bulk of the ship astern of us blocked our view of the quay. I kept waiting for the guard to appear and give the alarm, but he never showed.

The swinging of the bow and the absolute blackness of the night made an accurate estimate of drift impossible. For a bad few minutes I thought the current was carrying us eastward, toward Gaspar Grande, but that didn't make any sense. Finally, by ignoring the angle of the bow, and by reference to the ship's course from the dock, it looked like we would clear both Gasparillo and Gaspar Grande islands, if not by much. Thank God they were both steep-to, dropping off to deep water with no shallow shelves to trap ships. If we cleared them by at least a hundred yards, we wouldn't go aground.

The ship finally stabilized at a shallow angle to the wind, with the bow slightly to port. Gasparillo loomed closer, the bushes on its hilly top only slightly higher than our perch on the bow. I had misjudged our drift angle, or the current was slower here, because we were coming much closer than I first thought. I gulped.

"No good, Cap," Ramesh said. "Maybe we hit de rocks. Is de radio ready?"

"What, to call your dad? Yeah, it's ready. But let's wait and see."

I reached down and turned the walkie-talkie on. A burst of static until I turned the squelch down. Mamo's boat was drifting somewhere close by, its lights out.

The dark bulk of the island came inexorably closer. I clinched my jaw and waited for impact, for the sudden lurching and lifting of the hull as she struck bottom, but slowly and silently the ship drew past the island, still afloat. We came close enough to reach it with the line-throwing gun, but we never took the bottom. When I was sure we had cleared the tip, I stepped down to the forecastle deck and sat on the step with my forearms on my knees. "Not yet, by God," I whispered to myself. "Not yet."

"W'at dat, Cap?" Ramesh asked, still standing at the bow.

"Nothing. Looks like we made it. Now if we can just get past Gaspar Grande."

I stepped back up to the gunwale. The bigger island now filled the southern horizon, with house lights marking its western tip. A long backswell off the gulf set the ship rocking, and the smell of land faded. The sweat that dampened my shirt under the armpits was cold and clammy.

I hadn't brought binoculars. Ramesh and I scanned the dark water ahead with our naked eyes. Tiny lights burned in the distance, red and green running lights and faint yellow dots, but there was no way of distinguishing the tugboat. Then a deep rumble approached on the starboard side, a boat engine, and my heart jumped into my mouth. We rushed across just as a white-painted boat came up, rolling in the waves, and I started breathing again when I recognized the high bow and red mast of Mamo's fishing boat.

"Fadder!" Ramesh called. "What you doing, mon?"

Mamo grinned at us in the binnacle's red light. He waved and gave us the thumbs-up, then the boat sheered off and he took station a hundred yards away on the starboard side, slowing to our speed.

I glanced at my watch. Almost midnight. Fifty-five minutes since we'd undocked. We'd gone about two nautical miles. That was good . . . We were drifting at over two knots, which meant that we would reach international water before dawn. Not much before, but it didn't matter as long as we made it before a Trinidad patrol boat saw us drifting.

Now well out of danger of hitting an island, we left the forecastle and went back to the house. The starboard door was open, and the house was as dark as a cave. We turned on our flashlights and made our way up to the bridge, past the silent intermediate decks.

The wide, well-ordered wheelhouse rocked slowly as we drifted south. I unlocked the door to the starboard wing and dragged a stool out. Ramesh paced between the house and wing's bulwark. We said little to one another as we looked ahead for the tugboat and astern for pursuit.

Finally, at 5 A.M., with the night still black, dead reckoning—based on our speed going past Gaspar Grande—showed us nearing international water. There was a faint glow to the west-northwest, which must have been Gairia, Venezuela. There were no other landmarks. We could only wait for the tug to come up to us.

"Captain!" Ramesh called, a half hour later. "Lights coming!"

He pointed over the bow. I had sunk into a reverie on my stool. I jumped to my feet and pressed myself against the bulwark. The red and green lights of a vessel coming right at us showed dead ahead, about a point off the starboard bow. "Christ," I said, "I hope we're in international water."

"Dat boat's coming from international water, dat's for sure."

"Yeah, but a Trinidad patrol boat can go anywhere it wants as long as it doesn't enter Venezuelan water. Oh, Christ, I hope it's the tug."

"Want me to signal? What's the signal, two longs and a short?"

"Yeah, but wait. They're still coming . . . We don't need to signal yet, especially if it's not our tug."

The boat came on, still too far away to make out what kind of vessel it was. It was going too slow for a patrol boat at top speed, though, which was reassuring. We watched, eyes straining, as it came ever nearer.

Finally, the boat veered off to starboard and, as it came abreast, a flashlight flicked out the recognition signal, two longs and a short. We gave the answer, a short and two longs, and the boat turned to come up on our starboard side. It was still too dark to make out the boat's profile.

The boat threw up securing lines and we made her fast. Deck lights came on, showing the tug's high, fendered bow and long, low sides. The figures of men on deck stood out against the lights, dark Hispanics in ragged shirts and shorts. They had already hung tires over their port side, and the tires groaned and squealed as the two vessels rolled together.

Ramesh and I threw over a Jacob's ladder and went down to the tugboat. It was a large boat, about 150 feet long, with a wide, clear afterdeck and a three-deck house. Jack's crew came out of the house, black Jamaicans in coveralls. The captain, a stocky old man with a ball of white hair and a little Hitleresque mustache, introduced himself and the chief engineer. The chief was a thin man about thirty, young for a chief engineer, with café-au-lait skin and long, oiled hair that gleamed in the house lights.

"Captain," I said, "are we in international water?"

"Yasslr. De tug captain say we is fourteen nautical from de Trinidad coast."

"Good. Chief, do you have the air-start valve?"

The chief motioned toward one of the other men, holding a square parcel wrapped in brown paper, about the size of a dictionary.

"Good," I said. "Chief, I don't know how much fuel is on board. I'd like to get the ship under way before daylight, if there's enough fuel. Can you sound the tanks? You'll need at least a couple of tons to get through the strait." I looked at the captain. "Remember, you have the right of innocent passage through Venezuelan waters, but if you get in Trinidad waters and they see you, they can stop you."

"Do dey know de ship was took?"

"Maybe not, but they'll know as soon as it's daylight. That's why I want the ship as far away from here as it can get."

Ramesh pointed toward the eastern sky, already lightening. "Daylight coming, Cap."

"Yeah, I know. Okay, guys, let's get moving. Who's the tug captain?"

A barrel-chested Hispanic stepped forward. "I am the *capitan.*"

I said in Spanish, "Can you get your hose rigged now? If the ship needs fuel, we want to be ready."

"Si, Señor. No problema." He turned to his crew, three men standing a little apart from the ship's crew, and told them to rig the *manga por combustible.*

Some of the ship's crew climbed the Jacob's ladder. One of them lowered a light line and the crewman with the air-start valve secured it to the line. It soared up into the darkness and the last of the ship's crew climbed up.

By then, the tug's crew already had the fuel hose snaked across the deck and up the ship's side. I turned to Ramesh. "Where's your dad? Seen him yet?"

"Raght dere, Cap," he said, pointing off the tug's starboard side. In the faint gathering light, I could see the fishing boat's dim white shape a hundred yards away, bobbing in the swell. "I t'ink he's waiting for us to be raddy to get off."

I handed him the walkie-talkie. "Tell him to come alongside. If the ship doesn't need fuel, we'll be ready in a few minutes."

I climbed up the ladder and followed my flashlight beam down to the ship's engine room. As I went through the fireproof door on the lower accommodations deck, I could see darting lights and murmured voices. Just as I reached the second deck, above the main engine's giant cylinder heads, a loud whine broke the silence, followed by the clattering roar of a generator engine. A minute later, the engine room was filled with light from dozens of bulbs. The *Percival J* had come alive.

One of the men, probably an oiler, was already sounding a bunker tank. The tape came up showing the tank half full. "Don't worry about checking the tank tables," I told the chief, watching at my side. "That's enough to reach the other side of the strait. The tug'll follow you out. If you need more fuel to reach Curaçao, he can refuel you on the other side."

"Yassir."

I glanced toward the main engine. Two men were fitting the air-start valve to its bracket, the mounting bolts already threaded through the body. I ran up on deck and scrambled down the Jacob's ladder. The tug's captain and crew were still on the back deck. Now the fishing boat was rafted up to the tug's starboard side, all three vessels bobbing together. Mamo stood on the fishing boat's back deck, talking to Ramesh across the gunwales. He waved to me.

"*Hay sufficiente combustible abordo,*" I told the tug's captain. "You can pull your hose back on board. Follow the ship to the other side of the strait. If it needs more fuel there, make sure you're in international water before you stop to refuel."

"*Sí, Capitan,*" he said. "*Hay otro?*"

"No, that's it." I shook his callused hand. "Thanks for everything. Tell Jan hello for me. You and your crew have done a great job."

Now a gray light was filling the sky, although the sun had not yet risen. I scanned the empty horizon. No lights, no shapes, nothing. I called up to the ship's bridge, and the captain appeared at the wing. "Captain, how's the air-start valve doing? Any problems?"

"No, Cap, de chief jus' call. He say de valve ready to sta't."

"Okay, good. Be sure to stay on the Venezuelan side. Your chief will tell you whether you need to stop again for fuel before you reach Curaçao. Anything else?"

"No sar, dat's it. We see you on de odder side someday, eh?"

"Yas, mon," I called up. "We drink one lee beer togedder, okay?"

He grinned and waved and went back into the wheelhouse. Ramesh and I climbed over to the fishing boat and one of the tugboat hands cast our lines off. We gathered them in and the fishing boat sheered off.

We stayed at idle until the tugboat cast off and the ship's engine started. We were far enough away that we couldn't hear it, but I could see puffs of white smoke from the funnel, then a steady trail of blue smoke when it caught. The ship began to gain way to the north, with the tugboat trailing like an obedient puppy. Mamo turned toward Chaguaramas, out of sight over the northeastern horizon.

I was suddenly exhausted. Ramesh and I went in the cabin and I slumped onto the starboard bench, my legs aching. A dim light filled the cabin, and later, when I raised my head from my arms, the sun was up and the ship and tugboat were tiny dots on the vast rim of the sea.

I stayed in touch with Jack Jukes over the next couple of weeks. The ship had reached Curaçao, refueled without incident, and went about its tramping business. Mr. Jukes had called Captain Rami a few days after the extraction and offered to pay the yard's original estimate. After some vituperation about pirates stealing ships, Captain Rami accepted the agreed-upon amount.

I never heard from Mr. Jukes after that, but a couple of years later somebody told me that the *Percival J* had run hard aground off Anna Regina, Guyana. In 1999, a friend who had taken his ship to drydock in Georgetown told me that the wreck of the *Percival J* was still there, her hull completely exposed, blown high up into the shallows by successive South Atlantic storms.

CHAPTER SIX

ANNIE'S REVENGE

SOMETIME LATER, ANNIE Lindgren, the woman who'd brokered the *Cathy Jean* in Seattle, called me. She had a line on some scrap ships in Vladivostok and wanted to know if I knew anyone who wanted them. In fact, I did. A month earlier, a mysterious character named Dr. Chin had called me from China, looking for ships to scrap. So I found his number and set my alarm clock so I could call him during office hours in China. The connection was bad, but he said he was still interested, so the next day I had Annie send me the ships' broker sheets—one-page descriptions with general arrangement plans and specifications—which I then faxed to Dr. Chin.

He called me the following day, and he was excited. There were a dozen large factory ships for sale, each weighing more than two thousand lightship tons, and the seller, a Russian fishing company named Poporybprom, was selling them for a hundred dollars a ton. The world market price was around $250 a ton, so Dr. Chin's excitement was understandable. He wanted me to go to Vladivostok immediately.

I called Annie to see what kind of arrangements could be made. "One problem," I said, "is that neither of us speaks a word of Russian. How're we going to communicate with the sellers?"

Annie had a high, lilting voice at odds with her sturdy body, and a distinct northwest accent. "Well, let me see. I know a guy here that speaks Russian. He's a Bulgarian, works for a cement company in Tacoma. Will your guy pay for him to go? Say a couple of hundred dollars a day?"

"Maybe," I said. "Check to see when he can go and I'll see how we can get there."

We hung up and I called my travel agent. "You're in luck, Captain," she said. "There's a new service to Vladivostok by Alaska Air. Their first flight leaves on Monday. Vladivostok was a closed city until last month, you know. No foreigners were allowed."

I called Dr. Chin and got his permission to take the Bulgarian, then I called the Russian embassy in Washington and got instructions for a visa. Annie and the Bulgarian, whose name was Milos Lavroski, could get their visas from the Russian consulate in Seattle.

When I told my wife about the trip, she said, "You're going to Russia for two weeks with another woman?" Her tone was neutral, but when your wife asks you a question like that, you've got to tread carefully.

"Yeah," I said, "a big woman. She outweighs me. And there'll be a Bulgarian translator along."

She didn't say anything more about it. I got Dr. Chin to wire a thousand dollars for expenses and twelve hundred dollars for my airfare, and on Friday, my passport and a visa booklet arrived from the Russian embassy.

I arrived in Seattle on Sunday evening and spent the night in a cheap hotel near Sea-Tac Airport.

The next morning I met Annie and Milos at the Alaska Air counter. He was a big, soft man about forty, with wiry, graying hair combed straight back from a broad, lumpy face. He and Annie were about the same height and weight. The last time I'd seen her was just before the *Cathy Jean* sailed out of Seattle. I'd forgotten how big she was. She wasn't fat, just a big, sturdy, blond Swede.

The airplane had an interesting mix on board, mostly American businessmen looking to take advantage of Vladivostok's opening to foreign trade, with some Russian expatriates heading back for their first visits. We stopped in Anchorage, where a few more businessmen came on board, then took off through a dense fog that fell away as we gained altitude.

It was late afternoon when we landed in Magadan for fuel. The airport was a bleak, isolated collection of huts and hangars around a single runway, with a yellow terminal building standing stark against the knee-deep snow. After an hour on the ground, with the plane getting colder and colder, the pilot came on the intercom to announce that the fuel truck hadn't arrived, and we would have to get out until it did.

The passengers gathered their carry-on baggage and trooped across the tarmac to the terminal building. It was hot and bright inside, with rows of plastic-upholstered seats facing an Aeroflot counter. A dozen Russian men and women were waiting for us, all smiles. The stewardesses told us to sit and wait, and within minutes the Russians were circulating with ceramic mugs of scalding coffee and plates of thick-sliced black bread.

Just before dark we heard a grinding noise and went to the windows to see a Russian army tank truck pulling up alongside the airplane.

It was full dark when we landed at Vladivostok. A group of taxi drivers stood around the front doors, and after a bit of haggling, Milos made a deal with a diminutive Chinese man and we got in his Lada. "It's ninety dollars to town," Milos said apologetically. "That's the best I could do."

I whistled. "Jesus, I only brought a thousand dollars. Annie, how much do you have?"

She looked at me in shock. "I thought Russia was cheap. I only have about a thousand myself."

"Milos," I said, "ask the driver if there's an American Express office in town."

He asked, then said, "He doesn't know what that is, but he doesn't think so. He said there's no way of getting foreign money into Vladivostok that he knows of."

I gnawed on my lower lip and wondered what was going to happen if we ran out of cash.

The driver took us to a low, rambling hotel nestled in some shallow hills, but it was two hundred dollars a night, so we couldn't afford to stay there. The driver told Milos that the only reasonably priced hotel was the Hotel Vladivostok, which he didn't recommend. However, we couldn't afford anything better.

The Hotel Vladivostok was a high, square building on the edge of a cliff overlooking a narrow fjord, with a small portico in front. The lobby was ill lit and smelled of rotten meat.

The ladies at the counter—there were half a dozen of them—told us that foreigners were only allowed on the fourth floor. We got one room for Milos and me and another, across the hall, for Annie.

It was 10 P.M. by the time we got our luggage to our rooms; we agreed to meet downstairs for supper in the hotel's restaurant. When we got there, in a large, empty room cluttered with heavy old tables and chairs, the smell of rotten meat was stronger than ever. Milos ordered chicken stew for all of us, but it smelled vile, and we couldn't eat it. We had the waiter, a burly young man in a dirty uniform, take it back and bring us borscht, or beet soup. It was cheap and, as hungry as we were, tolerable.

During supper, Milos asked me what percentage of the money we paid for the ships he would get. I was astounded; I thought Annie had made a deal with him to work for two hundred dollars a day. No, he said, he wanted the two hundred a day plus a percentage of the purchase price of the ships. When I told him that I'd made no arrangement with my client for that, he accused Annie of trying to take advantage of him.

"Screw you," she said shortly. "You made a deal and you'll have to live with it."

His face darkened. "Screw me?" he hissed. "You say screw me? You will pay for that, you bitch."

She shoved her chair back. "How'm I going to pay for it, asshole? What do you think you're going to do?"

"Come now," I said, "let's calm down. Hell, we just got here. There'll be plenty of time for fighting later." I said it lightly, but they kept staring at each other across the table, tense and angry. "Look," I went on, "we may not be buying any ships at all. Why fight about it now?"

After we'd gone to our rooms, Milos told me, "Nobody says 'Screw you' to me. I'll show her. I'll fuck her in the Bulgarian way."

I chuckled. "Which way is that?"

"She will find out," he muttered. "I'll show her."

The next morning, we went down to the restaurant for breakfast, but the cashier by the door told us there was no food. To save money, we walked from the hotel to the waterfront, where the offices of Poporybprom, the owner of the ships, were located. The streets were icy, and we had to walk carefully down the steep slope that led to the bay.

It was a gray day, with dirty-looking clouds racing inland just above the old buildings. The people on the streets were bundled against the wind and kept their heads down. Milos's accent must have been distinctive, because the people he asked for directions looked at him strangely. They were pleasant enough, though, and with their help we finally found the Poporybprom building on the waterfront, across a wide plaza from a line of grimy vessels—some tugboats, a small cruise ship, a navy patrol boat—rocking in the low waves.

We went up a wide cement stairway to the second floor, where a short, fat woman sat behind a blond-wood desk eating something out of a folded piece of newspaper. Milos introduced us and she put her food in a drawer before going through a pair of high wooden doors. She came out and asked us to wait for the company's president, Mr. Tdeschenko, who would see us shortly.

Milos said to Annie, in a low voice, "I am going to get a share of any money for these ships. You must understand that."

She turned to face him. "You're nothing but a translator. What do you know about ships?"

"I know enough to stop this deal from happening if I don't get paid."

She reached out and jabbed a finger in his chest. "I'll break your fat neck if you try to sabotage this deal, asshole."

He knocked her finger away.

"You make big mistake," Milos spluttered. "You call me asshole." He grabbed her by the throat with both hands and started shaking her.

"Jesus Christ," I said, "cut it out."

Annie brought her knee up and kicked Milos between the legs. He had his feet spread, and she caught him right in the peach basket. His eyes bulged and he bent double. The woman behind the desk gave a little shriek. The doors opened and a tall, handsome man in a shapeless black suit stood there, a welcoming smile on his face. The smile froze.

Annie and Milos straightened and turned. Milos managed to say something in a strangled voice. The man stood aside with a small, polite frown and gestured us into the room. Annie strode in and I followed Milos as he limped after her.

We sat in square, heavy chairs in front of Mr. Tdeschenko's desk. By then, Milos had recovered his voice; he explained that we were the buyers for the fish-factory vessels the company was selling for scrap. The man nodded and pulled a fax from a pile at the side of his desk. Annie nodded to show that she'd sent it.

The company had eight factory ships for sale, laid up at a dock on Zolotoy Rog Bay. The man gave Milos directions and said we could inspect them any time we wished. The price—to be paid in U.S. funds—was a hundred dollars a light-ship ton.

There are several different tonnages assigned to every ship. Her deadweight tonnage is the weight of cargo she can carry—since it doesn't contribute to the ship's navigation, it's called "deadweight." Her gross tonnage is a calculated figure, generally based on her size, on which flag-state and port fees are based. And her light-ship tonnage is the actual weight of steel in the ship.

We made as graceful an exit as we could, Milos still limping. When we got to the street, an icy wind streaked across the plaza and bit our faces. Annie and Milos refused to look at each other.

"Look, you guys," I said, "I'm here to buy ships. Can you two cool it?"

"I'll cool it," Annie said, "if Milos's going to work for what he agreed to work for."

"Milos?" I asked.

"I'm not working for two hundred dollars a day," he muttered.

"Is that what you agreed to work for?"

"I don't care what I agreed to work for," he burst out. "Your Chinaman will pay one and a half million dollars for those ships and you want to pay me two thousand dollars? I can control this deal, you know."

I turned my back to the wind and buttoned my collar. "Milos, if that's what you agreed to work for, it's only fair that you stick with your deal. Otherwise you can go home and we'll hire a translator here."

He gave a short laugh. "Good luck. Nobody speaks English in this town. Hell, foreigners couldn't even come here until last month."

"I'll find somebody, by God," Annie said. "You can go back to the room and we'll go on without you."

"Now, now," I said, stepping between them, "let's just go look at the ships. Maybe they're no good and there'll be no deal."

After another tense moment, we went down to the waterfront and Milos got directions to the ferry terminal. It was too far to walk, so he led us to a taxi stand near the train station and we drove along the rim of the bay to a glass-walled building built on pilings out over the water. A small, white passenger ferry bobbed at the dock.

Yellowish scum caked the water along the bulkhead, and the ferry's waterline was stained brown. Plastic bags and rotting vegetable matter floated on the water's black surface. A couple of dozen passengers huddled on board, mostly old women bundled into tattered coats with knit shopping bags at their feet. As the city's waterfront receded, we could see cranes and warehouses stretching out of sight to the north, but there was no movement.

The ferry crossed the narrow bay and pulled up to an open quay at the foot of a rocky slope. A few taxis were waiting for the ferry, and we took one north on a narrow road that wound between the cliffs and the bay. Across the water, the windows of Vladivostok winked faintly through the haze.

We drove for an hour through thickets of stunted larches with snow banked against their bare gray trunks. Here and there wooden dachas in various stages of decay peered out from the forest. A small, ruined church with a great hole in its onion-shaped dome stood on the crest of a rocky hill. It was a wild, beautiful place, haunted—like all of Russia—by the ghosts of its lost glory.

Finally, shortly before noon, we emerged from the woods and began to switchback down to the shore. A long concrete pier stretched out below us, with the factory ships on its north side, squat and ungainly. Even from this distance I could see that they'd been laid up for a long time.

I had Milos ask the taxi driver to wait for us, since it didn't look like taxis went by here very often. We walked out on the pier. The haze was thinner and the sun warmer. I unbuttoned my coat and turned my collar down. Some smaller fishing boats were tied to the foot of the pier, high-prowed dories with houses aft, rust weeping from their fastenings. A burly, red-faced man sat on one foredeck scarfing in a piece of new wood on the port bulwark. He looked up from his hammer and chisel to nod to us.

A rickety steel gangway led from the dock to the first of the factory ships. "Careful here," I warned Annie and Milos. "If you go in the water it'll be tough getting you out."

We made our way on board and stood looking around. It'd been years since the ship had been to sea. Pieces of conveyor belt, rotting rubber hoses, and bent sections of support beams lay abandoned on the blistered steel deck. Everything was covered with dirt. We went into the house through an open steel door.

The interior was frigid and silent, and smelled of rancid fish oil. Tiny cabins with narrow steel bunks, three high, lined the corridors. We went up three decks to the wheelhouse. It was as derelict as the rest of the ship, with some decaying charts spread on the chart table, and huge, primitive radios and radars that looked like relics from World War I. But given that the ships were intended for scrap, that wasn't a problem.

I found a door that led to the factory equipment under the main deck. The vast, gloomy rooms were full of sinks and sorting tables. One room held a dozen giant boiling pots, with steam pipes stretching out below them like spider legs. Wrenches, rubber gloves, shovels, and ladles lay strewn on the floor.

We went topside, our nostrils still full of the stink of fish oil, and crossed to the next ship. It was virtually identical to the first. They were all sister ships, and in the same condition. The last one in the row was taking on water on the starboard side, and lay with a heavy list, straining her securing ropes.

"We'll skip that one," I told them. "I'd hate for it to break its ropes and roll while we're on board."

I made a cursory inspection of the rest of the ships, then we walked back up the pier. The fisherman was finishing the wooden insert on his bulwark, shaving it fair with an old-fashioned drawknife. He grinned at us, showing a mouthful of steel teeth.

On the way back, the driver said we had to find some gasoline. He turned onto a rough gravel track that led into a thick forest. I started getting worried and asked Milos to ask where we were going. The man said there were no service stations on the peninsula, and we were going to a place where the army sold fuel.

The road wound deeper into the forest, around stone outcroppings weeping with spring water and through steep valleys lush with green moss. We came to a wide place in the road where a big gray tractor-trailer was parked, surrounded by half a dozen soldiers in peaked caps. A crude sign propped against a back wheel said "76."

"What does that mean?" I asked.

The driver muttered his unhappiness. It meant that the soldiers only had seventy-six octane for sale. It was very bad for the engine, he said, but better gasoline was hard to find. Russian army vehicles were designed to run on the stuff, but car engines knocked and spluttered, and their valves quickly wore out.

The driver pulled up next to the truck and talked to one of the men, a pale, middle-aged officer with a battered face and corkscrew nose. Annie and I got out to stretch our legs. The young soldiers regarded her with frank admiration. One of them, a gangly boy with a thick crop of orange hair that looked as if it'd been cut with garden shears, said, *"Amerikanski?"*

Annie nodded. "Yes, *Amerikanski*. How did you know?"

Milos translated: "He says he could tell by our blue jeans. Russians can't afford American blue jeans."

When the tank was full, the driver paid with a fistful of rubles and we piled in. The car clanked and clattered, and the driver shook his head dolefully.

The ride across the bay seemed shorter than the ride out. We trudged up the steep streets to the Hotel Vladivostok without talking. A cold wind arrowed between the low buildings and eddied around the corners. From the hotel's parking lot, we could see whitecaps in the fjord far below. Half a dozen cars stood in the parking lot, including a long black Mercedes parked near the door. As we approached, a blond young man got out of the back of the Mercedes and called to us in English.

"Hello," he said, striding along the sidewalk with his hands in his pockets. He wore a long gray trench coat and the square-toed black shoes favored by Russian businessmen. "You're Americans, aren't you?" His English was good.

We stopped. "That's right," I said.

He came up and held out his hand. I shook it. His palm was warm and soft. "You're here to buy the factory ships, aren't you?"

I stared. "That's right. Are you with Poporybprom?"

"No, I'm with another company." He bowed to Annie. "How do you do, madam?"

"Fine," she said shortly. "Who are you again?"

Milos said something to the man in Russian, and the man answered in Russian. He turned to Annie. "I'm with the company that actually owns those ships."

"What about Poporybprom?" I said. "That's the registered owner."

He waved a hand. "Oh, they used to own them, but we own them now."

"I see," I said. I took out a business card and handed it to him. "Do you have a card?"

He put it in a pocket without looking at it. "No, sorry," he said easily. "But let's go somewhere to talk. My boss will make you a good deal on those ships, you know."

"We can go to the coffee shop here," I said.

He grimaced. "Oh, this place . . . Well, the smell, you know. It's not so good. There's a nice place on the waterfront . . . I can call Mel to come meet us."

I could tell Annie wanted to go someplace nice, but I didn't want to get in the Mercedes. I'd seen too many gangster movies for that. "Let's talk here," I said. "Your boss can come if he wants."

He had taken a couple of steps toward the car, as if he expected us to follow without question, but he stopped and came back reluctantly. "Very well, then," he said, and smiled, showing a line of perfect white teeth. Except for his close-set eyes, he could've been a male model.

We went into the deserted lobby and across to the restaurant. It still smelled of rotten meat, but not as badly. The Russian wrinkled his chiseled nose.

"And your name, sir?" I asked him.

"Andrei."

"Andrei what?" Annie asked.

He smiled at her. "Andrei for now. But let's talk about the ships. What have you agreed to pay for them?"

I held up a hand. "We can't go into that. As far as we know, we're dealing with the owners already. It would be improper to give details to a third party."

His smile got thin and wolfish. "I can assure you, we're not a third party, as you call it. We own those ships."

"Do you have any paperwork to show it?" I said. "I've seen their registrations, and they're registered to Poporybprom."

He snorted. "In Russia, that means nothing. Come to our office this afternoon and I'll show you that we own them. I'll send a car for you."

I shook my head. "Just give us the address. Milos can find it."

A waiter finally arrived, a peaked-looking young man with dirty fingernails. We ordered coffee. After he sauntered off, Andrei leaned over the table and said, "You don't have to be so suspicious. I know Poporybprom offered the ships to you for one hundred dollars a ton. We will sell them to you for eighty-five."

I glanced at Annie. She liked the idea. I didn't like it at all. "We'll talk it over," I said. "If Mr. Tdeschenko confirms that you own the ships, we'll talk to you about it."

Andrei sneered. "He's a fool. You'll see." He looked around. "This is a bad hotel. I know a better place. Do you want to check out today?"

"We've already paid for today," I said. "It's not so bad."

"You're on the fourth floor?"

I hesitated. He said, "That's the only floor for foreigners."

I nodded. "Yeah, we're on the fourth."

Our coffee came. It was weak and sour, as if it'd been brewed from yesterday's grounds. Andrei sniffed at it and pushed his cup away. "I'll send the car this afternoon," he said. "Say three o'clock?"

Before I could answer Annie said, "That'll be fine, Andrei. Thank you."

He stood abruptly and slung his coat over his arm. "*Au revoir,* then." He gave Annie a little bow and strode out.

I left some rubles on the table and we went upstairs. When Milos went into the bathroom, I slipped out of the room and went across to knock on Annie's door.

"Look, Annie," I said, "that guy's Russian mafia. It's written all over him. We'd better not get involved."

"And save fifteen dollars a ton? Hell, I'd deal with the devil himself for that."

"I don't think we ought to risk our lives just to save Dr. Chin fifteen dollars a ton."

"Come in," she said, and stood aside. I went in and she closed the door. "What are you talking about? Dr. Chin agreed to pay a hundred. You and I can split fifteen dollars a ton and get our commissions as well."

I shook my head. "We're working as brokers, Annie. Whatever price we get, that's what Dr. Chin gets."

She made a spitting sound. "You wussy. How would he ever know? Andrei'll give us an invoice for any figure we want."

I shook my head. "Nope, that's out."

She shook the bangs out of her eyes. "All right, let's wait and see. It might be bullshit after all."

There was a knock on the door. We looked at each other, then she opened the door. Milos stood there. "What are you two talking about," he demanded, "behind my back?"

"Milos," she said, "you're just a translator. We can talk privately any time we want."

"You're playing with fire now," he said. "You don't know who that man is? If you want to get out of this city alive, you'd better treat me right."

"Is that a threat?" she said.

He shrugged. "Not from me. But you'll see." He turned on his heel and went back to our room.

"Let me go talk to him," I said.

Milos was standing at the window looking down at the street. "What did you mean about getting out of this city alive?" I asked him.

He turned. "I know how to handle women like that. In the KDS, we put them in a cell with two feet of ice water in it. She would be a different woman in the morning, I guarantee."

"What are you talking about? What's the KDS?"

"One kind of police."

"The secret police? The Bulgarian KGB?"

"Forget it. She thinks I'm stupid because I have to pour cement in the United States. If she knew the truth, she'd be more careful what she says."

I sat on the bed. "Milos, we're getting in deep shit here, and you're in it with us. Be straight with me. What did Andrei tell you?"

"Nothing. He just said that he can prove that his company owns the ships."

"Uh-huh. It looked like you were talking about something else."

He gave me a guileless look. "I wouldn't lie to you, Captain Max. I like you."

At three o'clock we went downstairs. The Mercedes was already in the parking lot. The driver was a small-boned man with jet-black hair and flat little lynx ears pinned tight to his round skull. He gave a curt nod and pulled away. The big car swayed and bobbed as it went down the hill. He pulled into a parking lot behind a five-story building that occupied an entire block facing the bay.

The driver ushered us through a nondescript door and along a narrow corridor with a steel door at the end. It looked new. Two hard-looking men in belted leather coats and square shoes sat in a small antechamber. One of them knocked on the inner door and Andrei opened it.

"Ah," he said, "so good to see you. Please come in." The room was large, but sparsely furnished. A big, bald man with cauliflower ears sat behind a steel desk with a single file folder on it. He indicated the chairs in front of his desk without getting up. We sat down and Andrei stood behind us.

"I'm Mel," the man said, with a deep voice and a thick Russian accent. "I speak some English, so. How do you do?"

I said we were doing well. I gave him my card and he looked at it. "Very good, then, Captain Max," he rumbled. "So you wish to buy some ships for the steel, what you say, the scrapping?"

"That's right. I have a Chinese client."

"And he has the money? The cash?"

"Sure. But he'll want proper bills of sale. Of course he can only buy the ships from the owner."

Mel frowned and Andrei said something in Russian to him. He nodded and took a page out of the file on the desk. He slid it to me.

It was some sort of official document with a stamped seal in the lower corner. I pushed it over to Milos.

"It's a bill of sale," Milos said. "It's for fourteen ships, and it gives the names and registration numbers of the ships."

"What's the date?"

"Today's date."

I looked at Mel. "You bought these ships today?"

He gave me a smug smile. "Yes, we bought them today. You see, now we own them. But you will get a very good price. Now, how will your client pay? With cash?"

I took the page back and studied it. I couldn't read a word of it, but it looked official enough. "Your company bought these ships from Poporyb-prom today? It's very strange that Mr. Tdeschenko didn't say anything about that this morning."

Mel shrugged.

I said, "I'll have to check with the client. I'll call him this afternoon and let you know."

"This is my number," Andrei said. "You can call me at any time and I'll get the message to Mr. Mel."

Andrei led us out, past the toughs in the antechamber and into the hall. There were some boxes of files stacked in the hallway, and as I went by I stopped and looked at the papers in one of the top boxes. They were cargo manifests in the name of the Russia Pacific Shipping Company.

I looked at Andrei. "Is this building owned by Russia Pacific?"

"Yes," he said shortly. "Come, let's go."

Back at the hotel, Annie and I got out but Milos stayed in the car. I could see him talking to Andrei through the window. "That conniving skunk," Annie muttered. "He's up to something."

Milos glanced up and saw us looking at him. He climbed out and the car pulled away. "What were you talking to him about?" Annie demanded.

Milos gave her an innocent look. "I asked him if there was a restaurant around here with good food. I figured we might want to find someplace decent to eat tonight."

"Uh huh," she said. Inside, the same half-dozen ladies in their blue-and-gray uniforms were standing around doing nothing. It was amazing to me that there couldn't have been over a dozen guests in the hotel, but there were half a dozen women behind the counter.

When I called Dr. Chin, he was unfazed by the change in circumstances. "The price is very good. What do we care who we buy them from?"

"Because I think these people are mafia. When you get in bed with the devil, it's hard to kick him out."

"Oh, Captain," he said, his high, singsong voice vibrating in the wires, "the price is too good to let small problems get in our way."

Upstairs, I knocked on Annie's door. She opened it and I slipped inside. "Look," I said, "Russia Pacific is one of the biggest shipowners in the world. They must have eighty or ninety ships."

"So," she said, sitting on the bed, "that's good, right? Russia Pacific must have bought the ships from Poporybprom."

I shook my head. "So why would we be meeting a man holed up with bodyguards in a small room at the bottom of the building?" I leaned forward and rapped on the coffee table. "Because the mafia's taken over Russia Pacific. Mel's their man in the company."

She smiled. "Oh, that's silly, Max. You said Russia Pacific is one of the largest shipping companies in the world. How could the mafia take over a company like that?"

I stood up. "Okay, we'll see what Poporybprom says. If they say they sold the ships to Russia Pacific yesterday, we'll deal with Mel."

The next morning we took a taxi to the elevated walkway, where a knot of old women sold thin pancakes out of buckets. Called *blini,* the pancakes were layered with strawberry jam and pretty good. Then we went to the office of Poporybprom, but it was closed. A note with a black border was taped to the door.

Milos bent to study it, then he turned to us with a somber look. "It says the office is closed due to tragic circumstances."

"Tragic circumstances? That doesn't sound so good. Let's ask the lady downstairs."

The woman in the small office on the second floor was typing slowly on an ancient typewriter. Milos spoke to her; she replied gravely, still studying us. Milos turned to me.

"Mr. Tdeschenko is dead. He was shot last night."

I stared at him, then at the woman. "Jesus! Do the police know who shot him?"

He shook his head. "No, I don't think so. She says somebody shot him in front of his house. She doesn't know when the office will open again."

"So," I said to Annie, bitterly, "the mafia's not involved, is that right?"

"Hell," she said, "we don't know it was the mafia. It might've had nothing to do with those ships."

I started back toward the hotel. "Well, I'm not taking any chances. I'm getting out of here."

She and Milos hurried to catch up. "You're going back to the U.S.?"

"Damn right. I'm not going to deal with those murdering bastards." I glanced at Milos. "Do you know anything about this, Milos? Anything you haven't told us?"

He shook his head quickly. "No, no, nothing. I was shocked to hear it."

When we got to the hotel I called my travel agent in Louisiana; she said that Aeroflot had just started a service from Vladivostok to Anchorage. The first flight would leave the next day. I told her to make a reservation for me and to call my wife to bring a check for the fare. Then I went upstairs and knocked on Annie's door.

"Damn," she said. "I can't stand the thought of leaving those ships here. There's got to be something we can do."

"There is," I agreed. "We can get out while we're still alive."

"They're not going to hurt us. What good would it do them?"

"I don't know. But I'm not going to tell Dr. Chin to bring cash to this outlaw town."

"So the trip is wasted?"

"Yeah. That's better than getting wasted ourselves."

"Are we going to tell Milos?"

"I guess so. We've got to get him a ticket back. Or he can stay and use his return ticket on the Alaska Air flight next Monday."

I went across the hall and knocked on the door. No answer. I turned the knob and the door was unlocked. Milos was gone; his bag was gone as well.

"Milos's gone," I told Annie. "I'm going downstairs to see if he's checked out."

"That backstabbing asshole," she said. "I'm coming with you."

We rode the clattering old elevator down to the lobby and went across to the counter. The lady who spoke English gave us a worried look. "'Allo," she said. "Your friend, he go now, yes?"

"How long since he left?"

"Just now." She pointed to the door.

We rushed to the front doors in time to see Milos getting in the passenger seat of a little orange car. "Milos!" I yelled, as he closed the door.

He turned to look at us with a vicious little smile. The car jerked a couple of times—a bad clutch—and started away. He raised his hand and waved, a mocking gesture with just the fingers moving.

"Good riddance," Annie said. "I wonder where the fuck he thinks he's going."

"He's made some new friends," I said. "Some bad new friends. If he doesn't watch himself, he'll end up floating in Zolotoy Rog."

As we went back inside, the tall receptionist beckoned us over. She handed us our passports and said, "Look. Your friend take visas."

I took my passport and rifled through it. The yellow visa booklet was gone.

"Oh my God," Annie said. "There's no U.S. consulate here."

I turned to the hotel clerk. "Can you help us?"

She frowned. "Can you not call your friend, get your visa back?"

"No, we don't know where he's going."

She nodded. "Perhaps he not so friend, no? I will call."

She conferred with the other ladies, and then made a few calls, jotting down a number. She made some more notes and hung up. "You must go to this address," she said. She handed me a slip of paper with Cyrillic writing on it. "You must hurry. The office close at four o'clock."

I glanced at my watch. Two P.M. "Thanks," I said.

A taxi took us to a big yellow building with Cyrillic script on the cornice above the door. I made a gesture for the driver to wait.

The front doors gave onto a huge, wood-paneled room packed with people, almost all of them Chinese, clutching folders. They looked like they'd been there all day. The air was filled with a murmur of voices. Hundreds of eyes watched us curiously as we threaded our way toward the counter at the back wall.

Two peach-faced young men in blue uniforms stood there. I handed one of them the piece of paper and he read it slowly, his lips moving. Then he smiled and slipped through a rear door.

A few minutes later, the door behind the counter opened and the young man returned with a tall, dark man in a suit, his iron-gray hair combed carefully back from a high, broad forehead. He smiled at us, revealing two steel front teeth.

"I am Nikolas," he said, pointing to the piece of paper. "You are the Americans without the visa, yes?"

"Yes," I said. "Our visas were stolen."

"I am sorry. Please to come with me."

One of the young men lifted a corner of the counter and we followed the tall man through the rear door. It led to a long corridor with glass-fronted offices on both sides. Uniformed immigration officials sat behind tiny desks interviewing Chinese foreigners, small worried people leaning over the desks and pleading their cases. The tall man led us to a large office in the back and gestured for us to sit in front of his desk.

"Passports?" he asked. Annie and I handed them over. Hers was new, but he had to flip through mine to find my entry stamp. "You came on Monday?" he asked.

"Yes. On the Alaska Air flight."

"Ah, yes."

He talked for a few minutes on the telephone, then hung up. "Come," he said, "we must go to next office. No English there. I will come. It is necessary."

He put our passports in his pocket and ushered us out. "So," he said to Annie as we went along, "you are not married, so?"

"No," Annie said, and held up her bare ring finger, "no husband."

"Ah, so?" Then, politely, to me, "And you, Mr. Berger?"

I showed him my ring. "Yes, very married." I pointed between Annie and myself. "Business partners only."

He smiled again, with interest, as he opened a door that led into the foyer. "I Nikolas," he said to Annie. She made a simpering sound.

Nikolas looked around. "We must get taxi."

I pointed to our car. "That's our taxi." We drove down to the waterfront and stopped in front of a single-story building with rusty steel scaffolding across the façade.

The interior was hot and smelled of fresh bread. Nikolas led us up a stairway to a wide office overlooking the bay. A round, gray man in a gray sweater and a gray business suit sat behind a desk piled high with dun-colored folders. He smiled and shook our hands. He and Nikolas talked for a while and Nikolas handed him our passports.

He picked up his telephone and tried to make a call, but apparently without success. Nikolas said, to Annie, sadly, "The telephones are a problem. Sometimes you can make a call, and sometimes no."

She patted his arm. "We really appreciate your help, Mr. Nikolas. I don't know what we would've done without it."

He smiled at her like they were the only ones in the room. "Call me Niki," he said.

The little man finally got through to someone. They talked for a while, then he stood up and Nikolas said we had to travel to another office.

We all crowded into the taxi, and drove along the waterfront for a few more blocks, stopping in front of a large, gray building with a Soviet flag on a pole and groups of policemen standing around on the sidewalk, their automatic pistols holstered on wide black gun belts. I didn't dare turn around to look at Annie, but I had a sinking feeling.

Nikolas must have sensed our apprehension. "Not worry," he told Annie as we got out. "Only here to get proper paper. No problem with police."

"Thanks, Niki," she said. I don't know where she got that accent. Probably from *Gone with the Wind*.

The inside smelled of desperation and carbolic acid. A hubbub of noise and movement, with policemen coming and going and a few dispirited civilians sitting on benches. Nikolas introduced us to a grizzled, middle-aged officer in a tunic with golden shoulder boards. The officer led us to a desk in a corner, where he dictated something to a young policeman sitting behind a typewriter. The policeman filled in two forms in quadruplicate and gave Nikolas copies.

We all shook the officer's hand and, after dropping the gray man off at his office, went back to the immigration building. By then it was almost four o'clock. The crowd of Chinese had thinned considerably. Nikolas led us to his office, stopping on the way to hand the police forms and our passports to a plump, middle-aged woman with no front teeth.

Nikolas and Annie chatted while I sat and fumed about Milos's treachery. I couldn't see what he hoped to accomplish by stealing our visas, but I was glad that he hadn't stolen our passports. Now we just had to get out of town without running afoul of Mel and his boys.

The fat woman stuck her head in and handed Nikolas our passports and two yellow visa booklets. Annie and I thanked her profusely and she gave us a broad, toothless smile. "Now," Nikolas said, "the office will close. Perhaps a drink?" He looked at Annie. She hesitated. I was getting ready to kick her, but she said, soon enough, "That would be great, Niki."

He gave the driver directions and we drove to a bistro near the head of the elevated walkway. It was a small building with a painted sign on the window showing a cartoon leprechaun holding a giant whisky bottle to his upturned lips, four-leaf clovers dancing around his green bowler hat.

The building was hot and crowded, mostly with red-faced men. They turned to watch us come in—Russians have an instinctive ability to spot foreigners—and some of them raised their glasses to Nikolas. A few minutes later the gray man joined us, and a few minutes after that the grizzled policeman arrived, now in a blue sport coat and baggy green trousers. I told Nikolas to order us a round, and put a pile of rubles on the bar.

The barman, a scarred old man as wide as he was tall, put four shot glasses on the bar and filled them to the rims with vodka. One of the men at the bar spoke pretty good English. He was a trader from Yekaterinburg who'd come to Vladivostok to buy Japanese cars.

The policeman was an unregenerate Stalinist, and he was very unhappy about the criminal element taking over Vladivostok. He said that four of his men had been shot in the past year and that the police in the city felt like they were under siege. He said darkly—as translated by the trader—that under the old regime such elements would have been eradicated. The gray man nodded agreement and we all raised a toast to the old regime.

I don't know how many shots of vodka we tossed back, but by the time the policeman looked at his watch and said that he had to go, my head was swimming pleasantly. I and my drinking companions had covered world events, the North Korean threat to invade South Korea, and the relative worth of Japanese and European cars. We'd drunk toasts to Russo-American friendship, to Lenin (they prudently didn't propose a toast to Stalin), and again to Russo-American friendship.

I paid the bar tab with a large percentage of my remaining rubles and we went out into the nascent Russian night. A soft, gentle snow was falling, and the streets were already wet with it. Nikolas followed us out, holding Annie's arm, and she was looking distinctly unhappy. The trader had stayed behind. The policeman and the gray official and I exchanged bear hugs and they staggered off to catch a cab at the railway station. After some gentle argument, Annie and Nikolas said their goodbyes. He and I shook hands, and she and I started off up the hill toward the hotel.

"Man," she said, "that was tough. Niki really wanted to come back to the hotel with us."

"With you," I corrected her. "The man's in love."

"In lust. Well, I wasn't having any of that, I tell you."

"I thought he was good-looking," I said, to needle her.

"Steel teeth! You gotta be kidding."

"It's a status symbol," I said. "Really, except for that, he's a good-looking guy."

When we got to the hotel I stopped outside and counted my rubles. I had enough for the taxi back to the airport and only a few hundred more. "How much money you got?" I asked Annie.

She opened her purse and counted her bills. "I got about eighty dollars' worth."

"Christ," I said, "we haven't got enough for the rooms."

"We'll get one room," she said.

I chuckled. "Man, the ladies are going to like this."

The lobby was deserted, except for the ladies. When the tall lady saw us she gave us a questioning look, then smiled when I gave her the thumbs-up.

"We got new visas," I told her. "Thank you so much for your help."

"Yes, that is good, but there is something I must tell you." She hesitated. "Is not my business, of course. But some men came looking for you. One hour since now. Is not good, I think."

"What kind of men?"

"We call them musicians." She said something to one of the other ladies, who shook her head angrily and said something. The tall lady lowered her voice and bent over the counter. "Mafia."

"What did they look like?"

"One was not Russian. He speak Russian, but not. Small man, black hair, very short. The other . . . big Russian, very big. They wear leather coat."

I looked at Annie. "Mel's goons." I turned back to the lady. "Did they say what they wanted?"

"No, but they go to elevator and we do not want . . . we afraid to tell them no. No good call police, you know. But they come back down soon. I think they know your room numbers."

"I bet they did," I said bitterly. "Do you think we must go to a different hotel?"

She looked around. "You can stay, but we will put you on second floor. If they come back, we will say you check out." She gestured to the other ladies, who were following the conversation closely even though it was in English. "Nobody will say you are here."

I smiled and thanked her. "We will need only one room," I added.

Her pale blond eyebrows shot up. She gave Annie a delighted, conspiratorial look, which Annie returned stolidly. She said something to the other ladies, and they registered happy surprise. One of them went to the rack at the other end of the counter and took down a key. We had to turn in our passports, of course, but the tall lady promised that they wouldn't give them to anyone except the police. As Annie and I went to the elevator, they chirped and twittered behind us like schoolgirls at a matinee.

Our new room was a closet with two narrow bunks, a tiny deal table with two wrenched metal chairs, and a heavy porcelain sink under the window. There was no bathroom, so apparently the rooms on this floor were served by a communal toilet down the hall.

I washed my face in freezing water and started feeling a little more sober. Annie went down the hall and I lay on one of the bunks. There was only a thin gray blanket on it, but the room was warm and the radiator next to the sink clanked reassuringly.

Nobody inquired about us during the night. The day ladies were on station when we went downstairs, and I thanked them profusely for their help. The tall lady said she hoped we would come back soon, and said she was sorry we had had problems. She gave us a long, slim hand to shake. We waved goodbye to the ladies and went out.

The ride to the airport took most of our remaining money. We had a few bad minutes when the people at the Aeroflot counter couldn't find our reservations, but they soon got it sorted out and issued our boarding passes.

After about an hour, a young man in a white uniform came in and announced something in Russian. "Looks like it's time to board," Annie said. She finished her coffee and grabbed her bag. We lined up with the other passengers and went out into the cold.

A tractor pulled our unheated shuttle up to the plane, a giant jet with two engines on the wings and a third on the tail, like a Boeing 727 on steroids. There were only about a dozen passengers, and within minutes the door was closed. A few minutes later the plane took off and banked toward the north.

An hour later we landed at Khabarovsk, a dreary-looking city strung along a wide, gray bay, and the plane soon filled with laughing, jostling men. The noise level in the cabin shot up. "Miners," said one of the Russians who'd come on board in Vladivostok, from the seat in front of us. "They are going to Seattle. The company gives them a month of paid vacation in Seattle for eight months of working in the mines."

"That sounds like a party," I said. In fact, it already was a party, and some of the men were carrying half-empty bottles of vodka.

"Yes," the man said, craning around to talk between the seats. He was a dapper little fellow with shiny black hair parted in the middle. His English was heavily accented, but good. "The company puts them all in a hotel with guards to keep them in. Otherwise . . ." He tilted his hand back and forth. "Perhaps they will, what you say, run amok."

"I hope they don't run amok here," Annie said.

"Oh, no, they have minders." He pointed his chin toward a beefy young man in a white shirt and tie, standing in the aisle.

The stewardesses finally got the men settled in their seats and buckled up. The catcalls and boisterous laughter got louder. Bottles got upended and tossed aside. The plane took off and headed out over the dull gray ocean.

It wasn't until we got to cruising altitude that the serious drinking began. The stewardesses trundled a vodka cart down the aisle, pouring plastic cups full of the stuff. The cart went up and down, and the partying went on unabated.

Finally, after the vodka took its effect, the noise level dropped and the cabin got relatively quiet. A fast night came on, and then a fast dawn as the plane streaked toward the rising sun. I dozed off and on.

Clink. Clink-clink. I struggled into consciousness, looking around to see what was making the noise. Then, with a sinking feeling, I recognized it. The vodka cart. The cabin was filled with the faint red light of a giant new sun rising above the clouds and shining in through the left-side windows.

Men stirred. Glasses were filled. The laughter and noise began again. Annie and I begged off and took cups of strong, bitter coffee.

Not long afterward, the plane descended through the clouds and circled for a landing at Anchorage. The world was dark and forbidding under the low overcast, and dirty snow lined the runway as the plane touched down. A stewardess told the passengers who'd come on board in Vladivostok that we would be getting off first, and when we got our bags and went forward, I could see why. The miners were drunk again, and only half of them were awake.

A group of big men waited on the jet bridge. The dapper little man said, as we walked to the concourse, "They will carry off the men who can't walk. The authorities will clear them in asleep if they can't be awakened. They are used to them here. They get a load every week."

Annie and I had a long wait for the connection. At one point, I told her, "Did you know that Milos was in the Bulgarian secret police? He said they knew how to deal with women like you. They'd put them in cells overnight in ice water up to their knees."

"Asshole."

"This was after you kicked him in the balls. I bet that'd get you an execution squad in Bulgaria."

We were slumped in the hard plastic chairs in the concourse. She sat up suddenly. "The Bulgarian secret police?"

"That's right. That's what he said. I believe him, too."

She punched me lightly on the arm. "That's it, then. I'll get that asshole. You know who tried to kill the pope?"

"The pope?" I opened my eyes wide. "It was the Bulgarian secret police, wasn't it?"

"Right. And you know who arranged it?"

I chuckled. "I do now. What're you going to do?"

"Tell Immigration Services—INS. I'll tell them he admitted to us that he helped set it up."

"Christ," I said, "I hope I never get crosswise with you."

"I'll get that asshole back if it's the last thing I do."

And she did. A couple of months later she called me to say that she'd made friends with an INS agent who told her that Milos really had been in the Bulgarian secret police. The INS hadn't found anything indicating that he'd been involved in the attack on the pope, but he'd lied on his residency application, and he and his family were going to be deported.

She learned from her friend which flight Milos was leaving on, deported with his family back to Bulgaria. So she drove to Milos's house and waited in her car until he and his family came out with their baggage. A taxi pulled up to take them to the airport. His wife and children were crying. As he started to get in the taxi, she honked the horn. He looked up and saw her. She gave him a little wave with her fingers.

CHAPTER SEVEN

THE *PROFESSOR KURILOV* LEAVES PORT

AT ONE TIME IN my life, I got into the business of buying ships in Europe and sending them across the Atlantic for Haitian buyers. There were a number of us doing it, and although we were competitors, sometimes, if one of us found a ship and didn't have a buyer for it, he would pass it on to one of the others.

Among my competitors were Hans Dieter, an older German with tattoos covering his arms and chest, who'd been a roustabout and stevedore in his youth; Berto Pena, a pockmarked Cuban who looked like a character out of *Miami Vice,* with ropes of gold jewelry around his neck and a ring on every finger; Captain David Bruce, a hard-drinking New Yorker who'd run tugboats up and down the East Coast until he found his calling in the Haiti trade; and Bret Sullivan, a native Miamian with a brick-colored face, a bristly red crew-cut, and a bluff, confident manner.

Another man in the business, Captain Barry Butler, a Scot, became one of my closest friends. He has both an Unlimited Tonnage Master's License and an Unlimited Horsepower Chief Engineer's License, a rarity in the shipping industry. We'd met in Rotterdam, on board the *North Cape III,* a ship we were both looking at for clients. Barry's client bought her. The next time I went to Rotterdam looking for ships, I had the taxi driver take me by the *North Cape III*'s dock. She was still there; Barry had discovered that she had serious engine problems, and was still making repairs.

Barry, an aficionado of Captain Morgan Spiced Rum, has a calm demeanor and an easy laugh. He is a great drinking companion. Late at night in a bar in Puerto Quetzal, Guatemala, some years after we first met, he told me about his own adventures sneaking a ship out of San Andres, Colombia. It wasn't a happy experience.

The ship was a small break-bulk freighter that Barry owned himself, bought with the savings from a lifetime at sea. She'd carried a cargo to San Andres, and the receiver had allegedly bribed a local judge to have her seized. Barry had stayed in San Andres during the proceedings, hoping to fight the seizure in court. But when he learned that the judge had been suborned, and there was no hope of getting her back, he brought another crew to the island—San Andres is a large island hundreds of miles off the Colombian coast—and they sneaked on board in the middle of the night.

Unfortunately, the Colombian authorities had sabotaged the ship's main engine, and as they were leaving the port, it failed. Barry and the crew were taken off the ship, the crew were deported, and Barry was thrown in jail. The same judge sentenced him to fifteen years in prison.

He survived imprisonment on the island for two years only because the British government arranged for food to be brought to him every day. Then he learned from the British embassy in Bogotá, which regularly sent a consular officer to visit him, that his daughter in Scotland had died of a sudden viral infection.

He told me that upon hearing of his daughter's death, he'd lost his mind. The Colombians transferred him to a prison for the criminally insane—he didn't describe the conditions there, but I could imagine how horrific they were. Soon afterward, they gave him a "compassionate release" and sent him home to Glasgow. His wife had divorced him while he was in prison; he arrived home broke and alone.

Barry and I have become the closest of friends in the years since. It's hard to see in this calm, competent, jovial man someone who could have endured the kind of abuse and suffering he went through. Whenever I feel sorry for myself, I think of Barry, and I am ashamed of my weakness.

I located half a dozen ships in European harbors for Haitian buyers; each time I would spend a few weeks in port getting the ship ready to sail across the Atlantic, then turn the ship over to her new owner and fly home for a few weeks before heading out to search for another ship. Earlier that year, I'd started correspondence law school at Northwestern California University, and everywhere I went I lugged my law books. I spent long hours in hellhole ports reading primary texts like *The Theory of Law and State* and *Prosser on Torts*.

My wife was horrified. As a court reporter, my wife hobnobbed with the elite of the local bar; she was deeply ashamed of having a husband enrolled in correspondence law school. On the other hand, she didn't suggest that I quit work and go to law school full-time. To spare her embarrassment, I promised to keep my law school education a secret.

My modus operandi in buying ships was to locate a few for sale in a general geographic area, make a whirlwind inspection trip, and then find a Haitian to buy the most likely prospect. I found the ships through European ship brokers who would regularly fax me their lists of ships for sale. The Haitians had only a few hard-and-fast requirements: The ships had to be between a thousand and two thousand deadweight tons, they had to have their own cargo gear—Haitian ports don't have cranes, so a ship that can't load and discharge its own cargo is worthless in that trade—and, finally, they had to be cheap.

In the course of putting ships into service and getting them ready to cross the Atlantic, I'd lived in cities all over Europe. I'd made a lot of friends, and a few enemies. One of the men I'd encountered was a crooked ship seller named Brod van Half, a tall, pleasant-faced man who wore designer suits and operated out of a black Rolls-Royce. After the buyer paid the money, only to discover he'd bought a turkey, the Rolls disappeared, never to be seen again. I've met a number of men who've bought ships from him, and nobody's ever been able to find out where he lives, a sensible precaution on his part.

However, periodically Brod would send me his list of ships for sale, and a few times I went to look at them. Most brokers don't own the ships they sell, but Brod's technique was to buy ships with expensive problems, hide the problems as well as he could, and sell them, pretending that he was merely the broker, and not responsible for concealed defects.

Early one spring, I left for one of my ship-buying trips, flying to Amsterdam and taking a train to Rotterdam to inspect a fifteen-hundred-ton single-decker, the *Corinne Blanguette*.

It was a cold, rainy day. The ship was docked near the Euromast, a tall needle piercing the gloomy skies with a restaurant two-thirds of the way up.

I could see from quayside that the ship was a wreck, with wasted, corroded shell plating along the hull. I immediately lost interest. As I was about to walk to the tram for a ride back to the train station, to journey to the next ship, a long black Rolls-Royce pulled up next to the ship and Brod got out.

He was wearing a tailored raincoat over a vested brown suit, a jaunty homburg on his head, and carried a tan pigskin briefcase.

"Captain Max? What are you doing here?"

"I heard about this ship from Dirk Vallery. Are you the listing broker?" The listing broker is the one direct to the owner.

"Yes, yes, I'm the broker. Let's get out of this filthy rain. Please come on board."

We shook hands and I followed him up the battered, rickety gangway to the master's saloon. The accommodations were decent, but you can't carry cargo in the accommodations.

The crew were Egyptian, another sign of Brod's methods. Egyptians are considered the Haitians of European shipping: You don't put them on if you care about the ship. They work cheap, but they can't repair or even maintain a vessel.

I assured Brod that my client wasn't interested in the *Corinne Blanguette*. It didn't offend him, although he did offer me a secret commission if I would convince my client to buy her. When I demurred, he said that he'd just come to the ship to give the captain some papers, and offered me a ride to the train station.

On the way, he asked if I'd be interested in a really cheap ship in Brugge, Belgium. He hastened to add that it wasn't his ship, but belonged to a friend, the owner of a ship-scrapping yard who had to get rid of her in a hurry. He assured me, lifting his manicured hand, that he wouldn't even get a commission. I stifled a snort.

When we reached the station, he handed me a broker sheet, a single page with the ship's specifications that brokers fax to prospective buyers. The *Aldorf* was a neat little freighter, long and low, built in the mid-1950s, with the rounded house and graceful bustle stern typical of those days. A ship with a round stern is said to have a "bustle" stern, named after the Victorian dress style. I took the sheet and promised to ask my client if he would be interested in her.

The next ship on my list was in Lelystad, a quaint Dutch fishing village on the English Channel, windswept and desolate. The ship was a nice little freighter, but the owner had a completely unrealistic idea of her worth. He wanted five hundred thousand dollars for a seven-hundred-ton ship, and no Haitian would pay that. So I went to my hotel on the town's waterfront and looked at the *Aldorf*'s broker sheet again.

She was at a place called the Belgisch Scheepssloperij. The address was on the sheet. Early the next morning, I caught a train south and arrived in Brugge in midafternoon.

The train station was just inside a high, crenellated wall surrounding the medieval city. When I walked out onto the wide plaza that fronted the modern, glass-front station, it was like going a thousand years back in time. The ancient streets had clearly been made for horses and buggies, and even small cars had to negotiate them with care. The old houses had fanciful carvings in their stone façades and upper stories overhanging the street.

After a late lunch in one of the small open-air cafés, I caught a taxi and told the driver to take me to the Belgisch Scheepssloperij.

A wide circular canal surrounds the town's wall. We crossed it on a low bridge and followed the external road around the gentle curve that parallels the canal. Here the town's buildings were more modern, mostly stores and warehouses, with a good number of bars and restaurants lining the road. The canal's level was only slightly below that of the flat land, and the high sides of canal barges—some of them freighters and some tourist boats with bicycles lining their decks—rose high above the road as we passed them. Most were very old, old enough to have riveted hulls and houses, although the ones I saw—and most of the ones I saw in the subsequent weeks—were in good shape.

We turned away from the ring road onto a long, straight lane that ran north between tall, well-groomed poplars. Low, flat fields stretched to the far tree line. We went about a mile along the canal, as straight as a ruler, to an area of shipyards and warehouses between the canal and the road. Old ships and canal boats in various stages of disrepair lay canted against the bank.

Brugge is a very conflicted place; everything there has two names. Even the city itself has two names, depending on whether you're French or Flemish. Its French name is Bruges, with a soft *g,* and its Flemish name is Brugge, pronounced "Brugah." Since most of the people I came to know were Flemish, I have thought of it ever since as Brugge.

The driver stopped in a muddy yard in front of a small, prefabricated office building. A half-demolished fishing trawler, a bathtub-shaped boat as big as a small ship, was pulled up on the bank north of the office, her bow chopped off, her accommodations naked to the elements. Men with cutting torches swarmed over her. Farther up the canal, a despondent-looking lightship with her midships lighthouse tower still intact lay with a list against the rough bank, heavy rust streaks striating her bluff bows.

I paid the driver and carried my pack up to the office. It was warm inside, with wide windows overlooking the yard and the quay behind it. Two women, one middle-aged and the other young and pretty, sat at their typewriters. I said I was there to look at the *Aldorf,* and the young secretary leaned back and called toward an open door to the left, "Willem!"

An awkward, gaunt man in his shirtsleeves, about my age, appeared in the doorway, his brown hair sticking out in short, tousled spikes. He looked at me and spoke in good English, "Yes, what is it?"

I repeated that I was there to look at the *Aldorf.*

"Well, it's over there." He pointed past the lightship. The view in that direction was blocked by large pieces of the trawler that had been cut off and dragged ashore. "If you want it, come see me."

"How much is it? Mr. van Half didn't say."

"Just take a look. If you want the ship, we'll make a deal." He ducked back into his office. The secretaries gave me apologetic looks. I took my flashlight out of my pack, pushed my pack into a corner, and went out.

The wind was cold, but not as cold as it'd been in Lelystad. The graveled ground was soaked with oil, and oil stood in puddles along the unimproved verge north of the quay. As I passed the trawler, a front-end loader with a chain stretched to the hull pulled another piece free, and it fell with a crash to the bank. The cutters weren't even taking out the wooden inner ceiling—the hull's liner—and splintered plywood and frames fell with the steel into a pile on the ground.

Now I could see the *Aldorf.* She was a pretty little thing, with high bows and a low house, typical of old European freighters, although she was a true sea vessel and not what is called a river-sea boat. There wasn't a straight line on her. The forecastle dipped in a smooth arc down to the deck, and the front of the house made a graceful curve up to the round, sloping funnel. You could tell that she had been built in the 1950s, even without the rounded lines: The strakes—the plates of the hull—were welded to one another, but they had been riveted to the frames. The rib-band, the joint between the hull and deck, was secured with a triple line of heavy rivets.

European shipbuilders are a conservative lot. Although the United States had started welding ships as early as World War II—sometimes with disastrous results—Dutch and German shipbuilders used rivets until long after the war. By the early '50s they had started welding the strakes to each other, and around the late '50s they had gained enough confidence in this new-fangled technology to weld the hull to the frames. However, it wasn't until the early '60s that they finally trusted welding enough to use it to secure the deck to the hull. So you can tell about when an early European freighter was built by the degree of welding in the hull.

Riveting is a good, strong system of holding a hull together, but it has some serious drawbacks, chief among them the difficulty of making welded repairs. When you cut out corroded sections of the hull, the heat of the torch expands the steel around the cutting and "draws" the rivets. The resulting elongation of the rivet holes causes leaks that have to be sealed by laying welding flux around each rivet, a laborious process. Also, rivet heads, being harder than the mild steel plates they hold together, tend to corrode faster than the hull, and eventually the hull will have to be riv-eted. This would cost more than the ship is worth, so at that point a riv-eted ship has to go to the breakers.

This ship wasn't ready for the breakers yet, though. I wondered why she was at a breaking yard. The rivet heads were proud and well rounded, and none of them was drawn. A short gangway lay at a steep angle against the hull, and I pulled myself up. The deck was wavy but free of heavy corrosion. The ship had wooden hatch boards, but in the Haiti trade, this isn't so bad.

In most trades, the time it takes to open and close the hatches on ships with wooden hatch boards is a real problem, both in terms of manpower required and in the ability to close the hatches quickly when rain threatens.

One thing a cargo ship can't afford is to let rain damage the cargo. But Haitians have unlimited manpower to close the hatches, and it hardly ever rains in Haiti. And since the hatches are covered with tarpaulins, hatch-board ships are reasonably weathertight.

The tarpaulins over the hatches on the *Aldorf* were patched and frayed, but complete. The steps leading to the accommodations were thin but free of holes. The portside door to the accommodations was unlocked, and I went in.

The accommodations were a delight of curving wooden bulkheads and moldings. You never see that kind of carpentry in modern, fast-built ships. The wheelhouse was straight out of a prewar movie, with speaking tubes going down to the engine room and lower decks, and a massive brass bin-nacle supporting a giant wooden wheel. I turned the wheel. Incredibly, it was a mechanical linkage. You never see that anymore.

The engine room was the real jewel in the ship. At least by flashlight, it was clean and well ordered. It had a Werkspoor engine, which was no longer being manufactured, but for which parts were still readily available. One of the generators had its heads off, so it was being worked on when the ship was laid up, but generators are relatively easy to replace.

The hold was the worst part of the ship. She had been carrying corro-sive bulk cargoes such as fertilizer and salt—common cargoes in Europe—and the hull's inner surface was uniformly corroded, with some of the frames adrift from the shell plating. Any replacement of the plating would be complicated by the problem of drawing the rivets, but for a Haitian, who never plans to keep his ship more than a few years anyway, the major question would be price rather than hull condition.

The hold had a surprise. Two large tank trailers on wheels were chained to the floor, one forward and one aft. Hoses ran from them to a door that had been cut in the engine-room bulkhead. Such a door is strictly forbid-den by class requirements, as it compromises the ship's safety if the hold ever becomes breached to the sea. More puzzling, the tanks looked like they'd been there a long time. The ship couldn't have carried cargo with them in the hold, and they weren't big enough to hold liquid cargoes. Besides, carrying liquid cargoes in such an arrangement would have been illegal.

I went back to the yard's office. It was almost quitting time, and the cutters on the trawler were rolling up their hoses. The younger secretary was leaving, a bright scarf over her blond hair, and she smiled at me as she picked her way across the muddy yard.

The other secretary motioned me with a nod of her head toward Willem's office. I stuck my head in and knocked on the doorframe. He looked up with an irritated expression.

"What do you think? Want her?" Belatedly, he gestured toward a chair in front of his desk.

"She doesn't look too bad," I said cautiously, taking a seat. "What's the deal with the tanks in the hold?"

He leaned back and surveyed me. "I'll tell you about the ship. She's owned by a couple of Greek guys. They've been running cigarettes from here to South Africa. She's set up to make the trip nonstop."

I frowned. "Cigarettes?"

"That's right. Bloody great tax on cigarettes in South Africa. The boys would buy cigarettes here tax-free—for export—and discharge them off the South African coast into small boats. Made a fortune at it. Used to be a big trade smuggling cigarettes into England, too, but the Brits complained, and now the government's cracking down. So the boys want to sell the *Aldorf*."

"How much do they want for her?"

"Sixty thousand dollars."

"What? Does the main engine run?"

"Of course. That's the best part of the ship. Runs like a Swiss watch. They had to keep it in top shape to go from here to South Africa nonstop."

"That's awfully cheap." I had a thought. "She's not under detention, is she?"

"What kind of detention?"

"Port State Control."

He held up a skeletal hand. "No, no, they don't even know about her."

I nodded. I'd run afoul of Northern Europe Port State Control before. In the rest of the world, ships can come and go pretty much as they please, but in Northern Europe, Great Britain, and the United States, ships that call their ports, regardless of their flags, can be subjected to rigorous inspection by shore authorities, and if the inspectors find anything they don't like—hull condition, crewing, equipment, anything—they can detain the ship and prevent her from leaving. Since nobody can tell a country which ships can leave its ports, there's no appeal from a Port State Control detention, no matter how unreasonable.

Standards for ships vary wildly from country to country, and even from port to port within a single country. For example, the Miami Coast Guard is known to be reasonable about ship condition, but the Mobile Coast Guard inspectors are wild dogs. I knew a perfectly good ship that called Panama City, Florida, which is within the Mobile Coast Guard district, and never could get out. In desperation, the owner hired me to help, but nothing could get them to release the ship, even after the ship's own flag-state surveyor told them there was nothing wrong with her. I finally had to make a deal with the captain of the port whereby the ship would be towed to international water, with the understanding that she would never come to the United States again.

The problem in the United States is that ships are inspected by Coast Guard officers who may or may not know anything about ship construction or condition. Many are so-called "Ninety-Day Wonders" who come out of the Coast Guard's three-month training course—some of them from Iowa or Montana and have never seen a ship before—and are immediately able to go aboard ocean freighters in the nation's ports and bankrupt their owners.

Holland and Belgium also have reputations for being unreasonable about detaining ships, but for a different reason. It's well-known among port states that no one onshore will make a penny off a ship once it leaves. Tramp ships can go their entire lives and never return to a particular port. So everybody ashore knows that their only shot at making money off a ship is keeping it in port.

Even if a Port State Control inspector doesn't directly profit from detaining a ship in port, his relatives and friends, and even the general population, will. And since there's no appeal from an unreasonable detention, he's perfectly free to do it.

I wasn't sure that the *Aldorf* could withstand a rigorous Northern Europe Port State Control inspection, but, considering the price, it was worth the risk.

"I'll call my client tonight," I said, rising. "If he's interested, I'd like to take another look at her tomorrow."

He grimaced. "All right, fine. She'll be there." He got up and patted his pockets for his keys. I went out with him and the secretary behind me.

That night I stayed in a small hotel in the shadow of St. Salvatore Cathedral, a giant medieval pile dating back to the twelfth century. I walked around the old city and admired the neat little houses and chocolate shops. Then I had supper at a *frituur* place near the hotel, a small fast-food restaurant, washed down by some Stella Artois beers. I found it amusing that a bottle of water in the *frituur* shop was thirty-five Belgian francs, and a beer was thirty-two. Any country where beer was cheaper than water couldn't be all bad.

Before I went to bed, I called a couple of my Haitian buddies and told them about the ship. Both were interested, but one in particular, Robert Voisson, agreed to pay me to put her in service if she proved worth buying. I told him I would call after I'd made further inspection.

The next morning I was back at the breaking yard shortly before eight o'clock. There was a new ship at the quay, a trawler very similar to the one already half demolished, with the name *Vikunov XXI* on the bow.

When Willem arrived, I was able to look at some areas of the ship I hadn't inspected the previous afternoon, including the forecastle, forepeak tank, and steering flat. The biggest surprise came when I rummaged up an old sounding tape and sounded the vessel's ballast tanks. They were all full of fuel. That was very strange. You shouldn't put diesel in the ballast tanks because after that you can never put ballast water in them without causing an oil slick.

Except for the forepeak tank, every ballast tank in the ship was full of diesel fuel. I sounded the four bunker tanks, where the ship's fuel should normally be stored, and they were full of diesel as well. What was even more puzzling was that the ballast tanks weren't plumbed to the bunker manifold. In other words, the diesel in the ballast tanks couldn't be routed to the vessel's engines.

As I walked back toward the office, I saw that the name on the trawler that had just arrived had already been painted out, the fresh gray paint a poor match for the faded gray paint on the hull. I chuckled to myself. Now I knew what kind of breaking yard Willem was running.

I went into the office. Willem was standing in the front room, smoking a cigarette and talking to the secretaries. He took me into his office. "Mr. Bik," I said, "the *Aldorf* is full of diesel fuel. Every ballast tank on board is full of it."

He shrugged. "Are you complaining?"

"The ship can't carry ballast. Did the Greeks do that?"

He regarded me for a long time, then he got up and closed the door. "Captain," he said, "we cut up a lot of ships here. To take the fuel off the ships that come in would cost me a fortune. Can you believe it? I have to dispose of it as toxic waste, even absolutely good diesel. It's bloody ridiculous. This damned government . . . but I won't say more. If your client wants the ship, say so. If not, say so."

"Hold your horses," I said. "I've got to talk to him. But let me get this straight . . . I haven't checked the stability book, but a ship that size should hold about sixty tons of fuel in the bunker tanks and maybe a hundred and twenty tons of ballast water. Are you saying that you'll sell a ship with a hundred and eighty tons of bunkers on board for sixty thousand dollars?"

"Not me," he said blandly. "The Greek guys. Yes, they'll sell it for sixty thousand."

"Do they know you've been filling the ballast tanks with fuel?'

"Do you want the ship or not?" he said brusquely. "I have no time to play games. If you are finished with your inspection, talk to your client."

"Very well," I said stiffly, rising.

He rubbed his face. "Sorry. But please do find out. Otherwise I will sell her to someone else."

Mr. Voisson couldn't believe I could buy a ship with $100,000 worth of diesel on board for $60,000. "I don't know how good the diesel is," I told him. "Some of it could be old and contaminated. However, what I saw looked pretty good, at least on the sounding tape."

The next day I opened an account in a local bank and Mr. Voisson wired $70,000 to it.

Over the next week, I had the ship moved to a slip at the end of the canal, just north of the city, and started the work of getting her ready for her certificates. Mr. Voisson called a Honduran crewing agent and sent a captain and crew. My friend Ramesh was back in Trinidad working on his dad's fishing boat; I got Mr. Voisson to send him to the ship as bosun.

The captain and the rest of the crew arrived together, on a flight from Miami to Amsterdam. The captain was an old Portuguese man with a high, hooked nose and darting black eyes. A Colombian woman arrived with them, whom the captain introduced as his wife. Since he was about seventy and she was about twenty-five, I doubted that it was a marriage in any conventional sense.

The chief engineer was a short Czech man named Georg who'd been working on Haitian freighters. He didn't enjoy a good reputation. The second engineer, Mike Loft, was a big, puffy Irishman with heavy muttonchop sideburns and long, wavy black hair. He looked like Elvis in his last days.

I took an instant dislike to the captain, but in the interest of fairness—and considering that the owner had already paid his airfare—I set him to getting the ship in service. I gave him a list of jobs to get done on board and took the Colombiana to the local grocery store to stock up on provisions.

One of the first things I had to do was get a timing gear and chain for the Deutz harbor generator in the forecastle. The gear had broken in half and the failure had snapped the chain. Luckily, the engineers reported, the valves and valve stems were still okay.

I could have had the parts shipped, but both of the engine-room generators needed repair, and until I got the harbor generator working, we would be a dead ship. So I decided to save time and drive up to Rotterdam to get them myself.

The next morning I met Ramesh at the gangway. He was wearing an old, oil-stained boiler suit; his hairy feet still slopped along in the usual flip-flops. He led me into the forecastle. The engineers had the timing-chain cover off the harbor generator and were getting ready to install the new gear and chain. After I gave the engineers the replacement parts, Ramesh led me on deck.

"De cap'n buy plenty stuff yesterday," he said. "Did you tell him to buy dat stuff?"

"What kind of stuff?"

"Every kind of t'ing, Cap."

"All for the ship?"

"Yas, I t'ink so. But I fear he make monkey business wit' de chandler.

Dey go in his cabin and close de door. I t'ink maybe we have problem wit' him."

I patted him on the shoulder. "Thanks, Ramesh. How about the others?"

"Dat chief engineer drink all day long, Cap, but I t'ink he do his job. De second, I don't know yet. Him too fat for engineer, dough. We get to Miami, for sure he sweat all dat fat off."

"Yeah," I said, "I wondered about that myself."

I found the captain and cook in the master's saloon, drinking coffee.

"Captain," I said, "did you buy some supplies yesterday?"

"Yes," he said, and slid a long, handwritten invoice under a printed letterhead across the coffee table. "We had to have some supplies right away."

I glanced at the list. Almost everything was needed, but the prices were outrageous. I laid it back on the table. "I didn't authorize you to buy anything, Captain. I was planning to supply the ship myself. We don't need a chandler, especially at these prices."

His eyes snapped at me. "I am the captain. It is my responsibility to make sure the crew has what it needs. We didn't even have enough blankets and pillows."

"There are blankets and pillows on board," I said shortly. "Get the crew to gather up everything on this list. I'm giving it back to the chandler." I copied the number on the letterhead into my notebook. "I'll call him now. And I'm giving you a direct order: Do not buy anything for this ship without my authorization. Do you understand me?"

His lined, ancient face set hard. "I understand."

I went to the nearest pay phone (this was before cellphones became commonplace) and called the chandler's office. The secretary put me through to a raspy-voiced man with a French accent. "I delivered those goods on the captain's orders," he growled. "We cannot take them back."

"Then I won't pay for them."

"Then the ship won't sail from this port."

He had me there. The captain is always the agent of the owner, and whatever he buys the owner has to pay for. "All right," I said, "come by this morning and I'll pay. But I'm telling you now that you are not to supply anything else to this ship."

He hung up without replying.

At eight o'clock the crew went to work. I went to the forecastle to watch the engineers working on the harbor generator. By then, they'd gotten the Mercedes generator in the engine room working and the ship had power. The chief and second squatted in front of the Deutz, the second holding a flashlight as the chief tapped gently on the timing-chain gear to slide it onto the camshaft.

"How's it going, fellows?" I asked.

The chief stood up and wiped his hands on a rag. "Okay, Captain. We'll have it working in a couple of hours. Then we have to shut down the Mercedes and change some of the injectors." His breath stank of rum.

"Chief," I said, "can you come on deck with me?"

He handed the mallet to the second engineer and followed me out. The sun was rising above the line of trees along the road and burning off the mists. "Chief," I said, "I run an easy ship. I don't mind if the crew has liquor on board. But I can't have you drinking during working hours."

"I take a small drink every morning," he said. "That's all. I don't drink during working hours."

I shook my head. "I don't allow drinking before work, either. You'll have to do without your small drink every morning. If you can't obey that rule, tell me now and I'll make the necessary arrangements to get you home."

He stared at me angrily, his mouth set tight, then relaxed. "I don't need it," he muttered. "It's just my custom. Very well, then, I won't drink before coming on duty."

I finally got a tally of the bunkers onboard: thirty-eight tons in the bunker tanks, twenty tons in the tank trailer in the hold, and slightly over a hundred tons in the double bottoms. Diesel in Europe at the time was selling for two dollars a gallon, and there are 313 gallons in a ton of diesel, so we had just under one hundred thousand dollars' worth of fuel on board. At two tons' consumption for every twenty-four hours of navigation, we could steam for seventy-eight days without refueling.

After lunch on board, I went to the Belgisch Scheepssloperij office to see about the Deletion Certificate from the ship's ex–flag state. I was going to register the ship with Honduras, but I needed a Deletion Certificate from the previous flag state, Cambodia. Although I'd asked Willem for it several times, he still hadn't provided it.

"That's not my responsibility," he said shortly. "You bought that ship from the Greek guys."

"I paid you," I said. "The check was made out to Belgisch Scheepssloperij."

"That doesn't mean I must provide a Deletion Certificate."

"It might to a Belgian court."

His face flushed. "Are you threatening to sue me?"

"Look, Willem," I said, "you know a ship's no good without registration. You also know that no country—no legitimate country—will register a ship without a Deletion Certificate. What do you expect me to do?"

"All right, all right," he muttered. "I'll get it."

The chandler arrived at the ship shortly afterward, a fat man in tradesman's coveralls, driving a Citroën panel truck. I met him on the dock. "How much did you promise to pay the captain for that order yesterday?" I demanded.

His pig's eyes bulged. "Is you accuse me of monkey business?" he said in a thick French accent.

"I know what's going on here." I pulled out the invoice. "You charged me two hundred francs per bottle for dishwashing liquid. This is robbery."

He turned to go. "I will arrest zis ship. You no pay, I arrest ship."

"I'm going to pay. Just don't think I don't know what's going on." I scribbled on the invoice, "No further orders from this ship to be filled," and held it out. "Sign that and I'll pay."

He glanced at it, signed it, and handed it back. I calculated the U.S. equivalent to twenty-five thousand francs and shoved the money into his fat red hand. He stomped off to his truck and made a wide, squealing turn on the ancient stone wharf, trailing blue smoke.

That night as I pushed through the heavy wooden door of my hotel, I nearly knocked down the woman who ran the place, a slim pretty blonde of about thirty who kept her hair up in braided buns on the top of her head. Her name was Julie. She was leaving for the evening, and had a thick shawl around her thin face.

"Oh," she said, "you startled me." She smiled. "Have you had supper?"

We stood close in the narrow hall. "I ate at the *frituur* shop on the other side of the church," I told her.

"Yes," she said, "I am sorry we don't have a restaurant in the hotel, and there are very few restaurants around here open in the evening."

She had a large bundle tied in a blanket, either clothing or laundry. I held the door open for her and she went out.

Work on the ship proceeded by fits and starts. The captain was useless. He only worked when I forced him to, and then just enough to keep from getting fired. He tried to get some goods delivered to the ship on credit—in an effort to get kickbacks from other corrupt chandlers and suppliers—but Ramesh was able to scare them off. Once, Ramesh told me, the captain went into a fury, shouting and spitting at him, but of course he didn't dare raise a hand to the burly Trinidadian.

The end came when I got a call at the hotel one morning from Ramesh. "Captain," he said, "did you order tarps for the hatches?"

"Tarps? No, why?"

"There's a truck here unloading tarps. The captain says he didn't order them. He says you must have ordered them."

"Oh, Christ. Tell the driver we won't take them. I'll be right there."

When I reached the ship, two huge rolls of tarps were lying on the dock, about twenty feet long and three feet in diameter each. The driver was sitting in the truck's cab eating a doughnut. He spoke very little English but showed me an invoice for three thousand U.S. dollars for two heavy, rubberized tarpaulins. I stormed on board looking for the captain.

He was in the wheelhouse, making a big show of correcting the charts that I'd bought the previous week. "Captain," I said, "did you order those tarps?"

"No," he said, "but we must have new tarps, you know. The tarps we have are not good enough to cross the Atlantic."

"Nonsense. They're complete and watertight. Are you telling me you didn't order those tarps?"

His little rat eyes darted around the room and finally fixed on mine. "No, I didn't order them. I did talk to a man . . ."

"You're lying. You tried to have them delivered at six o'clock in the morning so they'd be on board before I got here."

I gathered the crew and we went down to the dock to reload the tarps on the truck. It was hard work, and by the time we'd gotten them lifted up to the truck's high bed, I was sweaty and gritty with dust. I went up to the master's saloon.

The captain was drinking coffee with his plump young wife. "Captain," I said, "I know you ordered those tarps."

He gave me a supercilious smile. "So what? The ship is not safe without new tarps. I have the authority to order whatever the ship needs to be safe."

I slammed my fist on the table. "You have the authority to get off this ship," I said. "You and your wife pack your gear and get off."

"Not without our salaries," he said calmly. "If you try to put us off without paying us, I will report it to the port authorities."

I paid them their salaries and airfare to Miami. The captain wrote out a receipt and stamped it with the ship's stamp. I went to get Ramesh. "Stay with that son of a bitch until he leaves," I told him.

I stayed on board until the captain and his wife took their bags down the gangway and went to the pay phone on the warehouse wall to call a cab. A few minutes later a gray Mercedes picked them up and that was the last I saw of them. But it wasn't the end of the trouble that scurvy old rat caused me.

That afternoon, while I was helping the ABs repair the stern capstan, a small white car with a crest on the door pulled up at the foot of the gangway. The capstan is a winch on the fantail that hauls in the ship's dock lines. A short man dressed in white slacks and a blue sweater got out and walked toward the gangway. He was carrying a small black-leather briefcase.

"Good afternoon," he said in British-accented English. He had a soft, pleasant face and twinkling blue eyes. "I'm with Port State Control, I'm here to inspect this vessel." He handed me a card printed in English. His name was Hans Polderman. We shook hands.

"Welcome on board," I said. "Would you like some coffee?"

"No, thank you. But perhaps we can take a look at the ship's documents."

It was the beginning of a bad afternoon. Mr. Polderman started writing in his notebook as soon as he started reviewing the ship's certificates, and he didn't stop until he left the ship four hours later. Most of the deficiencies could be rectified, like the nonfunctioning stern capstan and the lack of a belt guard on the harbor generator. But when he wrote, "Deficient hull condition in way of vessel topsides," I knew we were sunk.

"The hull's not that bad," I'd protested, as we walked along the hold floor. He played his flashlight over the corroded plating and held it on one of the wasted frames that had come adrift from the plating.

"This is not acceptable," he said mildly. "I'm afraid this ship will have to go into drydock."

My face fell. He said gently, "Is this your ship, son?"

I shook my head. "I'm just the superintendent."

He nodded. "There's a drydock in Zeebrugge. When she's on the blocks, give me a call—you have my card—and I'll come take a look at the work."

I nodded miserably. Back in the master's saloon, he took out an official detention form and began filling it in, writing in a small, precise hand. Ramesh stuck his head in, but I shook my head and he ducked out.

The detentions filled three pages. "You understand," he said, "that the vessel cannot move from this berth without our permission. However, you are free to take on bunkers and water."

I nodded. He gave me another kindly look and said, "You know, I wouldn't be here if we hadn't gotten a call. We don't normally come down to this little dock."

He got in his car and drove off. I stood there looking after him for a long time. Finally, Ramesh came up, his flip-flops slapping on the steel deck. "W'at is it, Cap'n? Who was dat man?"

"Port State Control. The ship's detained."

"What does that mean?"

I turned to him and said bleakly, "It means this ship will never leave this port. That pig of a Portuguese captain reported us. The inspector says we'll have to replace the shell plating before he'll let the ship leave."

Ramesh whistled. "Can de owner afford dat?"

"Probably not." I spat on the deck. "Even if he could, it wouldn't be worth it." I turned my back to the bulwark and leaned on it, rubbing my face. "All right, it's five o'clock. You and the crew can knock off. I need to go to the hotel and call Mr. Voisson. We'll see what can be done tomorrow."

As I pushed through the front door of the hotel, I heard Julie on the second floor, singing in Flemish. She had a beautiful voice. For some reason, the sound affected me, and I stood for a moment in the foyer, listening. Then her face appeared over the balcony, her hair backlit from the dim yellow bulbs in fake candelabra on the walls.

"Oh, Captain," she called down, "everything okay?"

"Oh, yes," I said, putting on a smile. "Just tired, I guess."

She came down with a broom and dustpan. "Have you had supper?"

I shook my head.

The staircase made a half turn at the bottom, with fan-shaped lower steps. She stood on the wide first step and brushed a strand of hair away from her temple.

"You must be tired of that *frituur* shop," she said softly, looking up. "Why don't you come to my place for supper?"

I didn't say anything for a moment. "It won't be much," she went on quickly." Perhaps just salad and sandwiches. But I have cold beer."

"That sounds great," I heard myself saying. "Thanks. It's . . . it's been a long day. I'd like that."

"I have some things to finish up," she said, slipping past me.

I hated to do it, but I called Mr. Voisson to tell him what had happened. He was an elderly man, and his old voice shook. "But what can be done, Captain?" he quavered. "Is all that money lost?"

"No, sir," I said, more firmly than I felt. "I'll figure something out. But we need another captain. Will you call your crewing agent in the morning?"

"Yes, of course. Thank you for all you've done."

I wasn't sure I deserved any thanks. We hung up and I went down the hall for a long, hot shower.

As Julie and I walked through the ancient streets, she asked, "How much longer will it take to get the ship ready to go?"

"Hard to say. A few more weeks."

"But you have been away from home a long time already. Does your wife not mind?"

"She's used to it," I said lightly.

In that light, with her shawl drawn tightly around her face, she was very pretty. "That must be very hard for both of you," she said softly.

My breath caught in my throat, so all I did was nod. We came to an alley and she turned me toward it with a touch on my elbow. "My place is right down here. That's one good thing about Brugge. Nothing is very far from anywhere else."

Her apartment was long and narrow, with high ceilings and a free-standing stairway that led to a loft running the length of the room. It was well-appointed, with Danish Modern furniture and large Impressionist reproductions on the walls.

"I'll start a fire," Julie said. "It'll only take a moment." She bent in front of a stainless-steel stove and filled it with kindling and some lumps of coal. Then she stood and brushed a wisp of hair out of her eyes. "How about salads and tomato sandwiches?"

It sounded a bit anemic to me, but I said, "Sounds great. May I help?"

"Please." She led me to the kitchen, a small square of black-and-white tiles in the back corner of the room. A glass-topped table and two stool-like chairs stood in the center of it. She put a head of lettuce, a cucumber, and a tomato on the table. "You can make the salad if you'd like."

She had a spicy balsamic dressing that made the lettuce salad delicious, and the tomato sandwiches, on butter-soft bread and spread with mayonnaise, were a treat. After supper we washed the dishes, then sat on the couch and listened to a strange album of African bells-and-drums music that was slightly hypnotic.

Finally, around nine o'clock, I told her that I needed to get some sleep, and levered myself up.

"Would you like me to walk back with you?"

"No, no," I said, stifling a yawn. "It's very easy."

She walked me to the door and hauled up on the heavy latch. "Then I will see you at breakfast."

I held out my hand. "Thanks for a wonderful evening."

I walked down the cold, dark alley to the street that led past the old cathedral to the hotel. My sleepiness was gone, and something was buzzing in the back of my brain, a restlessness, an anger at the old Portuguese captain and his treachery, a refusal to admit defeat. But I was too tired to think the problem through.

When I got to my cold room—I'd left the window open, and the damp night air had left dew on the dresser and night table—I snuggled into the deep, soft bed and thought about my wife and children.

The next morning I went to see Willem Bik at Belgisch Scheepssloperij. He'd delivered the Deletion Certificate to the ship a week earlier, and I hadn't seen him since. As I drove into the yard, another Russian trawler was docking behind the building, the pale-faced crew working in short sleeves on the deck. The dockworkers were using a forklift with the ship's bowline tied to it to pull the ship to the quay; I gathered that the ship's bow windlass wasn't working. The name *Professor Kurilov* was written in faded English letters on the bow.

Willem was his same brusque self. "So, Captain," he said, "everything okay?"

"No," I said. "I got a visit from Port State Control yesterday."

His eyebrows shot up. "From Antwerp? What on earth for?"

"I fired that old Portuguese captain, and I think he called them. Anyway, the ship's been detained."

"Holy Mother. Come into my office." We went in and I sat in front of his desk.

"I have an idea," I said, "but I need your help."

He threw up his thin, hairless hands. "You inspected the ship before you bought it. You knew exactly what you were getting."

"I'm not complaining about the vessel. She's a good little ship, especially for the price. But let me ask you this—how does Port State Control prevent ships from leaving? Do they tell the pilots not to take them out?"

He shook his head and picked up the box of cigarettes on his desk. "Not the pilots. The bridgetender at Zeebrugge." He lit a cigarette with a match and took a deep puff. "The bridgetender has a list of ships under detention. He won't open the bridge for them."

I had been to Zeebrugge to buy ship's supplies. I'd seen the bridge he was talking about. I pointed through the window. "What about that Russian ship? Is it detained?"

He grimaced through a cloud of smoke. "Of course not. Why would it be detained? I told you, Port State Control never comes here. If your captain hadn't reported your ship, they would never have known about you."

"So the *Professor Kurilov* could leave if she wanted to."

"That ship has come to the end of its days. There's no market for Russian trawlers. That's why we get so many to cut up."

"But the port authorities don't know that, do they? What would they do if my agent went to the harbormaster and asked for an outbound clearance for the *Professor Kurilov*?"

A slow smile split his face. It was the first time I'd seen him smile; it looked painful, and it didn't last long. "They would give it. They are just, what do you call them, bureaucrats? They are mostly concerned with the barge traffic in the port. We don't have foreign cargo operations in Brugge, so they don't pay attention to ships that clear for foreign ports."

"If I painted *Professor Kurilov* on the bow and stern, the pilot wouldn't find that strange?"

He shrugged. "The pilot will come from Zeebrugge. There are no pilots here. If he brought her in, he would know that it's not the same ship. But we always bring these Russian ships in at night, for reasons that don't concern you. If you go out during the day, you'll have a different pilot." Another long puff, another cloud of toxic blue smoke. "When will you be ready to sail?"

"A couple of days. I just need provisions and lube oil. And another captain, of course. The pilot won't ask to see the ship's certificates, will he? I've never had a pilot ask for certificates."

"No, he won't care about that."

I looked at the great gray bulk of the trawler's hull. The ship's crew were rigging a stage out over the starboard bow, getting ready to paint out the name.

"So the port has a record of the *Professor Kurilov* coming in today," I said. "In a couple of days they get a request for a clearance for her to depart. There's no Port State Control hold on her, so they issue the clearance. The pilot comes on board—he's never heard of the ship before and it's just another pilotage job—and takes the ship out. The bridgetender at Zeebrugge checks his list of detained ships, and she's not on the list. So he opens the bridge."

He shrugged. "It sounds quite normal. But what about me?"

I looked intently at him.

"I could call the harbormaster and tell him that the *Professor Kurilov*'s been cut up," he said. "You could have a problem then."

I could feel my face reddening. "You mean you want me to pay you not to contact the authorities?"

He lifted his hands in an equivocal gesture. "It's just a thought."

"Willem," I said carefully, "you made a shitload of money off the *Aldorf*. You got rid of a hundred and fifty tons of diesel that you couldn't pump ashore. Isn't that enough?"

He nodded and stubbed the cigarette out. "All right. It was just a thought. You can use *Professor Kurilov*. I won't say anything."

"Thanks." I stood up and we shook hands. "Call me when you've filled another ship with fuel," I said. "I might have a client for her."

A warm spring rain was beginning to fall as I left. I drove to the agent's office. It was a small, modern building just outside the town wall, on the bank of the encircling canal, with a wide plate-glass window overlooking the water. Piers, the ship's agent, and I sat in armchairs in the reception area. The bridge went up, and a few minutes later a long canal barge nosed through, a throng of young people in bright clothes lining the bulwarks.

"I don't see why it wouldn't work," he said. "But if you get caught, it could be trouble. Perhaps Port State Control will complain to the police."

"How could we get caught?"

"I suppose there's not much chance of it. I will do the paperwork if you want to try it." He coughed delicately. "There's an extra charge for an outbound clearance, you know. So far we've only charged for agency fees and clearing your crew in."

"How much?"

"Fifteen thousand francs. About five hundred U.S."

"Anything else?"

"Are you bringing in a new captain?"

"Yes, he's arriving today from Miami."

"Then there will be a small charge for putting him on the crew list. The secretary can add it up for you."

We stood up and I shook his hand. "Thanks, Piers. You've been a big help."

I waited for the secretary to draw up a final invoice, then I paid from my money pouch.

The new captain arrived that evening, a short, muscular Honduran with heavy, black-rimmed glasses and kinky gray hair. I liked him from the first, and he proved to be a good captain.

That week was full of last-minute tasks to ready the ship for the long voyage across the Atlantic. Getting groceries in Belgium isn't like going down to the local IGA and stocking up. If you want chicken, you go to the chicken store. If you want pork, you go to the pork store. If you want beef, go to the beef store. I spent hours rounding up food, tools, machinery spares, lightbulbs, fan belts, and a thousand other items. Every morning I went to the ship for lists of requirements from Georg, the chief engineer, and Ramesh, then spent the rest of the day looking for them.

Spring in Belgium brings one holiday after the other. It's maddening to realize, when you've got a lot of things to do, that today's another holiday and nothing can be done. Now it was the end of April, and today was the Feestdag der Blud—the Holiday of Blood—a religious festival that requires all shops to close at noon. I gave up and went back to the hotel.

Julie had persuaded me to let her do my laundry, as there were no coin Laundromats in the entire city, and I was almost out of clean clothes. I found her in the kitchen. When she heard me come in, she turned and flashed a brilliant smile. "Why, hello, Captain. Home early?"

"Can't get anything done," I growled. "Everything's closed."

"Yes, for the festival. Are you going?"

She was wearing her usual outfit, a sweater and pants with an apron over them. The fluorescent light washed the color out of her hair and gave her an ethereal quality, like the saints in sun-faded religious lithographs. She put a hand on my arm. "Come with me. There'll be bands and fireworks."

I opened my mouth to beg off, but what came out was "Sure, I'd like to."

"Come by about seven?" Then she laughed and said, "I must get back to work. The boss is coming at five and I want to leave before he gets here."

I went back to the ship for some last-minute arrangements, and returned to the hotel in time to take a shower and change clothes. Spring was yielding to summer, and it was a fine, warm night, full of the smell of wet dirt and young flowers. The sun was still high in the sky as I walked to Julie's apartment, bathing the houses' upper stories in a thick, creamy light.

Julie's hair was down, brushed into a fine blond cascade that flowed over her narrow shoulders. She wore a shiny long-sleeved shirt of some clingy material and a short black skirt over black knee-high boots. "Come in for a drink," she said.

I let her pour us glasses of red wine and we went out to sit on her tiny patio. A bay window overlooked it from another house, and when I looked up I saw a plump, elderly woman staring down at us.

"We have an audience," I told Julie. She looked up and waved to the woman, who waved and pulled her curtains together.

"Mrs. Kuipers," Julie said. "Her husband died last year. Now she will tell everybody I have a boyfriend."

The park was in the center of town, a maze of paths between hedges and well-trimmed bushes, overhung by silver-leafed trees that shone in the low floodlights. Small, gaily colored tents were scattered on the manicured grounds, some with musicians playing ancient instruments like lutes and zithers and others selling chocolates and pastries. Couples and families strolled from tent to tent, the children shrieking as they dashed about.

"Do you like it?" Julie asked as we stood in the middle of a small arched wooden bridge that spanned a dark creek.

"It's wonderful," I said. "What an oasis of peace."

A nearby musical group struck up a medieval tune. Julie slipped her hand around my arm.

Then another couple came up the path and, because the bridge was so narrow, we had to press ourselves against the railing to let them pass. Julie took her hand away to hold the top rail. About nine o'clock we walked back to her apartment. She asked me if I wanted to come in, but I said I would have a busy morning. We brushed cheeks and I waved as I walked away. She stood in the door for a moment, a slim silhouette against the soft light.

After I'd gone a few blocks, I remembered that I'd left my laundry, but I decided not to go back.

When I arrived at the ship the next morning, I asked Ramesh, "How are the stencils? Ready yet?"

"I finished dem last night. We don't have to do de life rings, do we?"

"No, but make sure the pilot can't see the ones with *Dieu Kapab* on them." That was the ship's new name.

"When do we paint on de *Professor Kurilov*?"

"I'm getting the clearance this afternoon. We'll paint them on tonight after dark. The pilot's ordered for eight in the morning."

He stroked his beard speculatively. "I hope we get away wit' it."

"A Belgian jail can't be as bad as the Port of Spain penitentiary, though, can it?"

A flash of white teeth. "No, sar. Maght be radder comfortable, no true?"

The morning was full of last-minute shopping and essential tasks. We had to seal up the hole in the engine-room bulkhead in case some wasted part of the old hull gave way and the hold started to flood, and it took a couple of hours to chock the tarpaulins down over the hatch covers. I'd waited until the last moment to get vegetables and fruit, so they would last as long as possible on the twenty-day voyage to Miami. In the late afternoon I called Piers and ordered the pilot. He wished us good luck and a safe voyage.

In the long twilight between eight and ten o'clock, we covered the three *Dieu Kapab*'s on the hull and got *Professor Kurilov* painted on. Her home port of Arkhangel'sk, on the stern, went on in a rush, but I figured it was good enough. After we finished, I took Ramesh to a cheerful little pub near the port, where regulars sat on slippery, plastic-upholstered stools and drank Stella Artois beer, and we swapped sea stories until about eleven. The real reason I did that, I admitted to myself, was so Julie would have gone home long before I got to the hotel. She knew the ship was leaving the next day, and I had a reservation on Sabena for the following evening. I would tell her goodbye at breakfast. It seemed safer.

*   *   *

The next morning, a light rain fell from a low overcast that scudded in from the English Channel. The morning colors were subdued, and the world was preternaturally quiet. There was little traffic, and the port was deserted.

I parked well away from the ship so that my car was half hidden behind a corner of the warehouse. The pilot arrived at eight o'clock and went on board. At eight-fifteen the ship undocked and turned north toward the twelve-mile canal that led to Zeebrugge and freedom.

I drove along as the ship steamed past the Belgisch Scheepssloperij and into the narrow canal. Every once in a while I would pull off and wait for the ship to pass.

Several low bridges lay between Brugge and Zeebrugge, but each one opened as the ship approached, and by noon she'd reached the last bridge. I was parked by a line of warehouses that fronted the ocean, and when the ship's high prow appeared on the other side of the last bridge, I stood on the high concrete seawall with my hands in my pockets, my collar up.

I had a few bad minutes when the ship came to a stop with the bridge still down. Traffic continued to cross. This was the bridge that controlled outbound marine traffic, and all it would take to stop the ship was a call to the bridgetender. But then bells rang and the yellow barriers started down. Another long minute, then the two halves of the bridge began to rise.

The ship slipped out into the channel, her bow heaving as she took the first short seas directly on her stem. Then the *Dieu Kapab* showed her broad, round stern and left a wide, flat wake into which a few seagulls swooped and dipped.

I called Piers a month later to see if there'd been any repercussions from the *Dieu Kapab*'s unorthodox departure, but he hadn't heard anything, and he didn't think Port State Control really cared.

After saying goodbye, I never talked to Julie again.

I made a number of trips to Europe that season and the next, and bought a couple more ships for Caribbean owners. One of them I managed for a short period of time, the *Valiant Progress*. I put Ramesh on board as chief officer. Then the owner and I had a difference of opinion on how the ship should be run, and I quit. I thought that was the end of it.

Then a couple of months later, I got a call from a man in Miami, asking if I'd heard about the *Valiant Progress*.

"I know the ship," I said cautiously. If the ship owed him money, I didn't want to get involved.

"She sank yesterday," he said. "Off the coast of Panama."

A chill ran through me. I could hardly speak. "Did anybody . . . was anybody . . . ?"

"Two men were lost. I think one was a friend of yours."

I was standing in the kitchen. I sagged against the wall. "Ramesh?" I whispered.

"Ramesh Chawla," he said. "It was in the *Miami Herald* this morning. And an oiler named Bwata Hastings. The rest of the crew were rescued."

My stomach heaved. Ramesh was my friend, one of the best men on the water I knew. I remembered Bwata as well, a happy, round-faced Ghanian boy with ten children. "How did it happen?"

"The article didn't give many details. Apparently the seas were heavy. The ship had just loaded bauxite in the Dominican Republic and was headed for the Panama Canal."

I thanked the man and hung up. It was a rainy December morning. I forced myself to walk across the sodden lawn to my office. The rest of the day passed in a gray blur; a week later I still couldn't believe it. I had a photograph of Ramesh tacked to the wall above my desk, a snapshot of the two of us on the dock in Brugge; every time I lifted my head from my computer my eyes were drawn to it.

I never really got over Ramesh's death. In time, I learned more about what happened; the sheer stupidity that had caused his death infuriated me. The captain, a diffident Brazilian whom I knew slightly—he'd come on board just before I quit management—had let himself get browbeaten into overloading the ship in the Dominican Republic. The ship had three thousand tons of deadweight cargo capacity; she had cleared out on a bill of lading showing 3,700 tons on board. She must've been loaded to the gunwales. The bill of lading was clear evidence that the ship had been "unseaworthy at the outset of the adventure," in the ancient language of ship policies, and the vessel's insurer had refused to pay the owner.

During the voyage to the Panama Canal, she had been caught in a heavy following sea, and, extremely low in the water, she'd taken a rogue wave over the stern that poured down the engine-room vents and shorted out some electrical circuits. With her steering disabled, she'd been broached by successive waves and began to settle. Finally, overloaded and adrift, she'd turned broadside to the seas and rolled over.

According to reports, everybody but Ramesh and Bwata had been able to get in the life rafts. One of the crewmen who survived had seen Ramesh clinging to some flotsam, but when he spotted the flotsam again, Ramesh was gone.

Many times in the years since, I've thought with bitter regret that if I'd never hired Ramesh as first officer on the *Valiant Progress,* he would be alive today. I tell myself that I couldn't have known that the ship would go down, and he would be lost, but the regret still surfaces in unguarded moments, a sick sense of loss in the pit of my stomach.

CHAPTER EIGHT

INTO THE STORM ON THE *DEVI PAREK*

A PAKISTANI SHIPOWNER contacted me the following January to help get his ship out of Honduras. He'd gotten my name and number from Captain Tiwali, the man who'd hired me as a port captain for Cartones del Sud. He was clearly desperate. His ship, the *Devi Parek,* had carried a load of rebar and steel profiles—building supplies—into the small port of La Ceiba, Honduras. During a storm she had damaged the town pier. She'd been under seizure for three weeks when he called me, and he was starting to despair of getting her free by legal means. He wired me the money to fly to Honduras.

I'd been to La Ceiba a number of times for Cartones del Sud. Jim Maher owned a banana-box factory there. I'd unloaded a number of ships with rolls of kraft paper for the factory, and had loaded a few ships with bales of cuttings from the factory for shipment to his repulping mills in South America. The port was as minimal as a port could be, consisting of a single dilapidated pier sticking out from the long, gently curving beach into open water. A narrow-gauge railway ran along the pier, primarily to carry boxes of bananas to the ships that loaded them for export.

The seizure sounded fraudulent. The captain had notified the port authorities that the wind and waves were slamming his ship against the dock, and had requested permission to go to anchor, but the linesmen hadn't arrived until the following day. During the night the force of the ship's movement had torn two bollards loose. The port authorities said the pilings under the pier had also been damaged, and so they billed the owner three hundred thousand U.S. dollars. I knew that pier well, and those pilings had been rotten since Simón Bolívar was a boy. It seemed to be another case of outright extortion in a port where "all power comes from the barrel of a gun."

As an open roadstead on a beach running east and west, the port offered no protection from the elements. During the winter, "northers"—storms coming down from the United States—would sweep across the sea and crash against the shoreline, making it impossible for ships to remain tied to the pier. During those times, ships waiting to load or discharge had to go to anchor nearby and hope the wind and waves didn't cause them to drag anchor and end up on the beach. That this was a real danger was borne out by the two ships already buried deep in the sand, abandoned hulks with nothing left but the rusted remains of their hulls and houses.

In 1998 I was in La Ceiba on another matter and found the pier cut in half. A ship at anchor on the eastern side had dragged anchor, slammed into the pier, and had torn right through it before ending up on the beach.

I took a taxi to the Ramada Inn, on the outskirts of town, deposited my bag, and took another taxi to the waterfront. This was one of those cases where I had no shore support, no one to look to for help. I sat on the beach and studied the ship. She was a trim-looking freighter of about three thousand tons, with two cranes and a square, modern house. She rode at anchor with her stern to shore under the press of a moderate northeast wind.

Rebah Ayub, the owner, had told me that there were two guards on board, but I couldn't see them. After about an hour, I walked to a restaurant and had lunch and a beer, then I went back to the beach for another couple of hours. To keep from being too obvious, I walked around the small downtown area, and at about 5 P.M. went back to the beach. I saw a couple of crewmen in blue boiler suits working on deck, but I never saw the guards.

At 6 P.M., four men in uniform, two with rifles, got in a small fiberglass patrol boat tied to the pier next to the guard shack. The boat went to the ship and the two men with rifles climbed up the pilot ladder. Two other armed men climbed down and the boat returned to the guard shack.

I caught a taxi and went to the hotel. Mr. Ayub answered on the first ring.

"The guards change at six o'clock," I told him. "Can you talk to the ship without the guards hearing?"

"Yes," he said. "It's a Pakistani crew, so I can talk to them in Urdu. What do you think can be done?"

"Well, the ship can't stay here long. The first storm that comes along is going to make her drag anchor. I think our best shot is to get ready for the port authorities to send her to Cortes. Why hasn't the P&I club issued a letter of undertaking?"

A ship's insurance is usually issued by a company called a protection and indemnity club, a term dating back to the days when men gathered in Lloyd's Coffeehouse in London to take on shares of a vessel's risk. When a ship causes damage to a dock, her P&I club will issue the port a letter of undertaking promising to pay whatever amount a court ultimately decides she owes.

"To get them to let the ship go?" he asked.

"Yes, of course. Who's your P&I club?"

"The Russian Club."

I winced. As a friend once said, "The Russian Club doesn't like claims." What he was saying was that the Russian Club couldn't be relied on to pay them. I doubted that any court in the world would accept a letter of undertaking from the Russian Club.

"All right," I said, "we've got to expect them to send the ship to Puerto Cortes. It's about a hundred miles west of here. It's the only protected port along this coast, and there's a big navy base there."

"But what do we do when it gets there?"

"We can't afford to let her get there. Too many navy ships and patrol boats. We need to take control of the ship on the way."

His reedy voice went up a notch. "What do you mean?"

I said quickly, "I mean we need to trick the guards into getting off."

"How?"

"I don't know. I'm thinking about it. Maybe we can fake a fire or something. I need to go on board. Can you call the ship to see if they can send the rescue boat in for me?"

"Yes, I can do that. The ship keeps radio watch on the SSB. I'll call them now and call you back."

I bought a Salva Vida beer from the bar and took it back to the room. It was a beautiful night, cool and breezy, with stars winking overhead in a clear sky.

Mr. Ayub called a few minutes later. "The guards stay in the crew's mess," he reported. "We've got some videotapes on board, and they watch them nonstop."

I called a friend in Houston and asked him to go to the Weather Channel. "I want to know when the next big cold front will be coming south," I told him. "There was one a few days ago, so there should be another one coming soon."

He called me back to say that an Alberta clipper—a big, fast-moving cold front—was sweeping across the Midwest. That was good news. I told him I would call him every day to check on its progress.

I called Mr. Ayub again. "There's a cold front heading south now. It should be here in a few days. I need to get on board tomorrow night."

"Very well, Captain."

He called a half hour later to say that the captain had said that the best time would be about midnight, after the guards fell asleep on the couches in the crew's lounge. We agreed to talk again the next night.

After a delicious, if expensive, dinner of *pescado al ajillo*—fish in garlic sauce—I went back to the room and read a few pages of Jim Thompson's *Roughneck* before turning in.

I spent a couple of hours on the beach the next morning, surveilling the ship and pier, and a couple of hours more in the afternoon. There were no beachfront restaurants, only decrepit slums. It's a beautiful beach, wide and continuous, yet all the restaurants and bars were clustered in the run-down city center, and the beach was fronted by tin-walled shacks. As an obvious gringo, I didn't dare spend all day on the beach, but I needed to establish the port's routine and the level of surveillance that the authorities maintained.

It wasn't much. Occasionally guards would walk out on the pier, but they didn't seem to be targeting the *Devi Parek*. It looked more like they were just stretching their legs. Except for taking the guards to the ship at 6 A.M. and 6 P.M., the patrol boat didn't leave the dock.

The weather continued fine throughout the day, with a moderate wind of ten to fifteen knots out of the northeast. After my afternoon surveillance, I took a cab back to the hotel and called Mr. Ayub.

"The launch will come for you at midnight," he told me. "Where do you want to meet it?"

"In front of the old freighter that's aground west of the pier. Tell them to wear dark clothes and run the engine at idle. I'll shine a flashlight when they get close."

"All right," he said. "I'll tell them. If there's any problem, go back to the hotel and call me."

I had supper in the restaurant and went back to the room to wait. I needed to get some sleep, but that was impossible. There were many things that could go wrong, and I couldn't help but consider each one of them at length. The worst would be that the guards would refuse to get off the ship and the captain would have no choice but to continue on to Puerto Cortes. In that case, I would have the choice of jumping overboard and swimming to shore—a risky proposition in a heavy sea at night—or going with the ship to Cortes and hoping I could stay hidden until the following night, when I could jump into the sheltered waters of Amatique Bay and swim ashore.

Finally, at 11 P.M., I took a taxi to a disco near the pier. After the taxi left, I walked across the street and down a sandy lane that ran westward. The houses between the lane and the beach were small and close together, each barricaded behind burglar bars. There were no streetlights, and the few passersby paid little attention to me.

I reached the end of the lane and plunged into the bushes. The old shipwreck was directly in front of me, blown by wind and tide high up onto the beach, its black hulk a spectral giant in the intermittent moonlight.

To my right, the pier was dark, with the only illumination a floodlight over the guard shack door. A faint thumping of music drifted up from the disco. I waded through the sand to the shadow of the wreck. It was 11:40.

The *Devi Parek* was a half mile offshore, her stern to me. At five minutes before midnight, a black dot appeared on the silvery water, and the wind carried the low mutter of an outboard engine. The surf carried the boat to the beach. I flashed a light with my fingers over the lens and ran down to the water.

It was a hard-bottom inflatable with two men in it, both dressed in black, their faces as dark as their clothing. Without a word the helmsman backed into the surf and turned the boat around. Still at idle, we puttered toward the ship.

The pilot ladder was down over the square stern. I got a hold on the ropes and started up. It was harder than going up a ship's side, with the spreaders swinging in space, but I managed to reach the bulwark and get my arms over the gunwale. Shadowy shapes pulled me on deck.

"To the master," I whispered to the two men on the afterdeck.

"Come, sah," one of them said. We went up to the boat deck and into the house. The hallway was bright after the dark night, and I could hear the sound of a television below. The master's saloon was open. The man who'd brought me up stepped into the light. He was a very dark man with a hooked nose and a sweeping black mustache. "The captain, sah," he whispered, and stood aside.

I went in. The captain was sitting on the couch reading a magazine, a short, bald man with a well-trimmed white beard and a round belly that strained the buttons of his shirt. He said something in Urdu to the other man and closed the door. "Capt. Max?" he asked.

"That's right. Are we safe here?"

"No, come with me." He led me through his head—past a spotless shower room and toilet—and into the owner's cabin on the other side. The two cabins shared the head. He closed the door behind us.

"The guards won't check here. Ahsan will keep watch outside my door." He gestured toward the upholstered bench against the port bulkhead. "Please sit. I'm sorry that I can't offer you supper or coffee, but it could be suspicious."

"That's fine," I said, sitting. "Tell me, what kind of guards do you have on board? Army? Police? Navy?"

"They're port police, I think."

"Smart guys?"

He shrugged. "They cause no trouble. As long as they get fed and have movies to watch, they are happy."

"Okay, now listen. There's a cold front coming down across the States. As soon as the wind comes up, I want you to tell the port authorities that your ship is dragging anchor." I looked around. The cabin was neat and well fitted, with a banker's lamp on the desk and comfortable chairs around the low coffee table. "This is a nice ship. They won't want to see her drive up on the shore."

"No, no," he said quickly, "we can't permit that."

"Yeah, but we have to make them think it might."

"Why is that?"

"We want them to send the ship to Cortes. Before you leave, I'm going to sneak on board and hide somewhere, maybe in here. We're going to trick the guards into getting off when we get to sea. As soon as they're off, we steam for international water."

"Yes," he said, "Mr. Ayub said we would do something like that. I'm not sure it will work."

"I'm not, either, but the only alternative is to let them have the ship. Which side is the powered lifeboat?"

"Starboard."

"Engine work?"

"Yes, yes. We had a lifeboat drill two weeks ago." His smooth, young-old face regarded me seriously. "But, Captain, I'm not prepared to risk my crew's lives in this, em, activity."

"I don't understand," I said. "What are you saying?"

The chief officer came through the master's head with a rolled-up chart. He nodded to me, handed it to the captain, and went back out. I unrolled the chart and studied the Honduran coast to the west. "Here," I said, pointing to the shallow bay that fronts the tiny town of Tela. It was about fifty miles from La Ceiba, halfway to Cortes. "This is where we'll put them off. There're no patrol boats in Tela—it's a very small village—so even when they get ashore there's nothing the authorities can do."

He pressed his thin lips together. "Captain, you are assuming that I will go along with your plan."

"That's right," I said, and I turned to face him. "That's exactly what I'm assuming. I'm acting on behalf of the owner. If you want to get off the ship, that's fine. But if you stay on board, you'd better cooperate. Is that clear?"

"No, it's not clear. Are you threatening me?"

"You're damn right I am," I said. "I can have you killed. It costs a hundred dollars in this country, and I know a guy that'll do it." I leaned toward him menacingly and continued in a low, hoarse voice, "I might even do it myself." I was bluffing, of course, but I had to convince him. He could ruin my plan and have me thrown into prison, to boot.

His voice trembled. "I have never been addressed in this way in my life. I cannot believe it."

"Believe it, Captain. Now call the chief officer to take me to the boat. I'm going ashore."

The chief officer was waiting outside the master's cabin. "Let's go," I told him. The wind was rising, and the ship was hunting to its anchor, snubbing up short like a half-broken horse. I went over the stern and down the pilot ladder.

The wind and waves carried us to shore. I thanked the dark figures in the rescue boat and waded to the beach. Only a few lights were still on in town; rather than thrash about in the bush, I walked along the line of hovels to the foot of the pier.

The guard shack was lit. The door was closed, and no shadows crossed its window. I waited a few minutes, then stepped up on the railway track and walked quickly away from the pier.

The disco was still thumping, with couples and brightly dressed girls milling about in the street. A half-dozen taxis sat in a line. I got in the back of the first one and told the driver to take me to the hotel.

The next day I rented a car at the airport and drove to Tela. The coast road was in poor shape; only half of it was paved, and the rest was a horror of potholes, ruts, and swampy low spots filled with muddy water. I followed a long line of buses and cars. Breakers crashed ashore and sent spume into the air. If this kept up, the master wouldn't have to pretend to the authorities that the anchor was dragging.

Tela is a small fishing village in a wide, shallow bay, with a few decaying tourist *posadas* and cafés around a tiny square, and a couple of open-air bars fronting the broken sidewalk on the beach. My main purpose was to make sure there hadn't been a coast guard or navy presence installed since I'd last been there. But the town pier was in even worse shape than I remembered. A storm had demolished it, and only the pilings were left, splayed like stumps of broken teeth. I drove back to La Ceiba.

I called my friend in Houston that night. He reported that the Alberta clipper had joined a cold front sweeping in from the Atlantic and was building into a full-blown norther. I called Mr. Ayub and he said that the master had called the port office to report that his anchor was dragging. The port captain gave him permission to start the main engine to maintain position. Then Mr. Ayub said, "Captain, did you threaten to have the captain killed?"

I chuckled. "Yeah, I did—it was a bluff. But I need his cooperation."

"Well done," he said. "I don't need a captain who won't protect the ship."

I had supper in the hotel's restaurant and finished *Roughneck*. Jim Thompson is best known for his hard-boiled novels—he wrote the book from which the movie *Bullitt* was adapted. But *Roughneck* is the true story of his desperate days and near-starvation during the Great Depression. It affected me profoundly. I went back to the room and lay in bed with my hands behind my head, thinking about my own family.

My paternal grandfather had died when my father was very young, in a sawmill accident; the family had had to turn to sharecropping. The whole family—my grandmother, my father, his brother and sister—had slept in one bed to keep warm, with newspapers piled between the two blankets they owned.

My mother's family wasn't much better off. My mother once told me that when she was in high school, she owned two dresses. When she put one on, she had to wash the other. But in spite of their poverty, my mother and all her sisters had graduated from college, and three of the four took graduate degrees. My father and his brother had become university professors.

All I'd had to do to get through school was play drums in rock-and-roll bands and occasionally tend bar between gigs. I'd never been hungry and I'd never had to pile newspaper on my bed to keep warm. It didn't seem fair.

The next morning the wind was blowing at a steady Force 5, and when I went to the beach heavy waves were crashing against the pier. Seagulls struggled to keep from being blown inland. The *Devi Parek* plunged in the swells.

At noon, I called my friend in Houston and learned that the Weather Channel was showing that the storm had crossed Cuba. I called Mr. Ayub and told him to have the master ready to send the boat for me that night. I would stay in the room until I heard from him.

He called back in midafternoon. "Captain, it's just as you said. The port is sending the ship to Puerto Cortes this afternoon."

"Christ," I said, "I can't go on board until tonight. Tell the captain to tell the port that he's having trouble with the main engine. After I get on board, he can tell them that the engineers have fixed the problem."

It was a long afternoon. I didn't go to the beach, but I glanced outside every few minutes to check the weather. High cirrus clouds raced southward and dust devils danced in the street. The wind was backing to the north.

I called Raoul Rojas, a friend of mine in Belize. We'd been best friends when I lived in Belize in the early 1970s, and now he owned a small resort on Bluefield Range, a group of islands about fifty miles southeast of Belize City. He and his brother, Roberto, had been lobster fishermen in their youth, and we'd spent our days diving for lobster and chasing vacationing British girls on Caye Caulker. Raoul and I had stayed in touch, and in 1981 my wife and I spent our honeymoon at his remote island resort.

"Raoul," I said, "I need a favor, *amigo*. I'm going to be coming north on a ship tomorrow morning, and I'm going to need somebody to come out to take me off."

"Take you off? W'at dat mean?"

"I don't want the ship to clear into Belize. Can you call an agent and arrange for a launch to come get a sick crewman?"

"Dat no problem, my fran'. I come for you in my lee dory."

"Okay. Let's meet right off English Caye. I'll call you back when I know what time we'll be arriving."

"Okay, fran'. I call de agent."

We hung up and I lay back down to snooze. In midafternoon I heard the sound of a marching band. A gaily painted truck came up the street, with street urchins running along with it. Behind the truck lumbered a small elephant pulling a high wagon with circus scenes painted on the sides. Horses with plumes of feathers on their bridles followed, and women in skimpy costumes walked behind them. A man in a cutaway suit and top hat stalked along on five-foot stilts, waving to the gathering crowd. God, I thought, if Fellini could only see this.

The little circus passed, dragging a tail of tired-looking trucks and children's rides on flatbed trailers; a long stream of men, women, and children followed in its wake.

At six-thirty, Mr. Ayub called again. "The guard was just changed. Only the two regular guards came on board. The port has told the captain to leave for Cortes as soon as the engine's fixed."

"All right," I said. "Tell the master to send the boat for me at nine o'clock."

I reached the beach at eight o'clock and hid in the brush until 8:50. The surf boomed, and spray flew across the lights of the guard shack. The wind had finally shifted to the north, and low, scudding clouds raced across the rising moon.

At nine o'clock a dark spot appeared on the crests of the waves. I lugged my suitcase to the water's edge and waited. The boat ran up onto the beach in a tangle of spume and spray, thrown sideways by the force of the breakers. Knee-deep in water, I threw my bag in and shoved the bow seaward. I slid over the bow, landing facedown on the floorboards. The helmsman turned toward the ship.

I fought for every handhold going up the ship's Jacob's ladder, my feet searching wildly for the steps. Strong hands pulled me on board. My bag came up on a light line. The chief officer appeared in the gloom and led me forward.

The master was waiting in his cabin. I searched his face for signs of treachery, but all I could see was a small, frightened man. He led me to the owner's cabin.

"Where are the guards?" I asked.

"In the crew's saloon, watching a movie."

"The same guards?"

"Yes, the same ones we get every night."

"All right, tell the engineers to get oil up. I want to get to Tela before dawn."

The wind was still rising. The ship reared like a skittish horse. "Should I report that we're ready to sail?" the captain asked.

"Yeah, go ahead. Set a course for Cortes once we get under way, but stay close to the coast."

"How're we going to get the guards off?"

"We're going to convince 'em that the ship is sinking. The engineers'll pump water out of the portside tanks. I want the ship to list to starboard so the powered lifeboat will be clear."

"Can't we put them in the port boat? I don't like losing the lifeboat with the engine."

I shook my head. "No, we can't take any chances. The wind'll blow them onshore, but it's better if they can steer. So we pump out the port tanks. And I want the quick-release dogs on the lifeboat tied back so it'll float free as soon as the weight comes off the hooks. Do you know what I mean?"

"Yes, of course. The hook guards."

"That's right. I want them tied back so the hooks'll slip off."

He looked at me with wonder. "What makes you think the guards will get in an empty lifeboat?"

"They will," I said grimly. "They'll be so scared they'll be glad to get in. And it won't be empty. The bosun, or whoever starts the engine, will be in it. He'll jump out as soon as they get in. The chief officer throws over the gravity brake and down goes the boat."

"You assume too much," he grumbled.

"We're going to do it. Now go on the bridge and send the chief officer to me."

He started to say something, but I gave him a hard look and he left.

A few minutes later the anchor chain clattered. The owner's cabin overlooked the deck. I pulled the window curtain aside; the mast lights showed small figures in yellow oilskins on the foredeck. One rang the foremast bell to signal that the anchor was up. The main engine coughed and rumbled to life.

The ship swung to the west and the pitching motion changed to a heavy rolling. With no cargo aboard, and with full ballast tanks bringing the ship's center of gravity down to its lowest point, we were in for a wild ride.

The chief officer knocked on the connecting door. I opened it and he came in, still wearing his slicker suit. I outlined my plan.

"All right," he said. He was a stolid, self-assured man, and his confidence cheered me.

"Where are the guards?" I asked.

"In the wheelhouse."

"Damn. Okay, it doesn't matter."

"What should I tell the crew?" he asked.

"Tell them that as soon as the ship takes a good list, they should start shouting and running around. We want to give the impression that the ship is about to sink. I don't think the guards have much sea experience, and they're going to take their cue from the crew's reaction. The crew should act like they're panicking."

"Okay."

"Make sure the hook guards are tied back. The boat's got to float free as soon as it hits the water."

"I understand. I'll do it myself."

"How's your bosun? A good man?"

"Very good, very experienced."

"So he starts the boat's engine, and as soon as the guards get in, he jumps back on board and you throw over the gravity brake."

"Okay. Anything else?"

"Yeah. Make sure the guards put life vests on. That'll make it harder to handle their rifles if they decide to start shooting."

"All right. I'll make sure of it."

I thanked him and he started for the door. Then he turned, silhouetted in the hard light from the head, and said softly, "Don't worry, Captain. I'll take care of it. The captain is afraid, but I am not." He went out and closed the door.

I went back to the window. The lights of La Ceiba fell behind. Car headlights flickered on the coast road behind the black sand dunes. By midnight the moon had disappeared. The wind continued to strengthen, and even through the window glass I could hear it whistling in the rigging.

We reached Tela at 2 A.M. The chief officer came through the master's head. "We're just off the eastern point of the bay," he said. "About five miles from Tela. The captain says we shouldn't get any closer."

"This is fine," I said, still at the window. I could see an orb of brighter sky to the southwest, the lights of Tela. "Everything ready?"

"Yessir."

"Tell the engineers to start pumping out the port tanks. Are the guards still in the wheelhouse?"

"Yessir."

"All right, I'm going to go up to the monkey island so I can watch the action."

He grinned, his white teeth gleaming in the light from the head. I followed him out and climbed the ladder to the monkey island, which is the seaman's name for the roof of the wheelhouse. I guess it's called that because, in a heavy blow, only a monkey can hang on there.

The wind stung my eyes and howled in the rigging. The ship rolled heavily in the long swells. She was starting to take a list. I'd figured it wouldn't take long, with no cargo to stabilize her. She leaned into the wind a couple of degrees, then a couple more. I glanced at my watch: 2:20. The lights of Tela were brighter, coalescing into bright points on the shoreline.

Another few degrees. There's a big difference on a ship between 5 degrees and 10 degrees of list. Ten degrees is dangerous, and 15 degrees means the ship's about to turn over. Now we were at about 7 or 8 degrees. The waves brought the ship nearly upright with every crash against the side, but she rolled heavily to starboard in the troughs.

Then the ship's alarm began to sound, a high, keening wail that cut through the night. Bells rang in the engine room, far below, and excited shouts filled the air. I couldn't see the lifeboats from the monkey island, so I decided to go down to the boat deck.

It was still deserted. I ran aft to the rescue boat's davit and crouched behind its inflatable hull. I could see the starboard lifeboat without being seen. It was over the side, and the bosun was cranking the engine. A puff of smoke, another, then the engine started with a clattering roar. Men poured out of the accommodations, their orange life jackets bright under the yellow deck lights. The guards came out carrying their rifles. One had a life jacket on, and the other was struggling into his. I was relieved to see that they were carrying M-1 carbines. Those would only be semiauto.

The chief officer was running around, pushing the men into their boarding positions. International safety regulations require that each man have a certain place to stand, his spot marked by a painted circle on the deck, and crewmen are trained to stand on these spots during lifeboat drills.

This was the critical moment. The chief officer shouted something, but the wind carried his words away. The ship rolled upright and the boat swung against the hull. The guards jumped.

Now! I almost screamed it. Now! Still the bosun hesitated. Then, at the last moment, he leaped across and cannoned into the assembled crew. The chief officer threw over the gravity brake and the boat dropped out of sight, the cables whining in their sheaves.

I craned my head over the side and saw the boat hit the water. The hooks fell away. The next wave carried the boat against the ship's hull, throwing the guards off their feet. The ship was still making way. The boat slid aft, banging and scraping. The guards' white faces—brown faces scared white—turned up. They were screaming at the crew, but they didn't raise their rifles. This was the moment I'd feared. I knew their light-caliber bullets wouldn't penetrate the hull, but the crew hadn't gone inside, and some were still looking over the side.

I stood up and yelled, "Get back! Get back!" The crew stared at me in astonishment. The chief officer's mouth made a round O as he realized that he'd forgotten to order the crew inside.

But by then the boat was sliding around the stern, rocking in the prop wash. No shots yet. I ran aft. The guards were hanging on with their rifles still on their backs, their eyes huge in their pale faces. The lifeboat whirled and took the next swell square on the side, rocking heavily.

I ran up to the bridge. The master was standing next to the quartermaster. "Ballast up the port tanks," I called through the door. "Turn north, straight away from the coast."

I grabbed the binoculars and ran down to the boat deck. Now the guards had put the lifeboat's engine in gear and had turned toward Tela. I ran back up to the bridge.

In ten minutes the ship was almost upright. The lights of Tela rose and fell off the starboard stern. The ship plowed into the head-seas at top speed, shuddering under the engine's thrust. I scanned the coast, but no boats were putting out. The lifeboat was making for Tela. It had its stern to the seas, so it had to be under way.

I had the radio officer patch me through to Whiskey Oscar Mike, the AT&T high-seas operator in Miami, and called Raoul. He answered sleepily, "Who dat, den?"

"It's Max," I said. "We're on our way, but I don't know when we'll get there. We're heading right into a big norther."

"You're telling me, my fran'. Dat naa'der somet'ing fierce. Plenty tree blow down tonight."

"Yeah, I know. I've been following it. Well, we should get through all right, but we might have to slow down. I'll call on VHF when we get close."

I handed the microphone to the radio officer and he shut the call down. The leading edge of the storm was already creeping down from the top of the radar screen, a bright white line of rain clutter, clearly defined, against the black background. That wasn't good: The more clearly defined the rain is on the radar screen, the worse it's going to be when it hits.

The second officer was on watch. "Are all ballast tanks full, Second?" I asked.

He was a slim, dark young man in a well-pressed uniform, a row of pens in his breast pocket. "Yessir, all full," he said.

"Forepeak tank?"

"Yessir."

"Does this ship have topside tanks?" Topside tanks are high tanks on the sides of the holds, just under the decks, that help to slow the ship's roll in a seaway.

"No, sir."

"Too bad. We're in for a rough ride, then."

He glanced at the barometer. "Glass is falling quick, sir. Navtex says winds'll be force nine."

I whistled. Back in the early nineteenth century, Sir Francis Beaufort, a British admiral, had invented the Beaufort scale to standardize descriptions of weather so seamen could have a common understanding of what a "breeze," or a "gale," or a "hurricane" meant. People today know that hurricane winds start at seventy-three miles per hour, but it was Sir Francis who set that limit. Force 9 winds would mean gusts up to fifty-five, maybe sixty miles an hour, and seas up to thirty feet high. We were in for a rough ride indeed.

A few minutes later, the leading edge of the storm struck out of the coal-black night, rain clattering against the windows like ball bearings. The captain appeared in the door to the after companionway, gripping the frame as the ship twisted and rolled. "It's too dangerous to keep going in this storm," he said. "We must turn for the lee of Roatan Island."

"Negative," I said. "We're keeping going."

He pulled himself up to the steering console, his face a sickly green in the console's light. "I'm the captain of this ship. I'm turning her east."

"Oh, yeah? We'll see about that." I went to the intercom and called the radio officer's cabin. "Sparks, come to the bridge. I want you to call the owner."

The captain stood by silently as the radio officer called Mr. Ayub in Pakistan. He was in his office. I told him that the master was determined to turn the ship around.

"Can you take command?" Mr. Ayub asked me.

"Yes. I'm an Unlimited Master."

"Then give me the captain."

I handed the microphone to the captain. "Captain," Mr. Ayub said, "you're relieved of command as of this moment. When Captain Hardberger leaves the ship, you'll resume command. Is that clear?"

The captain stood for a long minute, clutching the grabrail above the radio with one hand and holding the microphone with the other, his face working in anger. Then he said, in a strangled voice, "I understand, sir. I'll turn the ship over now."

The radio officer shut down the call. I told the master, "Make the proper entry into the log"—I checked my watch—"as of 0247 hrs. You can go to your cabin or stay here, but if you stay on the bridge you are not to interfere with my command of this ship. Is that clear?"

He drew himself up straight, but the effect was ruined by a sudden lurch of the ship that gave him a sharp rap on the side of the head from the lamp mounted over the radio console. He winced and staggered to the companionway door. "I will go to my cabin," he said. "You may make the necessary log entry." He stumbled downstairs.

The second officer and bosun stared at me in amazement. "Are you captain now, sir?" the second officer said.

"Yes," I said. "I'm entering it in the logbook now."

I made my way to the chart room and opened the ship's log to the current page. As carefully as the ship's wild motion allowed, I entered my relief of the captain and the time. When I went back to the wheelhouse, the rain was coming down so hard that the lights of the foremast were nothing but faint smears of yellow light.

"Spinning windscreen work?" I asked the second officer, then, to the bosun, "Take her off Iron Mike, Bosun."

The bosun switched the autopilot off and took the wheel. The second officer handed himself along the after bulkhead to the switch panel and flipped a switch. The spinning windscreen, a round, two-foot-diameter disk of glass set into one of the windows on the port side, started rotating. As it gathered speed it slung the raindrops off. By holding onto the forward rail, I could see through it as far as the forecastle. The world beyond the ship had disappeared. Massive waves burst against the bow, flying as far back as the midships mast house.

I glanced aft through the chart-room windows. The lights of Tela had already disappeared. At least the threat of arrest was well behind us. Suddenly the ship veered to port and the bosun had to rack the wheel hard a-starboard to bring her back. I hauled myself to the intercom and called the engine room. The second engineer answered.

"All ballast tanks full, Second?" I asked.

"Who is this?"

"Never mind who this is. I'm asking if the tanks are full."

"All tanks full."

"All right. Everything okay down there?"

"All okay for now."

The bosun spun the wheel, and even above the whistling wind I could hear the steering pumps whining as they fought to control the rudder. The ship dove down the backside of another giant roller and slammed against the sea. I glanced at the second officer. "Go to half ahead, Second."

"Aye, aye, sir." He pulled the throttle back and the thumping of the engine slowed. I was hoping to reduce the pounding, but with the slowing of water past the rudder, the bow fell off to port again and kept yawing. The bosun spun the rudder to the stop, but still the bow kept falling off. By then we were almost broadside to the waves. I shook my head and told the first officer to go back to full ahead.

"If we didn't have Honduras to lee, I'd turn and run," I said. "But now we don't have any choice. We've got to keep pounding ahead."

The second shook his head. "This is dangerous, sir. The ship's already had cracks in the bottom."

I stared at him. "Cracks in the bottom? She's breached to the sea?"

"No, no, we repaired them. But if . . ."

"Repaired them how? With cement boxes?"

He nodded. "But I don't know if they'll hold in this sea."

I staggered back to the spinning windscreen. The waves had built to tremendous heights under the murderous wind, and when the ship crested the next swell and plunged to the trough, the bow sank deep into the sea. White spume spurted into the black sky and swept across the deck.

The next wave was a rogue, a monster, that lifted the bow high above the wheelhouse. It hung on the crest, the whole ship shaking and groaning, then the flat bottom fell into the trough with a thunderous crash. The ship stopped dead in her track, trembling like a sick dog. The next wave caught her on the port quarter and broke solid over the bulwarks. We heeled heavily to starboard under the force of it.

Even with the helm hard a-port, the rudder couldn't bring it back. The next wave crashed into the side and heeled the ship farther over, sweeping across the deck. "Rudder hard a-port," the bosun announced tonelessly.

"Keep her there," I said, but I could already see that it wouldn't bring the bow back. Empty of cargo, with the forecastle high in the air, acting like a sail, the ship just didn't have enough rudder to fight the wind and waves.

"What're we going to do, Captain?" the second officer asked. "We can't turn to leeward, can we?"

"No, no," I said. "We can't afford to lose a single meter to leeward. We've got to get off the coast. If we have an engine problem . . ."

I didn't have to finish the sentence. Any interruption of engine power would carry the ship onto the beach, where the wind and waves would drive her high enough that she would never get off. As for taking to the lifeboat in that weather, it didn't bear thinking about.

"Let her fall off," I told the bosun. "See if we can come all the way around. And for God's sake don't let her fall off again. Not one degree."

"Aye, aye, sir." He spun the wheel to starboard and the rudder-angle indicator flew across the scale. The bow fell off and the ship took another wave flat on the port beam. The crest boomed against the empty hull. The ship rolled to 20 degrees, then 25 . . .

The three of us stared at the clinometer on the after bulkhead, willing the ship to come back. Ten more degrees and she might not recover, and that would be the end of it. But the ship finally stopped at 30 degrees, held there for a long, tense second, and started back to port.

With the weight of the ballast water deep in the double-bottom tanks, the ship had a fast, wicked roll, and in another second she'd whipped back upright, only to be met by another huge wave. The first officer and I were thrown off our feet; the bosun managed to hang on only because he had a death grip on the wheel. I scrambled to my feet and waited for the next roll.

But a series of lower waves followed, and the ship's bow came back into the eye of the wind just as another squall blanketed the deck in rain. Water squirted in through the cracks in the window casings, although we'd dogged them down as tightly as we could.

Two hours later, the storm front had passed, leaving a hard, steady wind and a thick drizzle. The seas were still twenty feet high, tumbling out of the north, but the crests were no longer being torn free and flung through the air. Here and there a light spot showed where the quarter-moon was trying to break through.

As the front fled south, the coast of Honduras and the big islands to the east, Roatan and Utila, emerged from the rain clutter on the radar. In three hours at full ahead, we'd made only ten miles offshore, but I didn't mind. At least we hadn't suffered an engine breakdown and ended up on the beach.

By dawn the rain had stopped, but the seas were still running high, big growlers storming out of the horizon and slamming into the ship. Every tenth wave was big enough to stop her in her track, shuddering and trembling. According to the GPS, we were making only four knots. At this speed, it would take thirty hours to reach English Caye, Belize.

I curled up on the pilot berth in the radio room and jammed my knees against the leeboard to keep from getting thrown out. After a while I dozed off, but it seemed like only minutes later that the second officer shook me awake. "Captain, we have a problem. There's water in the hold."

I sat up quickly, licking my cracked lips. "Which one?" I croaked.

"Number one."

Did it come through the hatch covers?"

"I don't think so, Captain. It's getting deeper."

I sat up and pummeled my face, trying to will myself into consciousness, and trudged into the wheelhouse. The first officer had come on the bridge, and he and the second were looking at a handwritten sheet of soundings. A well-run ship's routine includes twice-daily soundings of the ship's bilge wells—boxes below the cargo holds where any water that gets into the hold will drain—and ballast tanks. The soundings for the number-one hold showed about a foot and a half of water in it.

I looked forward over the deck. The seas were still running at about ten to fifteen feet, but the wind had dropped to a breeze. The ship was lifting sluggishly to the waves, though, and she was down by the bow.

I checked the sounding for the forepeak tank, in the bow. It was still full, so water hadn't drained out of it into the hold. If the forepeak—designed to add weight high, to slow the ship's roll in a seaway—were breached, its level would have fallen to that of the sea outside. The fact that the number-one ballast tank was full didn't tell us anything, since if it were breached to the sea and leaking into the hold, it would stay full.

I glanced at the first officer. "Have we started pumping the bilges?"

"No, sir. I called you as soon as the second got back with the soundings."

I went to the intercom and called the engine room. The second engineer was on watch; I told him to pump the bilges for the number-one hold.

The first and second officers looked at me as I hung up. "Let's see what happens when we pump the hold," I told them. "If there's communication between the tank and the hold, we'll see the water coming in."

"I checked the number-one hatch cover," the second said. "It looks tight."

"We must've broken one of the cement boxes loose," I said. "Has either of you been down in the number-one ballast tank?"

"I have," the second said.

"What's it like? Lots of rust?"

He nodded. "It's pretty bad, Captain."

"Any leaks into the number-one hold before this?"

"Not that I know of."

By then we were thirty miles from the Honduras coast, but still more than a hundred miles from English Caye, where we were to meet Raoul. I studied the chart. Going back to Honduras was out of the question, unless we wanted to risk arrest. Considering the circumstances of our departure, we could be facing legal trouble in Belize as well, but I preferred a Belizean jail to a Honduran one. I went back into the wheelhouse and told the AB, "Go sound the number-one bilge well again. I'll take wheel watch."

"Yessir." A minute later I saw him making his way forward with the sounding tape in his hand. It was hard to tell in the heaving sea, but it looked like the bow had settled further.

The AB returned with a long face. "Hard to say, Captain, but the water might be a little deeper."

"Do you think it's into the hold?"

"Oh, yes, sir, I think so. Want me to crack open the hatch cover so we can take a look?"

"Yeah. But just a crack. I don't want to wrench the cover in these seas."

He went out and I called the engine room to ask the chief engineer to come to the bridge. Then I told the first officer, "Make sure the lifeboat is ready for launching. Make sure every man has a flashlight. Also make sure we have at least two working walkie-talkies ready to take with us."

His eyes got round. "Are we sinking, Captain?"

"I think we're breached to the sea. We've been pumping number-one hold for an hour and the water's not going down. The AB thinks it's getting higher. I have the second engineer on his way, but if this keeps up, we could go down during the night."

"Jesus," he said. "Yessir, I'll take care of everything."

A minute later the chief engineer arrived, panting a little from the climb. He was a stocky, middle-aged man with a heavy gold chain around his meaty neck. "Chief," I said, "the pump's not making any headway against the water in number-one hold. Are you using the main ballast pump?"

He stared at me. "Where's the captain?"

"I'm the captain now. If you don't believe me, ask the first officer here."

The chief engineer looked at the first officer. The first officer grinned and said, "He's the captain, Chief."

"Are you using the main ballast pump?" I repeated.

"Yessir."

"Is it sucking all right? No leaks or cavitation?"

"As far as I can tell."

I looked over the bow and gnawed my bottom lip. "Is it sucking from both bilge wells?"

"Yessir."

"Any way of lining up another pump?"

"No, sir, and it's the biggest pump we have."

"What about lining it up on one bilge and putting another pump on the other bilge well?"

He thought. "I think we can do that. Yessir, that can be done. I can't use the other ballast pump, but I can line up the emergency fire pump on the other bilge well."

"Can we weld up the crack in the tank top?"

He grimaced. "No sir. The welding machine is broken."

"What? It can't be repaired?"

"No sir. It's been broken for a long time. It must be replaced."

"Christ, what are we going to do, then? Water's flooding number-one hold. We can't turn back, and at this rate, we'll go down in a few hours."

He shrugged. "I've asked the owner to replace the welding machine every time we go into port. It's not my fault."

"I don't care whose fault it is," I said grimly. "What about underwater epoxy? Is there any JB Weld on board?"

He brightened. "Yessir. We have two boxes of Red Hand."

Red Hand is a quick-acting brand of underwater epoxy. That would make the job harder, since we would have only a few minutes to get it in place, but it would have to do. I clapped him on the shoulder. "Bring them to me," I said. "Let's hope the crack's not too long."

He gave a half salute and disappeared. I went to the forward windows and watched as the two ABs undogged the number-one hatch cover. When they had it free, one went to the hydraulic control box on the starboard deck and pulled the lever. The two panels of the after assembly—each hatch cover had two after panels mated to a single forward panel—rose in the middle, at their hinged joint, until there was about a foot of clearance under it. I whistled to signal that it was enough.

I went down on deck. A weak yellow sun was rising out of the sea. I stepped up onto a coaming frame and looked down. The hold smelled of rotting grain—scraps of previous cargoes—and salt water. A foot of water sloshed back and forth on the hold floor, setting up crosscurrents in the brown, frothy wavelets. I shook my head and lowered myself to the deck. "Okay," I told the AB at the control box, "you can leave it open for now. Go get some rest, but make sure you have your life jacket handy. And make sure you know the quickest way to get topside if the alarm sounds."

He nodded somberly. I went back up to the bridge, where the chief engineer was waiting. "I've got two pumps lined up on the hold, Captain," he said. "How is it?"

"About a foot and a half, Chief. For sure we're breached to the sea."

"What happened?"

"We took a heavy hit during the storm. I don't know if you felt it in the engine room, but we slammed into a trough pretty heavy. Every time we tried to reduce rpm, the bow fell off and we started spinning around. Too much windage forward. When the bottom of the ship hit, either a cement box broke free or the hull cracked. As to why the water's getting into the hold, I don't know. Could be that the pounding also caused a crack in the tank top."

"Well," he said, wiping his face again and sticking the rag in his pocket, "let me know as soon as you know, one way or the other."

"Roger that," I said.

By 0800 hours, the hold had been pumped down to a few inches of filthy water sloshing about at the after end. Even from the deck, we could see where it was coming from. The tank top—the plating that forms the floor of the hold and the top of the double-bottom tank—had a wide crack just aft of the collision bulkhead. Water was spurting out of it a foot high.

I was standing on a coaming frame, holding on with my left hand, the first officer beside me. "The tank top wasn't leaking before, was it?"

"No, sir."

"All right. We're going to seal the crack with Red Hand. Underwater epoxy. The chief engineer is bringing it up now."

"Can we do it from the hold?"

"I doubt it. The pressure of the water in the tank might push it out. We'll have to stick it into the crack from the double bottom."

He took another long drag on the cigarette and didn't answer. I knew what he was thinking.

"I'll do it," I said. "I'm not going to ask anybody in the crew to go down there."

"It's too dangerous, Captain. That's a long way from the manhole."

"I know."

"It's not like going in the tank in port," he said earnestly, tossing the cigarette away half smoked. "If the hole in the hull opens up, or if one of the pumps fails . . ."

"I'll get out," I said. But then I had a sudden, stomach-clenching memory of the time I almost died in a double-bottom tank on the old *Erika*. My heart started pounding. My chief officer, Yussuf al Karim, and I had been trying to put a cement box over a crack in the ship's rotten hull when the bottom opened up. We'd fought our way back to the manhole with water flooding around us. We came within inches of dying. Ever since— even to this day, in fact—going into double-bottom tanks makes me queasy.

I shook my head. "It's our only shot." I started walking aft.

"You can't go down there alone," he said, from behind me. "I'll go with you."

"All right," I said. "Thanks."

We reached the bridge. The bosun sat on the starboard stool. "How's it look, Cap?"

"Not too good. There's a crack in the tank top forward." I picked up the intercom and called the engine room. "Bring up that underwater epoxy," I said, "and start pumping down the number-one double-bottom tank."

"I'll try, Cap," the chief engineer said, "but the fire pump bearing is already overheating. We need to shut it down as soon as we can."

"Can it run for another twenty, twenty-five hours?"

"No way, Cap. Maybe another two hours."

"Christ. We've got to get that crack sealed off, then. Bring up the epoxy."

The first officer and I stood at the forward windows without speaking while we waited. The second engineer came in and handed me the package of underwater epoxy. I opened the box and shook out the sticks of epoxy and hardener. They were about an inch thick and eight inches long. Kneaded together, they could make a rope about half an inch thick and about eighteen inches long, just barely enough to fill the crack.

Red Hand is fast-hardening epoxy, with a cure time of only fifteen minutes. If I didn't get it onto the crack before it started curing, there would be no hope of making it stick. After that, the ship could only make a desperate run for Belize, hoping to reach a beach where we could ground the ship before the hold filled with water and she took a nosedive into the sea.

"All right," I said, trying to ignore the knot in my stomach, "let's get it done. Bosun, can you and your men open the manhole?"

"Yessir. Who's going to go in the tank?"

"I am."

He shot a glance at the first officer, but the man kept an impassive face. "Very well, then," the bosun said, and went out.

The knot in my stomach angered me, but I couldn't make it go away. I told myself that there was very little risk of the hole in the hull opening up—that time on the *Erika* we'd been using a car jack to force a gasket against the hull, and that was what had opened the crack—but it didn't do much good. The shameful truth was that I'd become claustrophobic, at least in double-bottom tanks, and claustrophobia doesn't yield to reason.

Half an hour later the chief engineer called to report that the number-one double-bottom tank was empty enough to open the manhole. The first officer and I went down into the number-one hold. Six inches of dirty water sloshed against the after bulkhead. I waded through it and up the sloping tank top toward the men opening the manhole. One of the ABs was working on the last nut, and a minute later he had it off. The bosun stuck a pry bar under the cover and freed it gently, careful not to tear the rubber gasket underneath. The cover came up and they laid it to one side. Some gentle tugging got the gasket clear, and the bosun aimed his flashlight into the shallow tank.

Water was running aft, a lot of it, so the breach in the hull was forward as well. The sound of the pump suction was loud in the tank, gurgling and hissing. When I stuck my head down and shined my light, I could see the forward edge of the rusty brown water a dozen feet aft of the manhole, surging and receding as the bow rose and fell.

I pulled my head out. "The crack in the hull is well forward. It might have opened up at the same time the crack in the tank top started." I pulled on my gloves and looked at the first officer. "Ready, First?"

"Yessir."

I lowered myself down and crawled through the first lightening hole. The rims of the lightening holes were knife-edged by wastage, like the ones in the *Erika*.

A light flickered behind me as the first officer followed. The water running aft made ripples against my hands and knees. My clothes were already soaked, covered with rust and mud.

Another lightening hole, with razorlike edges. My heart was thumping wildly. I had to force myself through it. The crack in the tank top was still a dozen frames ahead.

We finally reached the area of the crack. I knew it was to port, so I worked my way past a couple of stringers—the longitudinal stiffeners—and saw a thin slice of light forward. I put my head through the next frame's lightening hole and saw that the water was coming from farther forward. The leak in the hull had to be right against the collision bulkhead, the "wall" between the forepeak tank and the number-one double-bottom tank. That made sense: When the ship slammed into the trough, the collision bulkhead had provided the resistance to flexing that caused the unsupported steel aft of it to tear.

Now we were in complete blackness. I shivered. If anything happened, it would take a long time to get back to the manhole . . .

"Let's see where the water's coming from," I said briskly, my voice echoing between the steel bulkheads. I crawled through another lightening hole. Now I could see a thick spray shooting up from the bottom and splashing against the tank top. When I reached the next lightening hole, my light showed a long, transverse crack in the hull that disappeared under the next stringer to port. That was one reason the hull had failed . . . the stringer was completely wasted away where it met the hull, leaving the bottom free to flex with every wave. Over the years, the flexing had fatigued the steel to the point that, when the ship slammed into the trough, it had finally cracked.

There was nothing we could do about the crack in the hull. Our only hope was to seal off the tank top and depend on it to keep us afloat.

"It's pretty bad, First," I said, pulling my head out of the hole. "At least a couple of feet long. Let's get that crack in the tank top sealed."

He worked his way aft, the soles of his shoes gleaming in my flashlight. When we reached the crack in the tank top, I crouched under it and took out the epoxy.

The first officer shined his light on the sticks as I peeled off the plastic wrappers. The epoxy was black and the hardener white, so the user would know by a uniform gray color that he had them properly mixed.

First I kneaded the two black sticks of epoxy together, then I looked at the crack and went through the situation in my mind. Once I mixed the epoxy with the hardener, there'd be no time for second thoughts.

"Wipe the steel clean around the crack, First," I said.

"Yessir." He took a rag out of his pocket and rubbed it around the crack.

"Good enough. Okay, here goes." I pushed the white sticks into the black epoxy, folding and squeezing the mixture over and over until I had a smooth gray lump in my hands. I rolled it between my palms into a two-foot-long snake and started pressing it against the crack.

The first officer held one end in place while I worked with the other end. Within a couple of minutes we had it stuck in the crack. "Okay," I said, "let's hold it in place for a while. Try not to move it."

"It's getting hot already, Captain."

"Yeah, it won't take long."

We squatted silently in the stinking tank, listening to the water rushing past and the pump suctions, far away. The ship rocked slightly, side to side; occasionally we had to brace ourselves as the bow lifted and fell.

The epoxy was getting really hot now, but I didn't want to let go long enough to put on my gloves. Then it began to cool, which meant it had gotten hard. "Okay, First," I said, "let's see if it stays in place."

We took our hands away. It stayed in place. "Let's get out of here," I said.

It was a long crawl back to the manhole. When I finally saw the light of the manhole, even from a dozen frames away, it was like a band of steel dropping away from my chest. And when I stood up and breathed in a lungful of clean, fresh air, I was lightheaded with relief.

I walked forward to examine the crack. Without being told, the bosun had flattened the bead of epoxy sticking up to hold it in place and help seal the crack, and by then it was as hard as the steel itself. "Looks good," I told the men. "All right, get that manhole bolted down and knock off."

The first officer and I went up on deck. As we walked back toward the house, he said, "That wasn't so bad, was it, Captain?"

"No," I lied, "it wasn't bad at all."

Back on the bridge, I called the chief engineer and told him to turn the pumps off. An hour later, the bosun reported that the double-bottom tank was full again, and he and I went forward to look down through the open hatch cover. No water running aft. The epoxy had sealed the crack. "Good deal," I said. "Now let's get this ship to Belize."

The wind continued at force 6 to 7 out of the north, and we didn't reach the approaches to Belize City until late the following morning. I had the first officer take the ship up the deepwater channel between Turneffe Island and the barrier reef. The air was so clear I could see whitecaps on the horizon, like the forced perspective of a primitive painting.

The seas fell off as we gained the lee of Turneffe. I took the binoculars out on the port wing. As we passed Bluefield Range, I could see Raoul's little resort on its sand-spit island. Actually, Bluefield Range is a group of nameless islets just inside the reef, and the resort was just a collection of huts built out over the water, connected by raised walkways, with a large, thatch-roofed dining room onshore.

At noon we approached English Caye, a small, brush-covered island dominated by a giant lattice-steel tower with a light on the top. There are two deepwater passages to Belize City, north and south of English Caye, and I could see Raoul's boat bobbing in the low chop on the north side. The first officer rang for stop engine and the ship slowed.

I got the captain on the intercom and called him up to the bridge. He appeared red-eyed and sullen. I hadn't seen him since he left the bridge two nights earlier. He gave me a belligerent glare. "It's your ship, Captain," I said. "I entered it in the log. Handover was at 1225 hours."

He grunted and went to the port door to look down at Raoul's boat, bobbing in the low waves in the lee of the ship. I shook hands with the first officer and bosun and shouldered my bag. As I went out, I stopped in front of the captain and said, "By the way, Captain, I just want you to know . . . if there's one thing I can't stand, it's cowardice."

His mouth worked, but no sound came out. I shouldered past him and went down to the main deck. The crew had a Jacob's ladder over the side, and after I climbed down, one of them lowered my bag to me.

Raoul stood at the stern of his boat, older and stouter than I remembered. He gunned the engine and turned toward the English Caye passage. A string of round white puffballs out of the ship's exhaust stack showed that she was under way again.

"What you doing, mon?" Raoul called over the howl of the engine. "You r'ally sick?"

"Of course not," I called back. "I just wanted to get off that ship without her having to clear in."

"But what will happen when de customs see you not r'ally sick?"

"Oh, I'll be sick, all right, but I'll make a miraculous recovery on the way to the hospital."

He threw his head back and laughed. Raoul had always been a handsome man, with a good mixture of Mayan Indian in his reddish complexion. He'd grown a respectable belly, but the legs below his shorts were still bunched with muscle.

Raoul docked at the customs wharf on the north side of Haulover Creek, and I climbed up holding my stomach. The agent was waiting, a small black man in a dress shirt and slacks. He and Raoul half-carried me to the customs house.

I sat in a chair in the first-floor waiting room, groaning, while the agent took my passport around to the various offices in the building. Finally, with my passport properly stamped, the agent shook our hands and left. Raoul called a taxi and told the driver to take me to the Belize City Hospital. The driver gave me a sympathetic look as I crawled painfully into the backseat.

I kept it up all the way to the hospital. Raoul told the driver not to go to the emergency entrance; when we got out in front, no one was looking. I straightened up.

"Thanks, buddy," I told Raoul.

"You don't need to check in?"

"Nah. If there's any question I'll say I suddenly felt better. Mother's Restaurant still open?"

He laughed. "You want to go to Modder's? Yas, mon, it still open."

"How's Mother doing?"

His smile faded. "Modder pass, you know. Maybe two, t'ree year back. Now his da'ghter run de place."

Mother was Belize's first hippie. He'd arrived from the States in the late 1960s, in a small trimaran, and had bought Mother's Restaurant, a big ramshackle building on the south side of Haulover Creek, near the swing bridge. Over the years, people had started calling him Mother. I never knew his real name, but I was used to seeing him sitting behind the cash register with a beatific smile and his long gray hair slowly turning white, and it was a shock to realize that even an institution as durable as Mother could fade away.

The restaurant was much as I remembered. I bought us the daily special, which was always fish and vegetables, and afterward I went with Raoul to the Theodore Hotel. Old Man Theodore was the father of one of our friends, and I always stayed at his little *posada* when I was in town. I was exhausted and went straight to bed.

I stayed in Belize another week—Immigration had given me two weeks in-country—and spent it out at Raoul's resort, drinking cold Belikin beers with him and his one-legged cook.

CHAPTER NINE

BATTLING PIRATES

NOT EVERY STORY has a happy ending, of course. In August of one year, I got a call from Ronald Joanuel, my Haitian friend. He said there was a ship at the Port-au-Prince dock that the port authorities wanted to sell, and she could be gotten for a cheap price. She was a sister ship to the *Sahira Rizvi,* a ship I'd extracted—recovered—from Rio Haina, Dominican Republic. I knew a man looking for a ship this size. I called him and he gave me the go-ahead to inspect the ship, wiring me my expenses to go to Port-au-Prince.

Ronald met me at the airport and we took a taxi to the agent's office. The agent, Robert Paillese, was a light-skinned man with wavy gray hair and a thick mustache that hid his mouth. His office was a hole in the wall near the port, behind a small bagged-goods warehouse. "Yes," he said, "the *PTA Concepcion.* A tragic story. Come, let's go get some coffee."

We went out his back door and across an alley to a workers' café with handmade tables and chairs. The fat proprietress brought a tray with small cups of café au lait and a plate of biscuits. "So your client is interested in the *PTA Concepcion*?" he asked.

"Possibly," I said. "I heard she had a fire in the engine room. It'll depend on the condition of the machinery."

He raised a hand. "It wasn't really a fire. It was an explosion, but there was no fire."

I frowned. "How is that?"

"There was no air in the bottles to start the main engine, so the chief engineer hooked up an oxygen bottle."

I stared at him in disbelief. "Only a madman would do that."

He shrugged. "He was Peruvian. The whole crew were Peruvian. Clearly it was a mistake."

"How many men were killed?"

"One, the chief. Well, three, ultimately. The second engineer and an oiler were burned, but they could have survived if Mr. Maldonado had sent the money to send them to Miami."

"What do you mean?"

"They were in the hospital here. You know the hospital here . . . it's not so good. They couldn't care for the men. But they could have lived. Every day for a week I called the owner and begged—"

"Wait," I broke in. "Did you say Maldonado?"

"That's right. That's the owner. Do you know him?"

"José Maldonado? I know of him. So what happened?"

"The men were in terrible pain. The doctors told me they had to go to Miami to live. I called Mr. Maldonado—José Maldonado—every day, trying to get him to send the money for them to go. The embassy said the paperwork would only take a few minutes. But they would have to go by special plane—a medical plane—and it would have cost a lot of money. I think twenty-five thousand dollars. Every day Mr. Maldonado promised to send the money, but he never did. Then the second engineer died, and the next day the oiler died." He finished his coffee. "A perfectly satisfactory result for Mr. Maldonado, I'm sure."

I heaved a deep sigh. "A grim story. What happened to the rest of the crew?"

"Some were able to get their families to send them money to go home. The others are still here. One died last month."

"He was burned?"

"No, he was the chief officer. He got sick and had no money to go to the hospital. He was living with a Dominican woman."

"I knew him," Ronald said. "A very nice man, very smart. But his family had no money."

I'd seen it a hundred times. Shipowners abandon their crews in foreign ports, and the crewmen have no money to get home. American citizens can go to the nearest consulate and get a suit of clothes, a good meal, and a flight home, all courtesy of Uncle Sam. But Latin American countries have no budget for this, and if the families can't come up with the thousand-dollar airfare—and most families can't—their husbands and sons are left to their own devices in some foreign country.

There's a wonderful organization, the Seamen's Church Institute in New York, which maintains a fund to repatriate abandoned crewmen, but they can only help the crewmen they know about. Many, many ships have come to grief in hellhole ports whose crews only got home through the tireless and generous efforts of the Seamen's Church. In one case, an extraction I did in 2004 that involved a stolen ship, the thief had promised to pay the Russian crew to steal the ship and deliver it to Haiti. After they did it, he abandoned them there. Ronald said that two men died of hunger and neglect before the Seamen's Church heard about them and repatriated the survivors.

Satisfied that the ship was worth inspecting, I asked when I could look at it.

"Tomorrow." He glanced at his watch. "It's too late today."

"Okay, I'll come by your office in the morning. Who has the claim against the ship?"

"There are several. About seventy thousand dollars to the port for dockage and light dues, and about ten thousand in medical bills. Another thousand in burial costs. And of course my agency fee."

"Of course. So the ship can be had for about a hundred grand."

"Well, it depends on who else is bidding, but we can make sure no one knows about the auction."

"How's that?"

"You know it's only necessary to publish the date of the auction in *l'Observateur*. I do not think many people interested in buying the ship will be reading the Port-au-Prince newspaper."

"True enough," I said.

After another cup of coffee, Ronald and I took a taxi to the Hotel Oloffson. I used to stay at the Holiday Inn downtown, but a couple of years earlier an American had bought the old Oloffson and reopened it. It had been the home of Haiti's first president, and in the 1950s it was the setting for Graham Greene's novel *The Comedians*, about life under Papa Doc Duvalier's brutal dictatorship. It'd also been the location for much of the movie of the same name, starring Richard Burton and Elizabeth Taylor. After it reopened in the early '90s, it became the hotel of choice for the foreign journalists who descend on the country like locusts whenever it's convulsed by riots or civil war. I like the place for its open-air ambience and the fact that few Americans stay there.

The next morning Ronald and I went to the port to inspect the *PTA Concepcion*. We had to walk a long plank over a gap in the pier that had been torn open by a careening ship the previous year. Now there were several derelicts at the dock, including one I recognized, the *Dieu Puissant,* a small shelter-decker that used to call Miragoane when I was a ship captain. Now Haitians were living on board, and she looked like she'd reached the end of her days.

The *PTA Concepcion* was at the end of the pier. She didn't look bad, but rust was starting to blister her deck. The engine room had several runs of scorched wiring, burnt oil on the main engine heads, and soot everywhere, but otherwise the machinery spaces appeared operational.

Having extracted the *Patric M* from the clutches of the Maldonados, I found the history of the *PTA Concepcion,* as revealed by documents in the master's saloon, very interesting. She'd been owned by Marbel Shipping of Piraeus, Greece, when she was seized in Callao, Peru, for cargo damage. The owner had fought the seizure, and survey reports indicated that the cargo damage claim might have been fraudulent. The charterer, Perumar Trading S.A., hadn't made the claim until after the cargo was completely discharged. The shipowner's surveyor had reported that there was nothing wrong with the wheat in the receiver's silos.

Some of the faxes from Perumar to Marbel had been signed by José Maldonado.

The court had ordered the ship to be sold at auction, and a company called Vapores Altamar—"High Seas Steamships"—had bought the ship. Most of Vapores Altamar's correspondence had been sent by a man named Luis Marin, but buried in the ship's class documents was a faxed request for an extension of the drydocking date that had been signed by—surprise!—José Maldonado.

The Maldonados had seized the ship and sold it to themselves.

I spent the rest of the day on the ship, then called my client to report that the ship was in acceptable condition for the price. He told me to go home and make plans to return for the auction, which was scheduled for September 21, 1996.

However, two weeks before the auction date, Ronald called to report that the port authorities had cut the ship loose and let her drift away. Hurricane Hortense was approaching the island, and the authorities were afraid that if the eye of the hurricane passed over the port, the ship would further damage the already-weakened pier. Adrift and unmanned, the ship had gone aground near Grand Goave, about fifteen miles west.

For many years her hulk was visible from the coast road, gradually getting smaller as Haitian entrepreneurs cut pieces off for scrap. In 2008, Ronald and I were flying over the coast in a light plane when he tapped me on the shoulder and pointed down. I looked out the side window. There was the hull of the *PTA Concepcion,* now reduced to a coffin-shaped outline filled with green water, just off the beach.

In the late '90s, a Turkish owner contacted me to get a ship out of port in Buenaventura, Colombia, so he wouldn't have to pay what he claimed was a trumped-up bill for damages to the port dock. After the owner had wired the money for expenses and my day rate, I called Cartones del Sud to see if Charlie Johnson was still with the company. Dolores told me he was loading coffee in Buenaventura.

He was working on a ship when I called, and it was a bad connection, but he said he would have a car meet me at the Cali airport. When I got out of Customs and Immigration, Charlie's man was waiting in the main hall with my name written on a sign.

We drove across town and over the mountains to Buenaventura, four hours away. The army had retaken control of the road since the days I'd been working in Buenaventura, and we had no trouble. Back in the old days, rebels maintained roadblocks where travelers were expected to contribute to their cause. But now army checkpoints stood every couple of miles, and pickup trucks full of soldiers patrolled the road between them.

When I got to the Hotel Estacion at 1 A.M., Charlie was waiting for me in the bar. A pudgy man about my age, he always wore a baseball cap with something about Vietnam on it, usually festooned with badges and pins. Tonight he wore a cap that said, "Southeast Asia War Games, Second Place." He pumped my hand with the merry hell in his blue eyes that I well remembered.

"Oh, hey, oh Lawdy," he said—something he said many times every day—"it's good to see you, ol' man. What you been up to?"

"Same old thing. Messing about with ships." I asked the bartender for an Aguila beer and told him to bring Charlie another bourbon and Coke, his habitual drink. I asked Charlie if he knew anything about the *Suna Akayya*.

"That's the ship that hit the molasses dock? Yeah, I heard about that. Why? You here about that?"

"Yeah. The owner hired me to see what can be done to get her out."

He took a sip of his drink. "I don't know, ol' man. She done a lot of damage. I heard the port wants a couple of million. Hell, they'd just put in new molasses tanks when she hit it."

At that moment I gave up the idea of extracting the vessel. I'd thought there was something questionable about the way the owner had described the situation—he'd said the ship had just "bumped" the dock, and had done no real damage—and I certainly wasn't going to help him avoid paying a legitimate debt. So what had started out as a recovery job turned into a night of reminiscing about previous adventures. By the time Charlie finally slid off his stool and declared that he was on his way home to his girlfriend, it was two-thirty and we were the last customers. The bartender brought us the bill gratefully and I paid it.

Charlie was a self-confessed redneck from Athens, Georgia. He refused to learn Spanish, and coordinated the coffee loading for Cartones del Sud by shouting English commands at the top of his lungs. The stevedores soon learned by inflection and osmosis what he wanted, and he was a good foreman. He took care of his men, buying them gifts and throwing parties for their families at the local park. They'd never met a gringo like that before, and they were devoted to him.

One time Charlie took a pistol away from a taxi driver. We'd caught a taxi from the port to the Hotel Estacion, a trip we'd made hundreds of times, and when we pulled up in front of the wide marble steps leading to the lobby, the driver tried to charge us twice the normal rate. When Charlie refused to pay it, the driver made the mistake of pulling an old black revolver out from under his seat.

I was still in the backseat. I yelled that the man had a gun. Before he could level it, Charlie had reached over and snatched it out of his hand. The man's face went as yellow as an old skull. But then Charlie laughed, climbed out of the taxi, and threw the pistol into the swamp. He took five hundred pesos out of his wallet, the proper fare, and threw them on the seat.

Once, while we were in a Cali restaurant, staying overnight for an early-morning flight to Miami, I told him, "Charlie, if I ever need somebody to cover my back in a knife fight, you're the man."

"Oh, hey, oh Lawdy," he said.

I never saw Charlie after that trip, but he called me a couple of years later. He'd gotten his Colombian girlfriend pregnant, and after he left Cartones del Sud and went home, he told his wife, Cathy, about his girlfriend and son-to-be. I'd never met Cathy in person, but she and I had talked on the phone many times. She was a pleasant woman with a Georgia accent as thick as Charlie's. Charlie told her abortion was out of the question, and that he would have to divorce her so he could marry Adelia and bring her and his son to the United States.

Cathy agreed to the divorce, and Charlie brought his new family to Athens, but the U.S. immigration authorities suspected it was a sham marriage, and they were watching the house that Charlie had rented for them, down the street from the house he and Cathy still owned. He restarted the welding business he'd had before going to Colombia, and got in the routine of leaving his new wife's house every morning to go down to have coffee with his ex-wife and plan the day's work. However, he had to spend every night with Adelia, or else she and his son would get deported. It was a bizarre arrangement, but Charlie was the kind of guy who made the world do things his way.

* * *

I took off the month of January 1998 to study for the bar exam. Never having attended a law class, I had no way of knowing how I would do, so I put my nose to the grindstone. I bought every bar-prep book there was, and spent every day holed up in my office, studying.

The California bar exam is a three-day affair, and no pushover. It was held in the Sequoia Center, a huge conference facility in the Buena Park area of Los Angeles. I had a typewriter I'd bought for the test, but I deliberately left my study materials behind. I figured that if I didn't know the material by then, no amount of last-minute cramming would help. At the time—I don't know about now—if you chose not to hand-write the test, you could only use a typewriter, so you'd have no way of preloading data into a disk or hard drive.

A thousand applicants were pounding away on their typewriters, sitting at long, cloth-covered tables in a huge room. You can imagine what it sounds like when a thousand typewriters get going at once. There was an elderly man at the back, at least seventy years old, and the rumor among the applicants, who tended to gossip during breaks, was that this was his twentieth attempt. At the advanced age of fifty myself, and also facing the horror of failure, I looked at the old man with awe.

I have a bad habit of assuming the worst. Many times, in dicey situations, I've assumed the worst. Of course, when I get through it, I have the pleasure of having survived against the odds, crying out joyously, "Not yet, by God, not yet!" But at the time it happens I get the same sick feeling.

In this case, my life wasn't on the line, but I assumed as I left the hall on the third day that I'd failed the exam. I was so convinced, I started studying for the next sitting as soon as I got home.

The results were to be posted on the California bar website at exactly 4 P.M. Pacific time on a given date. If your name appeared, you passed. If it didn't, you didn't. I was at home in Louisiana on that date. I logged on at exactly 6 P.M. central time, and there was my name. For a long minute I sat there, trying to figure out how the bar could have made such a glaring error. Then it sank in; I'd actually passed the California bar exam on the first try, without a single law school class.

I dashed through the rain to the house. We were having a couple over for dinner, friends we'd known from before our marriage. I ran through the dining room without a word to them and into the kitchen. Karla and Alex, now fourteen and eleven, were sitting at the breakfast bar engaged in one of their earnest discussions. I jerked open one of the bottom cabinets.

Many years earlier, when I taught flying, I'd had a lot of ex-military students, and it's a tradition in military aviation that when a pilot gets his wings, he gives his instructor a bottle of whisky. It's a gesture of respect and affection, and although I don't drink much hard liquor, I'd never refused one. So I had a dozen bottles of bourbon in the bottom cabinet, dusty and unopened. I yanked one out, unscrewed the top, and upended it.

I lowered the bottle, my eyes watering. My wife and our friends stared at me in astonishment. Karla and Alex, who'd never seen their father act that way before, were dumbfounded.

"I passed," I gasped. "I passed the damned thing." I capped the bottle and put it on the counter. "Damn! All that studying wasted."

A friend who was adept at that sort of thing put together a Web page for me touting my experience in cargo disputes and ship seizures. Shortly afterward, I got a call from a lawyer in London who represented the owner of a ship named the *Eagle Venture*.

His client was the victim of one of the oldest scams in the business. The ship had been under time charter to a murky outfit called Mediterranean Central Chartering, or MedCent, run by an infamous husband-and-wife team of criminals, George and Aila Mistilis, based in Malta. After the ship left Antwerp with a cargo of steel profiles for Port-au-Prince, the shipowner learned that the charterers had left the ship with a trail of unpaid debts from the Black Sea to Antwerp.

The scam works by taking advantage of the traditional way of handling ship expenses. In the old days, when ships traded regular routes and agents relied on their continuing relationships with owners and charterers, the agent would compile the ship's accounts after the ship left port and forward any outstanding amounts to the owner or charterer for payment. A dishonest charterer can run up charterers' debts—fuel, stevedoring costs, wharfage, light dues, etc.—and get the ship out of port without paying them. Then, at the end of the charter, the charterer disappears and lets the unpaid creditors seize the ship for the outstanding amounts.

This was MedCent's modus operandi. During a week of research, as I contacted the men I'd met during my years of putting ships in service in Greece, Italy, and Spain, I learned that the Mistilises had operated under dozens of different names—MedCent was only their latest incarnation—to charter ships and abandon them to unpaid debts. They had taken the *Eagle Venture* under charter in Istanbul, and had left a trail of debts in every port they sent the ship. There were more than $200,000 in unpaid port charges in Istanbul, Piraeus, Taranto, Cadiz, and Antwerp, and a $70,000 bunker bill owed to a Danish fuel supplier.

Part of the scheme was to keep the owners from knowing that the charterer wasn't paying its debts. So MedCent had been putting off the bunker supplier and the agents in the various ports with fabricated stories of wire transfers that somehow never appeared and promises to pay as soon as the next cargo was loaded.

Now the ship was on its way to Port-au-Prince, and when the owners discovered the trail of debts, they hired Peter Galloway, a barrister in London. Knowing that the ship's next port was Port-au-Prince, he'd found my website and called me.

The most interesting thing I found in the documents that Peter sent by email attachment were the bills of lading for the Antwerp cargo. The shipper was Peyton International, a trading firm out of Norfolk, Virginia, that frequently contracted for shipments to Haiti. I knew Peyton. As a ship captain, I'd carried cargoes for the company fifteen years earlier.

I called the man I knew in their office, Bill Monroe. I'd never met him in person, but he'd always seemed a fair and reasonable fellow. He didn't know anything about the string of debts. "Hell, Max," he said, "we'd never heard of MedCent before. We just needed to get that cargo from Belgium to Haiti, and they offered the *Eagle Venture*. What can I do to help?"

"Have you paid the freight yet?"

"Not yet. It's due day after tomorrow."

"How much?"

"Let's see." A rustling of papers. "Looks like two hundred and fifty thousand."

That was delightful. Peter had said that the total of all debts was somewhere around two-seventy. If the ship could get off with a twenty-thousand-dollar shortfall, the owners would be dancing on their desks.

"Look, Bill," I said, "I'm going to move for a Rule B attachment of the freight money, but I don't want to tie up other money as well. Is that money in a Peyton account?"

"Sure."

"Can you move it out of that account and into an account with no other money in it? That way when we seize the money we won't be seizing any of your other funds."

"Let me check with the accounting office. I assume it can be done."

"Better do it fast," I said. "I'm going to call a Virginia lawyer now. Call me back."

We hung up and I went to the Maritime Law Association website. I didn't know any attorneys in Virginia, but what I wanted was relatively simple, and I wanted to give the work to another maritime lawyer. I found a solo practitioner in Norfolk named Rod Markinson and gave him a call.

He said he'd be glad to do the seizure. Later that afternoon Bill called and gave the bank name and account number where they'd transferred the freight money, and I emailed the information to Rod. The next day he walked the complaint over to the federal courthouse and filed it, and the same afternoon the bank was served with the restraining order that kept them from disbursing the funds. Bill copied me on an email he sent to Med-Cent telling them why Peyton couldn't pay the freight money.

The next couple of days saw a blizzard of emails and faxes from Aila Mistilis to Peyton International and the owners of the *Eagle Venture*, threatening legal action and every other kind of retribution unless they got the money. She somehow failed to respond to the owners' enumeration of the unpaid charterer's debts, except to claim that MedCent had every intention of paying all debts, but that the company was prevented from doing so by the owners' completely unjustified action in seizing their freight money.

There was a hearing in the federal court in Norfolk the next day. Med-Cent had appointed a lawyer, but the judge ruled that there was enough substance to our claim to continue the seizure.

The ship arrived in Haiti a week later, and MedCent promptly had her seized on some trumped-up charge that would never have succeeded in any law-abiding country. The ship's owners called me to see what could be done, and I agreed to fly to Port-au-Prince.

Ronald met me outside of customs in Haiti and we took a taxi to the Oloffson. Then we went down to the waterfront to meet the ship's agent. The company was called Cariship S.A.; it was located in an old, crumbling building up the street from the U.S. embassy. The agent was a young Dominican named Emilio Barador. He swept some files off the chairs in front of his desk so we could sit.

"I don't know what to say about it," he said. "This is very unusual. The ship has not been seized for a cargo claim. There's nothing wrong with the cargo. We have started discharging already. The court papers say something about 'violation of the contract,' whatever that means. You should talk to the charterer's lawyer."

"Do you know who that is?"

He studied the arrest warrant. "Yes, a man named Yves St. Armond. Wait a moment."

He picked up his telephone and called somebody. They talked in Creole and he hung up. "Yes, that's the brother of one of the port officials. I knew I recognized the last name."

"Know anything about him?"

"Not much," he said guardedly. "I don't think he does much maritime law."

"What's his address?"

He scribbled an address on a piece of paper and handed it to me. I thanked him and Ronald and I went out.

"What do you think, Captain?" Ronald asked.

"This is a bullshit seizure," I said. "It would never be recognized by international law. However, that doesn't mean they can't keep the ship here for months waiting for trial. I'm going to see what can be done quick."

He frowned. "You mean . . . steal her out?"

I shook my head. "It's too early for that. I'm going to try something else first. Let's go see Mr. St. Armond."

The address was up the hill, near the Holiday Inn, a small office sandwiched between a warehouse and a transfer bureau, where Haitians can receive money sent from abroad. YVES ST. ARMOND, AVOCAT was lettered in a crude hand on the glass door.

I left Ronald in a nearby café and went into the office. It was hot, even with a wide-open window at one side. A round young man with a balloon of fat under his chin waddled out of a back room to see who'd come in. He was wearing a white long-sleeved shirt with crescents of sweat under the armpits and a grayish tie with red stripes. His tiny eyes were hidden by thick, black-rimmed glasses. "Mr. St. Armond?" I asked, holding out my hand.

"Yes, I am St. Armond," he said in passable English. His hand was soft and moist. "How may I help you?"

I handed him one of my new law cards. "I'm here to represent the owners of the *Eagle Venture*. I understand you represent MedCent Charterers."

He studied my card myopically, then turned it over to see if there were any hidden messages on the back. "Yes, that is my client. Please come into my office."

He led me back to another room, as small as the first, and hotter. An ancient fan with its blade guard missing rattled on the top of a scarred old filing cabinet with some of the drawer handles missing. The only ventilation was a small, barred window high in the wall. He sat down heavily, panting a little, and gestured for me to sit in the handmade chair in front of his desk.

"So," he said, "how may I help you?"

"The *Eagle Venture*. I want to get the seizure lifted."

His little eyes opened a bit. "You are ready to pay my client's claim?"

"I don't know what it is. Can you tell me?"

"Yes. Your client owes my client two hundred and seventy-five thousand dollars."

"For what?"

The question took him by surprise. "For what? For the money for the shipment of the cargo."

"That money is owed by Peyton International, not my client. Why don't you seize their cargo?"

"But did your client not stop that company from paying my client?"

"No, it was the court that did that. Look at the court order. My client couldn't do that unless the court ordered it."

"The court here will make the decision," he muttered. "Until then, the ship will stay."

I leaned back. "Mr. St. Armond, have you gotten paid yet?" He frowned. I went on. "The reason I ask is that your client never pays its bills. I have a stack of invoices they've left behind from Istanbul to Haiti. If they haven't already given you a retainer, you might have a hard time getting paid."

He smiled, his thick lips parting slightly over tiny, yellowish teeth. "Then I will get paid from the sale of the ship."

I shrugged. "You might not win."

I don't think he'd considered that. He leaned his huge belly against the desk. "What are you saying, Mr. ah, Har . . ."

"Call me Max," I said. "I'm saying you should look after yourself. Your client is a thief who has stolen money all over the world. I can show you their record. I'd hate to see you do a lot of work for nothing."

He leaned back and panted some more. "You are very concerned about my getting paid, Mr. Max."

"I'm more concerned with seeing that my client's ship leaves this port without unreasonable delay." I stood up. "Well, it's not right for you to work for free. If they don't pay, perhaps I can see that you get something for the time you've spent."

"Sit down, sit down," he wheezed. "Let me think about that." He fingered the top button of his shirt, feeling for it under the frog's neck of fat that overlapped it. I don't know why he didn't unbutton it. A sense of propriety, I suppose.

I said, "When is the first hearing in the seizure?"

"Tomorrow at two in the afternoon. In the Justice Court in Delmas."

I knew how Haitian seizures worked. Anybody at any time can seize any ship just by going down to the local justice of the peace and filing a claim. No supporting materials, no invoices, no affidavits, nothing. Just by paying the justice the filing fee and something under the table. And the most important aspect of justice court in Haiti, for my purposes, was that no records are kept. No transcript, no tape recording, nothing. There would be nothing later for anyone to review.

I pressed on: "I can tell you, my client has given me plenty of money to defend this case. We don't mind spending it in any way necessary to get the ship out of port."

I let that sink in. He was staring at the wall above my head. The damp circles under his arms had spread since I came in. I stood up again. "So I'll see you at the Justice Court in Delmas. I know where it is. In fact, I know the judge." That's wasn't a lie. I'd been involved in a seizure in that court some years earlier, and my client had lost because I didn't know then how things work in Haiti.

He struggled to his feet. "Mr. Max, let us resolve this matter. I can see that my client has a very weak case. Perhaps we will lose tomorrow. My client has not given me the proper papers to present a good case. But how can you assure me that I will be paid?"

"I'll bring the money with me. At the conclusion of the hearing, if the ship is released, I'll give it to you. What will your bill be at that point?"

"Fif—twenty thousand dollars," he said, promptly enough.

I held up my hands. "Now, Mr. St. Armond, your bill has to be tied to the work that you've done. All you've done so far is type up an arrest warrant for the justice to sign. No research, no document review, nothing. I think your bill should be around five thousand dollars."

He was in a hurry. "Eight thousand," he said. "This is my final bill."

"Fine. Eight thousand U.S. dollars in cash. I'll have it with me."

"But you will not need a receipt for your client?"

I shook my head. "My client trusts me."

We shook hands and I went out. He followed, grunting and huffing, and held the outside door for me. "Where will we meet tomorrow?" he asked.

"Here. I'll come here and then we'll go in separate cars."

"Very well." We shook hands again. His hand was slimy with sweat, and I had to restrain myself from wiping mine dry until he'd gone back inside. I found Ronald in the café drinking a Coke.

"It's all taken care of," I told him. "The ship'll be released tomorrow."

"How is that?"

When I told him, he grinned and clapped me on the shoulder. "Captain, you think like a Haitian."

"I can only aspire. Now, let's go to the Oloffson and drink some beer."

I had to scramble to get the money in time. I'd only brought enough money for expenses, but when I told Peter Galloway in London that I could get the arrest lifted for eight thousand dollars, he agreed to send the money by Western Union. He had enough sense not to ask any questions.

The money arrived at nine o'clock the next morning. We took a taxi to Mr. St. Ormond's office. I had the money in my small black-leather briefcase. St. Ormond was alone in his office. I opened the briefcase on the receptionist's desk and showed him the money. His little pig eyes looked it over carefully, then he nodded and we left for the justice of the peace office.

The courtroom was a plain storefront with a barred front door and a dozen folding chairs in front of an old steel desk. A Haitian flag printed on poster paper was tacked to the wall; some crumbling law books on a side table looked as if they would fall apart if they were ever opened. The judge was the same one I remembered, a loose-lipped old man with a squashed nose and a heavy tremble in his clawlike hands. He was the only person in the room.

The hearing was conducted in Creole. I don't have much French, but I could tell that Mr. St. Armond was telling him that his client had decided to drop the case. The old man didn't seem to like it, and he asked why the case had been brought in the first place. Mr. St. Armond said it'd been a mistake, but everything was settled now. Obviously unhappy that no more money would come his way, the justice finally took a form out of a desk drawer and filled it in. We all shook hands and Mr. St. Armond and I left.

Back in his office, I counted out eight thousand dollars and pushed them across his desk. He handed me the form. "This is the release. If your agent gives this to the port office, they will give the ship a clearance."

The case in Virginia dragged on for a couple of months, but the judge ultimately awarded the seized money to the shipowner, and MedCent disappeared from the scene. I'm sure the Mistilises are still out there, scamming unsuspecting shipowners, but I doubt that the owners of the *Eagle Venture* will ever fall for that one again.

Some time later, I got a call from another lawyer in London who'd won a judgment against a cruise ship in the Mediterranean. From his voice, he was an elderly man, and probably a smoker, but he sounded like a sharp cookie. "A colleague gave me your name," he said. "Peter Galloway. Remember him?"

"Sure. I did a little job for him a while back."

"Yes, he was quite complimentary. My problem is somewhat different." I waited. It was a beautiful summer day on the bayou, with early morning sunlight dancing on the placid water. He coughed delicately and cleared his throat. "I have a client who was injured on the *Regia dei Mari*. Have you heard of that ship?"

"Nope."

"She's an old girl, built in the mid-fifties. My client was on a cruise in the Mediterranean and broke her back. She's a paraplegic now. She was on one of the upper decks and a railing gave way. She fell two decks and landed next to the swimming pool."

"That's a sad story," I said. "What was the judgment?"

"Five million pounds."

I whistled. "How much is the ship worth?"

"She was an equestrienne."

"She was a what?"

"My client was a world-class equestrienne. She won the European Dressage Championship the year before the accident."

"Ergo the big award," I said. "Any idea what the ship's worth?"

"Last survey said ten million dollars."

"That's convenient. So what can I do?"

"Find the ship."

"It can't be that hard to find a cruise ship, can it?"

He coughed again. "In this case it is. Braga Lines went out of business last year and the ship was sold to a Greek. Now it's disappeared."

"Look in Egypt. That's where derelict cruise ships go."

"Oh, this ship's no derelict, in spite of her age. She went through a complete refurbishment in 1992. No, we think she's somewhere in Italy or Greece, but the new owner knows about the judgment. She's probably had her appearance altered, and I'm sure the new owner intends to run her under a new name."

"Flagged as a stateless vessel, in other words. So you want me to find her?"

"That's right."

"I can try," I said, "but it will take a couple of weeks. I'll need my day rate up front, and about five thousand in expenses."

"Where do I send it?" he said. He said he would email the ship's particulars, general arrangement plan, and some photographs.

I got the emails an hour later. The photographs were low-resolution and old, but good enough to identify the ship by. I printed them and the general arrangement plan. So a Greek had bought the ship. I called George Mitropoulis, a ship broker I knew with an office on Akti Miaouli Street in Piraeus. I'd bought a ship through him a few years ago, and he still sent me brokers' sheets occasionally, although by then I was more or less out of the business of buying ships in Europe.

"'Allo? 'Allo?" George said. "Who call, eh?"

"Captain Max," I told him. "Max Hardberger. How're you doing, George?"

"Oh, Captain Max! Long time no hear from you. Are you in Greece?"

"No, I'm in the U.S., but I'll be coming to see you soon. I'm looking for a ship, and I thought you might be able to help me find it."

"A ship to buy? Very few small ships around here anymore. You and your friends have bought them all."

"No, a cruise ship. I've got a client who wants me to help find it. The *Regia dei Mari.*"

"I remember that ship. She belongs to the Braga Line."

"Used to. She was sold to a Greek last year."

"Is that so?" I heard him light a cigarette and blow smoke into the mouthpiece. "She could be anywhere, then. Greeks have ships all over the world."

"I think she's in the Mediterranean. The owner's trying to change her identity. There's a judgment against her."

"Is that so? Okay, I'll check around. When will you get here?"

"Tomorrow night. I'll come by the office on Thursday morning."

"I'll be here."

Greek customs were perfunctory, as usual, and with carry-on luggage only, I was the first passenger out of the Athens terminal. I caught a taxi to my favorite hotel, the Hotel Posidonia in Glyfada. It didn't take long, and after I stowed my bag in my room I walked down the hill to the Glyfada waterfront for supper. The air smelled of flowers and olive trees.

I'd had a long nap on the plane, and Glyfada is a party town, so I dropped by some of my favorite bars. One of the ones I used to frequent was a chess bar in the basement of a shopping center. You could always find a man waiting for a game. An old man in a tweed sport coat sat behind a board at the back of the room, playing a puzzle; when he saw me looking around he gestured me over. He didn't speak a word of English, but that's the beauty of chess.

We played a long, hard-fought game, which he finally won through a cautious strategy of attrition.

When I left, the street was just beginning to come alive. Athens is a late-night town, and the restaurants don't get crowded until about 10 P.M. Many a night I'd made my way home at 2 or 3 A.M. past the bustling open-air bars and restaurants, with cars jostling for parking spots and packs of well-dressed boys and girls laughing and chattering along the sidewalks.

At eight the next morning, I was on Akti Miaouli Street in Piraeus. The ferries that arrive from the islands every night were lined up along the dock with their stern ramps down, getting ready for the day's run. Traffic was, as usual, heavy and chaotic. George Mitropoulis's office was in a dingy building a half block up the hill from the waterfront, on the third floor. The elevator didn't work.

Mitropoulis was sitting behind a desk reading the faxed brokers' sheets that had come in during the night. He hadn't changed a bit—he still had the same pudgy, pale face with a peppery grenadier's mustache. He poured me a tiny cup of Greek coffee, loaded it with sugar and cream, and laid it on the front edge of his desk. Then he opened a large hardbound book and turned it around. "Is this the ship?"

The book held photos of hundreds of cruise ships, some of them old, black-and-white photos of long-gone ships with plumb bows and high, straight funnels, and some of them new, sleek, arrow-bowed cruisers with long, black-tinted windows. He put his finger on a ship called the *Rhapsody,* which was apparently the ship's build name. I recognized it immediately as the *Regia dei Mari.*

"That's the ship," I said. "Do you know where she is?"

He shrugged. "No, but I know where she might be. Do you know Abelakia?"

I shook my head.

"It's between Piraeus and Perama. It's a place where people take ships for rebuilding. Maybe ships that need new names and need to lose their old names, eh? I asked a friend of mine where he thought a Greek owner might take such a cruise ship, and he said there are a couple in Abelakia that could be your ship. I thought we might go take a look."

"Sounds good to me." I finished my coffee and Mr. Mitropoulis hunted around in the piles of paper on his desk until he found his cellphone, a big square relic with a thick black antenna. We went out and he locked the door.

His shiny black Mercedes was parked behind the building. We drove up the hill and away from the waterfront, dodged through the tangled streets of the old city, and rejoined the waterfront on the other side. The winding street followed a high wall that separated the shipyards on the waterfront from the road, the masts and superstructures of ships at the docks visible above it.

A street led off to the left, and we turned down it. A line of ships appeared in various stages of disrepair, with at least a dozen cruise ships among them, their sides streaked with dirt and their decks littered with wreckage. They were all docked stern-to, with gangways leading down to the quay's crumbling concrete.

I had the photos of the *Regia dei Mari* laid in my lap as we drove along, but none of the ships seemed to match. "Doesn't look like she's here," I said.

"Don't be so sure," he said. "Remember, this is where ships come to hide. Perhaps her profile has been altered."

We reached the far end of the street, where the end overlooked the wide bay dotted with ships at anchor, and he turned around. We drove back slowly. Some of the ships had men crawling over them and the hot light of welding torches sparkling along their decks. One had a huge hole cut in her side, with a deck barge alongside, and men were throwing furniture out of the hole and onto the barge.

With the ships all lined up stern-to at the dock, so close to each other that they needed fenders between them, it was hard to see anything except the sterns. None of the photos that I had of the *Regia dei Mari* had been taken from astern, so there was little to go on. We rolled past one ship with a high, graceful bustle stern under raked, slanting windows that vaguely resembled hers, but the *Regia dei Mari* had an open fantail and this ship had a raised poop deck.

The term "poop deck" comes from the Roman ships that carried small religious statues, or *puppis,* on their raised sterns. Over time, a raised stern came to be called a "poupe" deck, then a poop deck.

There was a name on the stern in Greek letters. "The *Royal Palace,*" Mr. Mitropoulis said. "What was the *Regia dei Mari*'s build name?"

"*Rhapsody.*"

Then it's not the same ship. Look, her build name was the *Alegria.*"

I chuckled. "That could be a new build name."

He stared at me for a moment, then shook his head at the thought of such base trickery. I sorted through the photos I'd printed and selected a page with some interiors. "I'm going on board," I said. "I doubt that they tore out the whole interior, so I might be able to identify her by these."

"Maybe not such a good idea, Captain. The men on board could be pirates. If they catch you . . ." He drew his finger across his throat.

I grunted. At that moment, two men carried a length of railing down the gangway and laid it on a pile of paneling and ship parts on the quay. I took my camera out of its case and got out. Mr. Mitropoulis's worried face followed me across the dock.

The gangway was steep and homemade, and the hand-ropes were loose, but I managed to reach the gunwale and jumped down to the afterdeck. There was nobody in sight. I went forward along the starboard walkway. I could hear the sound of a welding torch, and men's voices. Somebody was hammering in the bowels of the ship.

The walkway led past a restaurant that filled the width of the stern, the interior in disarray, dimly seen through tinted windows. The walkway opened onto a swimming pool, now drained, with deck chairs stacked against the far railing and lashed together. The teak deck planks were bleached gray and cupped at their edges, and tiles were missing in the pool's border. I didn't have any photos of this area.

I saw two men on the other side, aft of the pool, standing next to one of the fairings that supported the upper deck. They had their backs to me. They'd already cut away the fairing forward of it with a cutting torch, and had a piece cut out of this one. I ran up to the boat deck. Here the lifeboats lay in their cradles in a long line, each with its rope boarding ladder coiled on deck under it. The passageway ended at a steel door in the forward bulkhead.

The door was unlocked, but its hinges shrieked. I jumped back to hide behind a vent, but nobody came out. I tiptoed back to the door and slipped inside. The door led to a hallway that ran athwartships, across the width of the ship, with cabin doors on both sides. Another hallway led aft on the ship's centerline. I could hear voices in the distance, but the hallway was deserted.

The hallway ended at a sweeping stairway with heavy mahogany railings, a deep-pile carpet padding the steps. The stairway led down to a restaurant ringed with alabaster statues of naked goddesses and gods with fully formed genitals. Bingo. I had a photo of the restaurant. I studied it. The same shameless statues, the same Corinthian columns at the back of the room.

I heard voices and jammed the paper into my pocket. Two men came in, one of them carrying an electric drill. I froze. They did double takes and one of them spoke to me in Greek.

"Where's the boss?" I said. "I'm from the buyer." My voice didn't sound so firm to me, but I put on a brave face. "Do you speak English?" I thought about turning and running, and that's probably what I should have done, but I decided to bluff it out.

They raised their voices, still speaking Greek, and I kept saying that I was from the buyer. One of them came up and pushed me. I knocked his hand away. The other man said, "Hey, hey," and they argued for a moment in Greek. The man with the drill put it down and took out a walkie-talkie. He muttered into it.

Three men, led by a swarthy young man in designer jeans and a loose shirt, came running out from the portside hallway and piled to a stop in front of me. "Who are you?" the young man asked. "What are you doing here?"

I raised my hand. "What's the matter with you guys?" I said in an aggrieved voice. "I'm from the buyer. I'm supposed to inspect this ship."

"Bullshit," he said. He had a high, straight nose, the kind of nose you see on ancient Greek statues. His thick lips twisted in scorn. "This ship is not for sale. You talk bullshit. You will come with us."

"I'm not talking bullshit," I said hotly. "I'm a surveyor. I was told to do a prepurchase survey on the *Princess . . . Marina*. The *Princess Marina*. Isn't that this ship?"

Another couple of men came up, burly workers in dirty boiler suits. One of them held a length of pipe like a weapon. The young man stared at me uncertainly. "The *Princess Marina*? No, this isn't that ship."

"Hell, I thought that's what the name on the stern said. I can't read Greek. What's the name of this ship?"

"The *Royal Palace*. So why you come on board without permission? Why you no ask somebody?"

"There was nobody around."

The men crowded around me, hostile and suspicious. "Take everything out of your pockets," the young man ordered me.

This was serious. If they found the page of photos, the jig would be up. "I'm not going to do it," I said. "If you think I'm trespassing, call the police. But you're not going to search me."

He gave me a measuring look. I knew they weren't going to call the police. I said, "Look, I have a fax from the owner of the *Princess Marina* giving me permission to inspect her. Why don't you come down to the car and I'll show you?"

He hesitated. I pressed ahead. "Why are you being so suspicious? What's going on here, anyway? What do you have to hide?"

That did the job. "All right," he said. "We will go to your car. But if you are telling bullshit, you will be sorry."

"Come on," I said, "let's go."

He took two men and escorted me aft along the starboard walkway to the gangway. One of the men went down first and waited at the foot of the gangway as I climbed down, the young man and the other worker following me closely. Mr. Mitropoulis's face stared at us from behind the car's window. The car was facing toward the main street. That was important.

"Come on," I said confidently, and walked quickly toward the car. I needed to put some distance between us. They fell slightly behind. I went around to the passenger side and opened the door. They were on the other side. Mr. Mitropoulis still had his window up.

I jumped in and reached across to lock his door. "Go! Go!" I said, "Let's get out of here!"

The young Greek's eyes got wide. He jerked on the driver's door, rocking the car. Mr. Mitropoulis started the engine with a roar and slammed the car into gear. One of the men was coming around to my side, but he had to jump out of the way as the car leaped forward. In an instant we were halfway to the main road.

"What happened? What happened?" Mr. Mitropoulis asked. "Did they know what you were doing?"

I looked back. The three men were standing on the quay looking at us, but they didn't have a car, and there was no use running after us on foot. We turned the corner and joined the traffic on the road to Piraeus.

"It's the same ship," I said, taking out the crumpled sheet of photos. "I found this restaurant."

"You're lucky," he said gravely. "If they had known what you were doing, they could have killed you and thrown you overboard." I started to smile, but he said, "You should not think this is something funny. I can tell from looking at those men. They are Greek mafia. They would kill you and not think anything about it."

"Then I must thank you for saving my ass."

Back at his parking lot, I shook his hand and hurried down to Akti Miaouli to catch a taxi back to the hotel. I used the hotel fax machine to send a handwritten report to the London lawyer, with the hotel's phone and fax numbers, and waited for an answer.

He called a few minutes later. "I've hired a lawyer in Piraeus," he said.

"The police should be on their way to the ship now. How'd you find her so quickly?"

"I've got a friend here who knew where that kind of thing is done," I said. "The ship was in the first place we looked."

"Well, it was good work nonetheless. Please stay there until I call back, in case we need something else done."

I lay around the room reading for the rest of the day. Late in the afternoon he called to say that the police had seized the ship and put the workers off. Nobody had been arrested, but the investigation was ongoing. In any event, there was no chance that the ship could be slipped out of port, so I could go home.

A year later, the London lawyer sent me a faxed copy of a magazine article about the *Regia dei Mari*. It turned out that the ship hadn't had a new owner after all. According to the lawyer, Braga Line had been owned by a Greek named Michael Kouris, and after the judgment, he'd sold the company's three cruise ships to a sham Maltese company. Then, through a complicated series of transactions, he'd allegedly secretly sold the *Regia dei Mari* back to himself. He was never arrested, but the ship was sold at auction for 6 million, which went to satisfy the equestrienne's judgment.

CHAPTER TEN

GREEK EASTER ON THE *FONTANKA SAGA*

I N 2000 I WAS asked by a fellow member of the Maritime Law Association to find a ship for him and some other lawyers to buy. They'd been making money hand over fist from a dot-com company they'd invested in—something to do with file management—and they wanted to buy a ship.

By then, my buddies and I had just about sucked all the little freighters out of Northern Europe, so it took a couple of months to find a bargain. However, in late March of that year I got a brokers' sheet from Mr. Mitropoulis on a neat little Hungarian-built freighter named the *Fontanka Saga*. The vessel was laid up in Drapetsona, Greece, a suburb of Piraeus, and the price of two hundred thousand dollars was better than right. I forwarded the email to Greg Powers, my lawyer friend, and he circulated it among his investor partners. A couple of days later he sent an email asking me to go take a look at her.

I landed in Athens late at night and went right to the Posidonia. I knew the restaurants only a few blocks away would be open and bustling, but I was too tired to go out, so I went to bed without supper. The next morning I had a light continental breakfast at the hotel and took a taxi to Drapetsona.

The *Fontanka Saga* was tied stern-to at an old stained dock next to a line of decrepit trawlers. She was a nice-looking ship, a traditional house-aft freighter with union-purchase derricks—cargo gear with two booms per set, so that one swings out over the dock and the other stays over the hold—and three hatches with MacGregor covers.

An Alfa Romeo sedan was parked at the foot of the gangway. As the taxi pulled up next to it, I saw a huge dent in the starboard stern quarter of the ship's hull. The steel had not been torn open, but it was crushed over a diameter of about eight feet, and set in about a foot and a half. The ship had hit something, or something had hit the ship, with a great deal of force.

It was a cold morning, and I hunched my shoulders against the wind as

I hurried along the starboard side of the house and through a steel door. The hallway was lit and a generator thumped down in the engine room.

I went up to the master's deck and along the hallway toward an open door. A big man in slacks and a rayon shirt stood bending over the desk with another man, a small, white-haired man in a boiler suit, at his side. I knocked.

The big man had a square, pale face under a shock of thick black hair. The small man was about sixty, with the sharp features of a fox. The big man said, "Yes? Captain Hardberger?"

"Yes." I stepped forward and shook their hands.

"I'm Vladimir Dubrovich," the big man said. "This is Petro, the chief engineer. Would you like some coffee?"

"I'd love some," I said. "It's cold this morning."

"Yes, a Greek spring." He picked up the intercom and spoke in Russian. Then he said something to the chief engineer and Petro, with a little bow to me, went out. "Please, let us sit. The chief and I were talking about the ship's wiring. Some little problem with the motor generator."

We sat facing each other across the coffee table. The master's saloon was small but well-appointed, with wood paneling and upholstered chairs bolted to the floor. Vladimir was a soft bear of a man, with a pleasant face and a ready smile. He spoke excellent English with a strong Russian accent. "So you have come all the way from America to inspect my little beauty?"

"Yes," I said, looking around. "She does look like a nice little ship."

"I have spent a lot of time and money on her, but now my wife and I are going back to Odessa and I need to sell her. Did Mr. Mitropoulis send you any information on her?"

"Yes, a broker's sheet. She was built in Hungary in 1977? A Sulzer engine?"

"That's right."

"Three holds and hatches?"

"Yes, with MacGregor hatch covers."

That was the biggest drawback about this little ship, the fact that she had three hatches and holds. Back in the day when ships mostly carried general cargo, it made sense to divide up the ship's carrying capacity into different holds, to segregate the various cargoes. However, in the last twenty years, containers have taken over the general cargo market, and break-bulk freighters—the kind of ships I deal with—are more often relegated to carrying homogenous cargoes. It's easier to load homogenous cargo into one large hold, with one hatch, than it is to maneuver it into a number of smaller holds. However, if you can buy a 1,500-ton freighter for two hundred thousand dollars, you can overlook a relatively small disadvantage like that. At least she had MacGregor hatches.

Of all the tasks facing a ship designer, hatch design is the most challenging. In the fifty years since ships have gone from wooden hatch boards to steel hatch covers, designers have tried every different type and combination of hatch covers, and, unfortunately, no truly satisfactory system has yet been found.

The problem lies in the contradictory requirements of watertight sealing versus openness of access. For cargo operations, you want a hatch as large as possible, so cargo can be lowered directly into the hold. However, the larger the hatch, the heavier the hatch covers and the harder it is to make them seal against rain and spray.

Wooden hatch boards are actually a good way of obtaining a weathertight seal, but as ships grew larger, they became impractical. They have to be opened and closed by hand, which is time-consuming and labor-intensive. Once they are closed and covered by tarpaulins, they are generally more tightly sealed than even the best type of MacGregor hatch cover, but the time it takes to open and close them was the real reason they went the way of the dinosaur. Charterers don't like having to pay ship hire while hatches are being opened and closed—delaying the loading and unloading of cargo—and there's also the danger of getting caught by a sudden rain shower that will damage the cargo in the hold.

The first type of hatch cover to follow wooden hatch boards were simple rectangular panels, called pontoons, that were lifted off or lowered in place by the ship's cargo gear, and, when opened, were stacked one upon the other. Given their size, there is no other place on a ship to put them. This system has two disadvantages: one is that you cannot open the entire length of the hatch, because they have to be stacked somewhere, and the other is that, in any water except dead calm, lifting and lowering heavy hatch covers with a crane can be dicey and dangerous.

The next type of hatch cover was called the chain-pull MacGregor. Although hatch covers are made by a number of different companies, the

MacGregor company of Scotland was the first to invent a mechanized system of opening and closing steel pontoons, so the name has become generic. Chain-pull MacGregors use small wheels on the sides of the pontoons that roll on tracks along the hatch coamings.

The great advantage of this system is that it allows the holds to be fully opened, with the covers rotating and stacking vertically forward and aft of the hatch. The disadvantage is that it is a complicated and delicate mechanism, and as the hatches' wheels, axles, and chains get old and tired, they get harder and harder to open and close. Also, because each pontoon has to be relatively small, the large number of seams between the pontoons make it hard to obtain weathertight matings.

Several innovations have followed. The most common is the hydraulic bifold hatchcover, in which large hydraulic pistons push up hinged pontoons at the ends of the hold. These covers seal better than chain-pull MacGregors, and also provide a completely open hatch, but they require a massive hydraulic system. And if the system ever blows a line or seal under the cover, the hydraulic fluid spraying over the cargo will bring its own cargo-damage claims.

On very large ships, those with decks wide enough to take them, side-rolling hatch covers are the best answer. These covers join in the middle, and each hold has only two covers that pull along tracks to the sides. The hold is completely open, and on ships this size, the hatch coamings are high enough to permit men to pass under the open covers. However, on any ship smaller than about forty thousand deadweight tons, it's counterproductive to have decks that wide because they limit the size of the hatch.

One would think that engineers, who sent men to the moon forty years ago, would have been able to come up with an answer to this problem by now, but they haven't. And I certainly don't have it.

Our coffee came, delivered by a blond young man in an apron. He nodded to me and set the coffee cups on the coffee table. Vladimir ladled cream and sugar into his cup and looked surprised when I lifted my cup to my lips unadulterated. "Hoh," he said, "you are a real man, who can drink Greek coffee with no cream or sugar."

"Yes," I said, "it makes me tough."

He laughed, showing a mouthful of square white teeth. After we finished our coffee, he took me on a tour of the deck. The ship was in amazingly good condition for her age. Union-purchase derricks are not the best system, but they have the advantage of simplicity. They are slightly faster than swinging derricks—cargo gear with a single boom that swings from over the cargo to over the dock—but they're slower than cranes. Today you will find no type of gear on ships except cranes, but they are complex and prone to mechanical problems.

The steel of the ship was excellent. Except for the huge dent in the starboard stern, the vessel was ready for her annual inspection. The accommodations were also nice, although Spartan. The ship had been built during the Soviet era, when Hungary was a satellite, and the Soviets were never big on luxury in the quarters. However, it did have a sauna on the lower deck, complete with cedar strips lining the walls.

Vladimir showed me some other interesting aspects from the ship's Soviet days: not only did it have the complete *Works of Lenin* in a bookcase built into the starboard hallway, behind glass, it had a secret radio room for the ship's political officer, or commissar. At the far end of the commissar's cabin, a panel swung away to show a very small compartment with an ancient radio console against the starboard bulkhead. According to Vladimir, the commissar on all ships of that era was also an intelligence officer and was expected to report back to his controller all information of intelligence value from the foreign ports where the ship traded. Now the commissar's room was being used for storage.

The ship's crew were all Russian. The captain was a very old man, slim and dignified, with a Cossack mustache. The rest of the crew were mostly young men, pale boys who grinned and scuffed their feet and gave me shy smiles when we were introduced.

We finished our inspection by lunchtime. Vladimir insisted that we pick up his wife and go to a restaurant for lunch. His Alfa Romeo looked like a sedan, but the motor growled like a sports car's. Vladimir drove fast and well. When the streets were clear, he rocketed between the old buildings and took corners with screaming tires. In heavy traffic, he grumbled and fumed.

His office was in downtown Piraeus, on the main street. He squealed to a stop against the curb and we went up an outside stairway to the second floor. His wife, Irina, was a strikingly beautiful woman, as big as he, with high Slavic cheekbones and Mongol eyes. She gave me a large, firm hand to shake.

Vladimir poured us three shot glasses of vodka as an aperitif before we went out for lunch. I don't drink much hard liquor, and never before lunch, but it seemed churlish to refuse, so I tossed mine down. I will admit that, when we went out into the blustery wind, the vodka made a nice warm feeling in the pit of my stomach.

We had lunch in a Chinese restaurant on Akti Miaouli Street. Irina spoke English as well as Vladimir, and it was clear that she was the business head in the relationship. Vladimir let her do the talking and drank most of the ceramic jug of hot sake that they ordered.

After lunch, we dropped her off at the office and Vladimir and I went back to the ship. I spent the afternoon taking notes and photographs. He wanted me to have supper with them and their two children, but I begged off and took a taxi back to Glyfada.

I reported to my client that night. I told him it was a good ship and, for the price, an almost unbeatable bargain. The only problem, I warned, was that shipping was in a slump and cargoes were getting harder and harder to find. However, he and his fellow investors were flush with cash and determined to buy a ship, and they wanted to go ahead with the deal.

The next morning I met Vladimir on board again, and after some friendly haggling I got him to sell the ship for $150,000. He promised to have the dent in the stern repaired before the sale. He called the crew into the master's saloon and asked them if they wanted to go with the ship to the Caribbean. Except for the captain, who wanted to retire, the rest of the crew wanted to go.

That afternoon, Vladimir would not take no for an answer when he invited me to eat with the family. I went back to the hotel to clean up—I had worn an old boiler suit to the ship, and I was greasy and dirty after crawling through the double-bottom tanks and poking about in the engine room—and he and Irina came to pick me up.

They and their two daughters lived in a nice apartment on the Piraeus waterfront, with a balcony overlooking a small marina crowded with exotic powerboats. The girls were about eight and eleven years old, bright, vivacious preteens full of questions about life in America. Both of them spoke English perfectly, with hardly a trace of their parents' Russian accents.

After a long meal, followed by several glasses of vodka, I said goodbye to Irina and the girls and Vladimir drove me back to the hotel. He insisted on walking up to the door with me, and when I tried shaking his hand, he grabbed me in a big bear hug that almost lifted me off the ground.

The next day I flew back to the United States. I had some law work that had to be done, and my client needed to make financial arrangements before we bought the ship. It had been a warm winter, and I arrived in New Orleans on a beautiful spring day. Back in the office, I got to work on other business and started making arrangements for the purchase of the *Fontanka Saga*. I stayed in email contact with Vladimir, and a week later Greg wired him the purchase price. A good part of my law practice was setting up Belizean companies, mostly for shipowners, and within a few days I had a Belizean bearer-share company in place to take ownership of the vessel.

Two weeks later I was on a flight back to Athens. I landed just before dark and took a taxi to the hotel. I had a late supper of fried calamari—squid, a Greek delicacy—and turned in early. The next morning I took a taxi to the ship, where the repairmen were still hard at work fixing the dent in the stern. Vladimir's car was parked at the foot of the gangway.

The work was almost finished. They had cropped out the crumpled steel and replaced it with a welded insert, and when I climbed down into the steering flat—the compartment that holds a ship's steering system—a half-dozen men were fitting and welding new frames to the shell plating.

The job was complicated by the fact that the ship had a beautiful, rounded bustle stern. To do the repairs, the men had had to heat and shape the plates, and were now cutting curved strips to make the framing.

Vladimir and Irina insisted that I have supper with them that night, and after supper he and I chatted while I played chess with their elder daughter, Lina. And, of course, we downed a few shot glasses of vodka.

The next morning the desk clerk, a lean Greek woman with her hair in braids, handed me a fax from Greg, asking me to call him. It was the middle of the night in Chicago, so I put it in my pocket and went to the ship. The welders were finishing the stern repair when I arrived, doing some grinding on the welds and gathering up scraps of steel.

Vladimir wasn't on board. I spent some time getting to-buy lists from the chief officer and chief engineer, and chatting with the electrician, who was the only man onboard who spoke good English. He was a tall man with a bodybuilder's frame, his muscular arms bulging his boiler suit's sleeves, with pale blue eyes and an angular jaw. He'd served on many British-owned ships and had learned his English at sea.

Vladimir arrived to pick up the captain and take him to the airport for a flight to Moscow. The new captain was scheduled to arrive that afternoon, a Ukrainian from Odessa. When Vladimir got back, it was early afternoon, just after 8 A.M. in Boston. I called Greg.

"Any chance we can sell the ship back to the Russian?" he asked.

"What? What's the matter?"

"You seen the news?"

"No, not since I got here. What's going on? World war?"

He didn't laugh. "We've lost everything. The bottom's fallen out of the dot-com market. FileIntegra's down to eighty cents a share."

"What's FileIntegra?"

"That's the company we bought. It's dropped from eighty dollars a share to eighty cents a share in one week."

"Holy Christ! What are you guys going to do? Vladimir's not going to buy the ship back. He and his wife are moving to Odessa and going into the real-estate business."

"Can you sell it to somebody else?"

"Well, I don't know about selling it here. It's worth a lot more money on the other side of the Atlantic. I can sell it to a Haitian if we can get it to Miami. But what about bunkers and the other costs of getting across?"

"How much do you need?"

"I need twenty thousand for bunkers. Mr. Mitropoulis has a cargo lined up in Cadiz, Spain, but we need the port fees there, since the charterer won't be paying the charter hire until three days after we leave."

"Well, you can try. I can tell you, though, we don't have any money. We were going to sell shares for the expenses of getting the ship across, but that's out now."

I handed the phone back to Vladimir. "Bad news?" he asked.

I told him what had happened. "Yes," he said, "I saw that on the news.

They're calling it the 'dot-com collapse.' Your friends had money in these dot-com stocks?"

"Yeah. That's where they got the money to buy the ship. You wouldn't want to buy her back, would you?"

He shook his head emphatically. "Even if I wanted to, Irina wouldn't let me. Mr. Mitropoulis might be able to sell her for you, though."

"Well, we can make a profit if I can get her across the pond. They haven't got the money for bunkers, though. Or provisions or anything else."

Vladimir clapped me on the shoulder. "I will help you," he said. "I will not let you fall down now. Come, let's go to the office and have a drink."

I stifled a grimace. I wouldn't have minded a beer, but I didn't want any more vodka. However, after Vladimir's promise, I felt that I had to keep him happy, and having a shot of vodka was what made him happy.

The next two days were a blur of activity. Vladimir got a Norwegian bunker supplier to advance us fuel on credit—to be paid out of the charter hire from the Cadiz cargo—and he loaned me the money for food and other housekeeping supplies.

By the time the ship was ready to go, it was Thursday, April 16. We had to rush around for last-minute supplies and repair parts like madmen, because the next day was Good Friday, and nothing, but nothing, can be done in Greece on Good Friday. By noon we had everything done, and Vladimir was about to call the agent to order the pilot when he got a call from Irina.

He clicked off the phone and turned to me. We were in an electrical-parts store buying relays for the derricks' electric motors. Piraeus is probably the best port in the world for outfitting a ship. Earlier, we'd gone to a large store near the waterfront that specialized in hatch cover gaskets. That was all the place carried—large gaskets, small gaskets, U-shaped gaskets, corner gaskets, every kind of gasket any ship could need. I'd never seen a hatch cover gasket store before, and I was suitably impressed.

"That Greek asshole that repaired the stern," he said. "He came with the bill today. He wants seventy thousand dollars."

"What? Just for repairing that dent in the stern? What was the agreement?"

"Seven thousand."

"Did you have a contract in writing?"

He looked abashed. "No, that's not how we do things here. He came on board and we make an agreement. Just on a handshake."

"He can't win in court, can he? No judge'll give him seventy thousand dollars for that repair."

He shrugged sadly. "I don't know what a Greek judge will do. They don't like Russians here. They don't like anybody but Greeks. But it doesn't matter. Even if I win in court later, he can keep the ship from leaving now."

"Oh, shit. He's had the ship seized?"

"Not yet, but he told Irina he would keep the ship from sailing until it's paid."

I looked at my watch. "It's one o'clock on the day before Good Friday. Do you think he can get a judge to issue a seizure order now?"

"Maybe not. I think all the judges will be drunk already. Let me call the agent."

He called the agent and a few minutes later the agent called him back. His jovial face turned red, and there was no trace of a smile on it now. "That bastard has gone to the coast guard and told them not to let the ship sail," he said. "We can't clear out now until Monday."

"And on Monday morning he'll have a court order in place."

"Probably."

"Well," I said, "you and Irina have done a hell of a job. We couldn't have gotten out without your help. I doubt that my client will survive this, though. We just don't have the money to fight a lawsuit, especially against a Greek in Greece."

"I think I will have him killed," Vladimir said solemnly. For a moment I thought he was serious, but then he smiled. "No, that's too good for him. I will see that he gets nothing. For a Greek, that's worse than death."

"Any ideas?" I knew we were a long way from open water here, much less international water, and I didn't see how the ship could sneak out past the coast guard office in Perama. I'd been there before. The opening in the long breakwater that surrounds the ports of Perama and Piraeus is just off a coast guard base located at the end of a large pier called the Germaniki Scala, or German Pier. It'd been built by the Wehrmacht during the German occupation in World War II. If the coast guard had agreed to stop the ship from leaving, I didn't see how the ship could thread its way from the dock, down the waterway, across the crowded harbor, past the coast guard base, and out through the breakwater, all without a clearance.

"Yes," he said. "I have an idea. Ships are not allowed to take on bunkers in the port except at the bunkering anchorage. And the bunkering anchorage is just inside the breakwater."

"Go on."

He threw a heavy arm around my shoulders and hugged me to him. "Come," he said. "Let's go see the agent. He's a friend of mine, a wonderful man. Best Greek I know."

I paid for the relays and we left. The agent's office was a small, cluttered office in a nondescript building half a block off Akti Miaouli, Piraeus's wide waterfront boulevard. The agent, Stelios Thales, was a tall, languorous man with a tobacco-stained mustache and a great, high, hard belly. He looked like an anaconda that'd swallowed a peccary. "Come, my friend Vladimir," he said, before we could get into the details of our problem, "let us go downstairs to discuss the matter."

Downstairs was a long, narrow bar crowded with Greek businessmen drinking lunch. We took a tiny table where our knees bumped against one another. We had to bend over to avoid the elbows of standing drinkers and hurrying waiters.

"I know that man," Stelios said. "He has a bad reputation in this port. Why did you hire him?"

Vladimir threw out his huge hands, narrowly missing the head of a man at the next table. "I didn't know. I asked a man I knew, a ship's engineer, and he recommended the man. I'd never heard of him before."

"Well, it's a problem. If the coast guard said they'll stop the ship, then they probably won't let it go past their base. They keep a patrol boat right there, you know."

Vladimir leaned close, although with the noise level in the bar, he couldn't have been heard a foot away. I could hardly hear him myself. "What about getting permission to go to the bunker anchorage? The ship doesn't need a clearance for that, does it?"

"No," Stelios said. He smiled suddenly. "You can just order a pilot for that. Then the ship can sail from the bunkering anchorage to the lighthouse."

Vladimir's heavy face wrinkled in a deep frown. We sat silently for a moment. Stelios threw back his glass of ouzo and drained it. He'd bought a round of the stuff, and although I can force vodka down if necessary, I find ouzo virtually undrinkable. My glass sat untouched in front of me.

Stelios's smile stayed on his lean, crafty face. "But there is one thing I have to do tonight. I have to take some whisky to the coast guard station."

Vladimir brightened. "Why is that?"

"I do it every Good Friday. Perhaps I can do it early this Easter. When would you want to take the ship out?"

"If we can get bunkers on board in time, we can do it about midnight."

Stelios shrugged. "Perhaps I could get delayed. Perhaps I could arrive at the station just before midnight. Of course we must drink a few drinks when I arrive. It would be rude of me to do otherwise."

"Of course." Vladimir laughed, punching him lightly on the shoulder. "And we wouldn't want you to be rude to the coast guard."

"Fine, then," Stelios said, waving to a waiter for another round. I lifted the glass to my lips and made a manful effort to get some of the bitter stuff down. "I will get the whisky today. I usually take ouzo, some retsina, some Metaxa. There will be five or six men there at that time of night. I'll make sure to have a bottle for each man. Should I order a pilot for six P.M.?"

Vladimir had already made the arrangements with the bunkering company. He looked at me, and I nodded. The drinks came and a new shot glass of ouzo appeared next to my half-full one. I made another try at it and got most of the rest down. It was getting easier, I had to admit.

"Six P.M.," Vladimir said. "The ship will have oil up."

They drank their second drinks quickly. I had to leave most of mine. Stelios threw some bills on the table and we pushed our way out. We shook hands at Stelios's door and headed back to the ship.

Vladimir and I drove to the airport to pick up the new captain. A short, wide man with a thick black beard, he had a bone-crusher handshake and an intent look in his eyes. We took him to the ship and got him settled in, made sure everything was ready for the voyage to Cadiz, and went to Vladimir's office. Irina wasn't there, and Vladimir had to go out on some other business, but he gave me one of the spare cellular phones he kept in the office and said he would keep me posted on events.

Irina came back in the late afternoon and poured us a couple of shots of vodka. I still had a headache from the ouzo we'd had instead of lunch, but the vodka miraculously cleared it away. The strong black coffee that she brewed in the little kitchen at the back of the office also helped. Vladimir called to announce that the pilot was ordered for six o'clock, and the ship would be at the bunkering anchorage by seven-thirty, with fueling to be completed by ten o'clock.

He got back at five and the three of us had another shot of vodka to fortify ourselves for the night's festivities. We went to a restaurant on the south side of the harbor, an open-air establishment under strings of gaily colored lights suspended from awnings that fluttered and snapped in the night wind. We had a couple of platters of fried, finger-sized pieces of octopus, then huge plates of grilled fish and french fries. I couldn't take any more vodka, and they graciously let me drink beer, a delicious Greek pilsner called Mythos.

After a leisurely supper, we dropped Irina off at their apartment and Vladimir and I drove to Perama. Traffic was light. Everybody had already left work, and it was far too early for respectable persons to head to the bars. We went to a restaurant halfway up the steep hill that overlooks Perama harbor, one of several on the narrow street, each at the top of steep steps cut into the cliff face.

The dining area was almost empty, but the long, narrow bar with a glass wall facing the sea was half full of early drinkers, most still in their business suits. We took stools at the end of the bar, where Vladimir nursed a vodka and I sat with a beer. The Germaniki Scala stretched out into the harbor right below us, the coast guard station at the end a white cube against the dark water. Beyond it, the lights of anchored ships twinkled, and, far to the right, the bright, blue-white beam of the lighthouse swept the black sky.

At eleven o'clock Stelios came up to us. By then the bar was packed; we didn't see him until he'd shoved his way through the clots of laughing, gesticulating men. "Everything is okay," he said. "Come, let's go out on the balcony."

He ordered a drink and we followed him through the swinging glass door. Two couples were climbing the steps, the women talking loudly in Greek. It was cold and windy, and we were the only people on the balcony.

Without the bar's lights reflected in its glass wall, we could see the entire Perama harbor spread out below us. "My friends in the coast guard office were very happy to get their whisky," Stelios said. "I stayed for one drink, but I think they will continue without me. They did not seem to be watching for ship movements."

"Where is the bunkering anchorage?" I asked. "Can we see it?"

"Not from here. It's behind that hill, the one with the antenna on top." He looked at his watch. "We should see the ship in a few minutes."

We leaned on the rail for a while without speaking. I zipped my jacket and turned my collar up. A gaily lit cruise ship or ferry—in Greece, the two are sometimes indistinguishable—appeared in the distance and steamed in past the lighthouse. It disappeared behind the hill on its way to the downtown docks in Piraeus. A large container ship, spotlights illuminating its high, square funnel, navigated slowly past the Germaniki Scala and turned seaward.

A few minutes past midnight, Vladimir straightened. "I think that's the *Fontanka Saga*," he said. "Look. She's the right size."

A small freighter, visible only as a green running light and weak yellow house lights, was steaming slowly into view. "Yes," Vladimir said, "I'm sure that's my little ship. Your little ship."

"Now let's see what the coast guard does," Stelios said. "We must pray they do not pay attention to her."

Silently, we watched the ship steam past the Germaniki Scala, not more than half a mile offshore, and thread its way between the lights of the anchored ships. The coast guard patrol boat sat at the pier across from the coast guard station, but its lights were out and there was no smoke from its exhaust stacks.

The ship's lights dwindled as she turned her stern to us and slipped away. By the time she reached the lighthouse, she was only a single pinprick of yellow light, and after that her lights disappeared into the night. Or perhaps the master had turned them off. Stelios turned and raised his glass. "To the *Fontanka Saga*," he said. "And to a successful voyage to the New World."

We drank the toast and went inside, where we had another drink before going down to the street. Vladimir wanted me to go to his house for more drinks, but I was exhausted, and I was finally able to persuade him to let me go to the hotel. As usual, he insisted on driving me himself, but luckily the bar was closed, and he was content to give me a tight hug across the seat and let me get out.

"You call me and tell me how it goes," he said. "And you must come back and visit soon."

The *Fontanka Saga*, renamed the *Anka Saga* to save trouble repainting the hull names, reached Cadiz without incident, loaded machinery parts for Veracruz, and went into the general cargo trade in the Caribbean. Vladimir called to say that Irina had convinced him to pay the Greek repairman seven thousand dollars, although his personal preference was to give the man a seven-thousand-dollar beating.

Greg asked me to manage the ship, but ship management is a full-time job, regardless of the ship's size, and I was too busy. So he and his buddies hired a man in Cape Canaveral, Florida. I ran into Greg at the next Maritime Law Association meeting, in San Francisco; he told me that FileIntegra's stock had fallen to a penny a share. They'd sold the ship to a Haitian a few weeks earlier. The last I heard of her, she was laid up in Freeport, Bahamas, with a ruined main engine.

Later that year, Vladimir and Irina came to visit me in Lacombe. They rented a hotel room near my house and we had a rolling party for a week. My wife was a little taken aback by the heavy drinking, and prudently didn't join in.

Vladimir and Irina were impressed by my daughter, Karla, then fifteen. One night, while we were sitting around my dining room table tossing back shot glasses of vodka, Vladimir proposed to my wife and me that we arrange her marriage to Irina's eighteen-year-old brother. "Vladimir," I protested, "does Dimitri speak English?"

"No," he said, with the ponderous sobriety that marked all of his drinking sessions, "but together they will learn the language of love."

My wife didn't find it funny, but when we told Karla about it, she burst out laughing. For years afterward she and I joked about her "learning the language of love."

Vladimir and Irina moved back to Odessa shortly after that, and made a fortune in real estate. We stayed in email contact, and Vladimir recently sent me a photograph of the family. Irina is still a beautiful woman, and their daughters have grown into stunning young ladies.

CHAPTER ELEVEN

A MEXICAN BROTHEL AND
THE *PETRO CHEM IV*

ABOUT SEVEN YEARS ago, I received an email from a Spanish ship-owner whose tanker had been seized in Mexico. The *Petro Chem IV* was a products tanker, built with segregated compartments designed to hold different kinds of liquid chemicals. She'd been on a voyage in ballast—without cargo—from Rotterdam to Coatzacoalcos, Mexico, when she ran over a fishing boat.

According to the owner, the ship's master had done nothing wrong. The bridge was properly manned and the vessel's radar was in good condition. However, as the ship was transiting the Bay of Campeche, at about 3 A.M., she'd struck a small, unlighted fishing boat at full sea speed. The boat had sunk and two of the three crewmen had died. The ship stopped immediately and put over its rescue boat. One of the fishermen was found clinging to flotsam, injured but not seriously. The other two men were never found. The injured man was brought on board and the master immediately reported the accident to the Mexican authorities. He was instructed to take the ship to Ciudad del Carmen, the nearest port.

On arrival, the ship had been seized and the captain taken to jail. The crew was taken off and put under house arrest—at the owner's expense, of course—in a local hotel.

The master and crew were Spaniards, and the Spanish government had protested their arrests, but to no avail. However, after the surviving crewman testified that, at the time of the accident, the fishing boat had been drifting without lights due to a generator failure, the master and crew were deported to Spain.

The ship's radar was tested and found operational. It wouldn't have picked up a small wooden fishing boat anyway, but still the Mexican authorities refused to release her. An auction had been set for February 26,

2002. The owner had been advised by his Mexican attorney that the auction was going to be rigged so a Mexican company would get the ship for next to nothing. That was why the court had refused to accept the P&I club's offer to post a bond so the ship could leave.

· I'd flown over Ciudad del Carmen before, in my days of delivering aircraft to Latin America, but I'd never landed there. I remembered that the town was located on an island just off the coast, west of the Yucatán Peninsula, connected to the mainland by a long causeway. I did some Internet searching and found a Continental flight connecting through Mexico City.

I could see the tanker as the plane banked low over the island on its way to final approach. It was about five thousand tons' deadweight, easily the biggest ship at the dock. The only commercial port on the island was on the southwestern side, protected from open water by its western tip, and there were several smaller vessels at the T-pier west of the tanker. We continued east for a final approach to the long runway that parallels the island's north coast.

I'd made a reservation at a hotel called the Guacamaya, which was on the town's main drag. It was a reasonably nice place, with the lobby done in a vaquero theme, with cow skulls, saddles, and coiled lassos mounted on the walls.

By then it was late afternoon, and the winter sun was low in the western sky. I took a taxi to the commercial pier. The street dead-ends at the pier, in an area of bars and restaurants catering to locals. I paid the cabbie and sauntered across the street to an unpainted kiosk selling snacks and candy. I bought some peanuts and strolled down a side street that ended in a high chain-link gate, closed and locked. On the other side of the gate was an unused waterfront with a few pieces of machinery strewn about on the stained and chipped concrete; across a narrow strip of water, the bow of the *Petro Chem IV* loomed high in the sky. A closed and shuttered warehouse blocked my view of the rest of the ship.

I went back to the main street. The pier's two guards sat in metal chairs in front of the tiny guard shack, leaning back with their chairs' front legs off the pavement, pump shotguns across their laps. They paid no attention to me.

I walked up the next side street and reached a narrow lane that went back to the waterfront. Small houses, each with steel cages over their windows and doors, presented only their rough and poorly troweled faces. Two ragged children played in the street with a homemade toy wheelbarrow that held a dirty stuffed dog. They broke off to stare at me with sooty faces.

The lane stopped at a ragged stump of broken asphalt sticking out over a crumbling waterfront. The dirt had washed away, and pieces of asphalt that had broken off lay scattered on the narrow strip of sand. Hundreds of empty soft-drink bags lay like dead jellyfish along the shoreline.

Now I could see most of the ship, with only the bow hidden behind the warehouse. The stern rose high out of the water, and beyond it I could see the outer corner of the sunken barge to which the ship was secured. She was a good-looking ship, well painted and free of corrosion or panting. *Panting* is the surveyor's term for the indentations between the frames that you often see on the sides of older ships, caused by repeated heavy contact with docks.

The dying sun painted her white house pink. I knew there were no crew members on board, and it didn't look like there were any guards, either. I wasn't surprised. The ship was only fifty yards from the guard shack, and the authorities probably figured that the guards would hear anything that happened on board.

A man came out of a door behind me, a potbellied man with a Zapata mustache. He stared at me suspiciously. *"Buenas,"* I said, and walked back up the lane. He went back in his hovel.

The sound of pulsing disco music greeted me as I walked toward the street that ended at the pier. I stopped at a small gasoline station and leaned against a light pole. The music was coming from a bar across the street, painted purple. A sign painted on the stucco front said CAIMANO BAILANDO; above it was a crude painting of an alligator on its hind legs, dancing with a nearly naked woman. Musical notes floated around their heads. A wide balcony overhung the entrance to the disco, shadowing its purple-painted glass door.

Back at the hotel, I called Mr. Alemano, my client, and reported what I'd seen. "What do you think, Captain?" he asked. "Can you get her out?"

"I think so. It's a very quiet dock, so starting the engines is going to be a problem unless I can create some kind of covering noise. The crew's going to have to sneak on board. Will your crew do that?"

"Sneak on board? What would happen to them if they got caught?"

"They'd go to jail."

"No," he said emphatically, "they will not do that. Can you find a crew to do it?"

"I can put one together," I said, "but it'll cost money."

"The ship is worth fifteen million dollars," he said. "Tell me how much and I'll get the money to you. But what is your plan?"

I told him. He sounded skeptical but finally agreed to send the money. I said I'd call back when I had the crew ready. We agreed that they would deliver the ship to Belize, the nearest foreign country, and his crew could take over there.

I called Barry Butler and outlined my requirements. "I've got a chief engineer," I said. "I need a good captain, a pretty good second engineer, and some good oilers and deckhands."

"Let me see what I can do," he said.

It took a couple of days, but we finally rounded up a crew willing to sneak the ship out. I called my German friend in Haiti, Otto Volmer, and made arrangements for Mr. Alemano to send him a ticket from Port-au-Prince to Ciudad del Carmen. Otto was an alcoholic, but he could find his way around an engine room blindfolded, drunk or sober. I'd once seen him chase a Haitian mob off a ship by charging them with an upraised monkey wrench, so I had no doubts about his bravery.

Barry was able to supply the rest of the crew. He had a captain who was willing to do it, a Bahamian named Perry Merriweather, whom I'd heard of. He was known on the Miami River as the captain who'd beaten a crackhead half to death for trying to steal the outboard motor off his rescue boat. I didn't hold that against him.

Two days later my crew were installed in a couple of low-budget hotels that catered to Mexican tourists, a few blocks from the pier. They'd checked in separately and were under strict orders not to be seen together.

I brought the captain and chief engineer to my hotel room and briefed them on the plan. They'd never been to the pier, so I described it. "It's a very quiet area," I said, "so we're going to have to do this carefully." I turned to Otto. "Chief, I'm going to need you to sneak on board with me tonight to check out the engine room. We'll have to swim, but it's not far. Can you swim?"

"Of course I can swim," he said. "How far will it be?"

"Oh, maybe fifty meters. Not far. There's a sunken barge next to the ship, so we won't have any trouble getting on it. I hope there's a ladder over the side of the ship, but I can't see that side. It's one of the things we'll have to check out."

The captain was about fifty, with a grizzled skullcap of close-cropped hair and deep crow's feet at the corners of his eyes. He had hardly said a word since I'd met him. "Any questions, Captain?" I asked.

"No."

"Okay. We'll report to you tomorrow morning. Everything okay with the crew?"

"Of course."

I went to a department store in a mall near the hotel and bought four waterproof flashlights, two inflatable swim rings, and a spray can of flat black paint. Back in my hotel room, I inflated the rings and spray-painted them black. Then I opened the window to get rid of the smell.

After a light supper, I lay in bed and read until 10 P.M., then I took a taxi to Otto's hotel, carrying the swim rings and flashlights in a small bag. He had a room with the second engineer. He was already wearing dark clothes. We went out and down the street. He was drunk, but you wouldn't have known it except by smelling his breath.

Car traffic was light, but the street was crowded with people, sitting around, chatting in groups, gathered around cars with the radios blaring. I knew we stood out as gringos, but since the pier was the major point of departure for vessels going out to the hundreds of rigs in the Mexican offshore oilfield, I figured that the sight of foreigners walking toward it wasn't so unusual.

We passed the disco on the corner. Music was blaring, a blend of hip-hop and salsa, with screeching horns and a heavy, unvarying, computer-generated backbeat. Two girls stood on the sidewalk in front of the bar, one in a miniskirt and the other in red hot pants with a wide silver belt. On the second-floor balcony, another girl leaned on the painted steel railing smoking a cigarette, wearing a pair of skintight Capri pants and a spandex top that clung to her pendulous breasts.

I nodded my chin toward the place as we passed. "Whorehouse?"

Otto chuckled. "I thought it was a nunnery."

The lights on the pier made dim pools of yellow light at regular intervals. An old supply boat at the end hadn't been there that afternoon. The two guards at the foot of the pier stood talking to a young man on a bicycle.

We turned down the side street and I slowed as we reached the lane. It was deserted and had no streetlights. "Come on," I said, and we walked quickly to the far end. Televisions and radios blared from the open windows on both sides, but nobody looked out. I jumped down to the narrow beach and Otto followed me.

Once in the shadow of the high cinder-block wall that encircled the warehouse, we stripped off our pants and shirts and put them in a plastic bag. I stuck the bag in a crevice under the wall and handed one of the swim rings to Otto. We inflated them and stoppered the mouth tubes, and I slung the bag over my shoulder.

The water was cool, but not cold. My feet stumbled on submerged pieces of broken pavement, then found smooth sand. The water rose to my waist and I struck out with the ring around my chest, dog-paddling toward the dark bulk of the ship.

Now the guard shack came into view. I felt horribly exposed, with the lights along the pier shining out over the water. We were only about thirty or forty yards from the guard shack. I turned my head away and kept swimming. I cut a quick look behind me. Otto looked okay, although he was breathing heavily through his mouth.

I paddled around the stern of the ship and reached its shadow. Otto caught up and joined me next to the sunken barge. "You okay?" I whispered to him. He nodded.

One end of the barge was underwater. The deck rose gradually, covered with algae and too slippery to scale. We paddled around to the far side, in shadow from the pier's lights, and found some welded staples covered with barnacles. I was able to pull myself up with nothing worse than some tiny cuts on my fingers. I hung my swim ring on one of the deck cleats.

Otto came up behind me, a pale wraith in the darkness. I unzipped the bag and took out the two flashlights. I handed Otto one and we crept across the deck toward a Jacob's ladder hanging down from midships.

The ladder's spreaders knocked against the ship's hull as I climbed. Otto came up and I helped him on deck. We went across to the starboard side. Now the guard shack was clearly visible off the starboard bow. One of the guards sat in front of the door. I couldn't see the other.

We went aft and into the house. Spidery ladders led down to the upper machinery deck, where our flashlights played over the main engine's heads. Otto moved ahead and went aft to inspect the turbo. He then continued down to the lower deck and checked the engineer's control station. His flashlight followed the air-start line to the valve on the forward end of the engine. Then he went from one generator to the next. Finally he led me aft to the steering flat, where he inspected the pumps and rams that controlled the rudder. He turned and said, his voice echoing in the silent compartment, "Looks ready to go. Even got thirty bar in the air receivers."

"Okay. Let's go up to the wheelhouse."

He followed me to the bridge. It was wide and well fitted. Here, high in the air, we could look down to the guard shack's roof. A thin sliver of moon was rising above the warehouse. We would need luck as well as skill to get the ship out, but at least we didn't have a full moon. An overcast sky would have been better, but the sky was clear and forecast to remain so.

I checked the ship's controls. Everything looked in order. She was only ten years old, young for a freighter, and tankers are usually in better condition than dry-cargo ships because they're subjected to more rigorous inspections. We padded downstairs and went out on the main deck. A gentle breeze wafted out of the northwest, smelling of dust. The supply boat I'd seen earlier had its running lights on, and as I started down the Jacob's ladder it pulled away and turned westward.

We crossed the barge and swam back to the bank without being seen. After getting dressed and deflating our swim rings, I stuck my head up above the level of the lane. It was quiet, with only a couple of televisions still on. Most of the windows were dark.

The music from the disco was louder, and a gang of young people stood in front of it. We walked in the other direction, where the street was dark and quiet; nobody paid any attention to us.

I had a long talk with my client the next morning, then called Raoul in Belize. "Hey, good buddy," I said, "I'm in Ciudad del Carmen and need some help. I need somebody who speaks Spanish to go to a disco here and rent it for the night." I gave him the general outline of my plan.

"You want me to do it?"

"If you can. I don't have anybody here I can trust."

"How much do it pay?"

"How about a thousand dollars for a one-day job? Well, two days including driving from Belize."

"Dat's okay. I'll do it. When you need me?"

"Tomorrow. Meet me at my hotel." I gave him the necessary information. "Try to get here in the afternoon so you can talk to the disco owner before dark. One more thing . . . I need to talk to an agent in Belize. We're going to need to change the crew somewhere, and Belize is the best place. Can you give me the number of the agent you used when I came in on that ship from Honduras?"

"Sartainly." He put the phone down, then picked it up and read off a number. "Dat's my fran Otoniel Jones. He's a good man, true t'ing, but don't say nottin' 'bout stealin' de ship out of Mexico, eh?"

I called Mr. Jones and told him I wanted to change a ship's crew at sea, without clearing in.

"Why you no want to bring de ship in, eh?" he asked.

"To save money. I need to change the crew, but there's no reason to pay port charges just for that."

"Hmm. Radder unusual, you know, but I t'ink no problem. W'at you want is just to bring in de crew from de ship. De new crew dat get on, dey don't need anyt'ing in dere passports to leave de country."

"Good. Can you make the arrangements? Maybe there could be something in it for the immigration man who stamps the crew in."

"Dat always help, no true?" He laughed. "All raght, Cap. I see w'at can be done. You call me back dis addernoon."

We hung up and I went downstairs for lunch. I visited my crew in the afternoon to make sure everybody knew his role. Then I went across the causeway to the public beach on the mainland and found a store that sold small inflatable boats. I bought two bright yellow six-man boats and took them back to the hotel. There I inflated them, spray-painted them black, and deflated them.

I called Mr. Alemano and told him the replacement crew would have to get to Belize by the following day, because the ship wasn't going to be clearing in, and I didn't want her steaming around offshore acting suspicious. He promised to have them there on time. Then I called Mr. Jones. He said his friend in the immigration department would clear my crew in, but it was going to cost a thousand dollars. I whistled.

"Dat's a bargain, mon," he said. "De man risk his job, true t'ing. And de crew will have to come to the sout' side. Raoul will bring dem in his dory, but dey can't go to de town dock. De man will meet dem dere and stamp dere passports."

I thanked him and promised to have the immigration man's money when Raoul and I arrived the next day. Then I lay on my bed and dozed until Raoul arrived. He was wearing a lime-green guayabera shirt and his habitual khaki shorts, a big grin on his brick-red face. "Well, my fran'," he said, "w'at kind of trick you play now, eh?"

Over lunch and beers, I told him the situation.

"W'at you need me for, den?" he demanded. "You can rent de disco you'self, no true? Not dat I don't want de money, true t'ing, but why you need me?"

"There's going to be hell to pay when dawn comes and the port authorities find the ship's gone. This ship's worth fifteen million dollars. The police are going to investigate the ship's disappearance, that's for sure. If a gringo rents the club the same night, they could tie me to it. You're a local, just throwing a party, and nobody will think there's a connection."

"But how do dat help you in taking de ship out? I don't understand, mon."

"It's for the sound of the ship's engine," I said. "That's a very isolated dock, at the end of a street. Without the disco, it'd be as quiet as a graveyard. We have to start a generator before we can start the main engine, and that's going to be loud. I need you to have the disco put speakers out in front and turn them up all the way."

"What if somebody make complaint 'bout de nise?"

"We only need ten minutes, just long enough to start the generator and main engine. Do you have a cellphone?"

"Yas, mon, all de time." He pulled out an old-fashioned phone with a stubby antenna.

"Good. If you have any problems or delays, let me know by cellphone."

After we finished lunch, we got in his old truck and drove by the disco. It was closed, but a couple of girls were lounging on the second-floor balcony in skimpy outfits, smoking cigarettes. "Dat look like one lee whorehouse, my fran'," he observed.

"Yeah, disco on first floor, whorehouse on second. It's a match made in heaven."

"Dat wery interesting," he said, eyeing the girls as we passed. One of them waved, her red fingernails gleaming in the sun.

I chuckled. "Good cover, eh? And as soon as the ship's gone, you can do what you want. Turn here. I want to check something out."

He turned left and I had him drive past the lane. A dog lay sleeping in the middle of it, and two boys sat on their bicycles at the far end. "That's where we're going into the water," I said. "The crew and I will take inflatable boats to the ship."

The high stern of the tanker loomed above the warehouse roof. "Dat de boat?" Raoul asked.

"That's it."

He whistled. "Dat one big boat, mon. And you t'ink dey no see it gine out?"

"I'm hoping they don't. There won't be much moon, and I'm hoping the guards on the pier won't be able to see beyond the lights."

He grunted and turned down the next street. We went back to my hotel and I put him in my room. Then I took a taxi to the captain's hotel and gathered the deck crew in his room. I went over the plan until I was sure everybody knew his role. "Cut the dock lines as soon as the generator starts," I told the captain. "Don't wait for the main engine. And try to do it as quietly as possible. No loud voices, no noises. And don't wait to test the steering. Just go."

I gave him instructions to steam for Belize City and wait for the new crew just off Turneffe Island. Then I walked down the street to Otto's hotel and gave him the engine-room gang's instructions. There was a half-empty bottle of rum on his table and an empty glass of melting ice cubes in front of him, but his faded blue eyes were bright and focused.

"Get the main engine started as soon as possible after the generator starts," I told him. "I know you've got to get oil up, but don't take any more time than necessary. The second you get oil pressure in the bearings, start the engine."

"I will waste no time, Captain," he promised.

I told him I would come to get the black gang—the traditional name for an engine-room crew—at eleven-thirty.

Back in my hotel, I gave Raoul five hundred dollars to rent the disco. He came back to the hotel an hour later and said, "De mon t'ink I crazy, for true. He no want to close de disco, but I tell him no matter, keep de disco open, I just want hold pa'ty in front wit' de speakers. I gib him one hundred dollar for to put de speakers in front, an' he happy."

He tried to give the rest of the money back, but I told him to keep it as a down payment on his fee. We went downstairs to the bar and had a couple of beers, then went back to the room and lay on the bed watching bad Mexican soap operas. The sun moved at a crawl across the clear western sky. Finally it sank behind the low trees on the island's western tip. We went down for a quick supper, and back up to the room. I was antsy, thinking about what lay ahead. If the guards noticed the ship leaving, if we were caught, a few hours from now I'd be in a Mexican prison. It was a sobering thought. Did my plan really have any hope of succeeding? I couldn't watch television any longer and started pacing between the bed and the bathroom.

"Mon, dat makin' me narvous," Raoul complained. "Stop dat."

I sat on the bed and rubbed my face with my hands. "I wish midnight would hurry up. It's the waiting that gets to me."

Eleven o'clock finally came. I stuffed the boats and paddles in the duffel bag, made sure the flashlights were working, and led Raoul down to his truck. Traffic was heavy with Friday night revelers—as the main Mexican port for the offshore oilfield, Ciudad del Carmen was full of workers flush with cash—and the downstairs bar at the captain's hotel was full. The lobby was busy as well, with people coming and going; the crew were able to get their bags out without being challenged by the receptionist. Anyway, the night was already paid for.

The other hotel was smaller and had no bar or restaurant. But the reception desk was deserted—the crew were able to walk past with their bags unobserved. The men sat on their luggage in the back of the truck as we drove to the waterfront.

We could hear the disco as soon as we crossed the canal and turned onto the street leading to the pier. A crowd stood in front, spilling across the sidewalk and into the street. I'd been worried that it would look strange with speakers out front and nobody there, but I needn't have worried. There must've been fifty discoers in flashy clothes milling about.

I had Raoul turn a street early, to avoid passing in front of the disco. Nobody would be suspicious then, but a truck with nine foreigners jammed in the back could be remembered later. A small kiosk stood on the next corner, with a short round woman selling food off a barbecue grill and a few men standing about eating. They watched as we went past, but there wasn't anything we could do about that.

The lane was deserted, with only a few dim house lights casting shadows across it. We were far enough from the disco. I had Raoul pull over.

"Go to the disco," I told him. "Make sure they keep the music loud for another hour. I'll see you at the hotel later."

His face was in shadow. "Good luck, my fran'. Be car'ful, eh?"

The men sat tensely in the truck's bed, watching me. I looked up and down the street. "Okay," I said to the captain, "let's go."

I lugged the bag with the boats across the street with the men right behind me. We hurried along the lane, our footsteps echoing between the house fronts, until we reached the end of the pavement. I jumped down to the sand and moved off to the right, toward the port. The disco's music was muted here, but still loud.

When I had the men clustered around me, out of sight from the lane, I took out the boats and we started inflating them. They were small boats, and it didn't take long.

A fresh wind was blowing from the north. The flimsy boats wriggled like live fish, and we had a hard time making way toward the ship. But I didn't mind. The wind would help carry the sound of the ship's engines away from the guard shack.

The moon was waning; tonight it was only a sliver, with Venus burning near its lower cusp. The stars glittered like diamonds. Finally, after a long five minutes, we reached the ship and pulled up next to the sunken barge. The crew climbed up the staples one by one and crouched silently on deck.

We were hidden from the guard shack by the bulk of the ship as we went up the Jacob's ladder. The men knew their jobs and dispersed without discussion. The chief officer led a gang forward to cut the bowlines. Another gang went aft. The captain and I went to the bridge and Otto and his men slipped down to the engine room.

The captain switched the engine console on, the instrument lights glowing on his square, bearded face. A generator in the engine room started with a whine and a rumble.

I clapped the captain on the shoulder. "Good luck," I told him. "I'll be talking to you on the VHF when you get to Belize."

I ran to the main deck and slid down the Jacob's ladder. Standing on the bow of the sunken barge, just ahead of the bow of the ship, I could see the roof of the guard shack, but I was too low to see the guards. I didn't dare climb up on the pier, though. The generator was horribly loud, even with the wind blowing the sound away.

The five minutes that it took to get oil up seemed interminable. I climbed down into one of the inflatable boats and crouched down with just my eyes above the barge's deck. If the guards hear the engine start, I told myself, I'm dead. If I try to swim back to the lane, they'll see me and start shooting. I thought of my children, growing up without a father . . .

"Christ," I muttered to myself, "get a grip on yourself."

A deep thumping joined the clatter of the generator, and balls of black smoke puffed out of the main engine's exhaust stack. The bowlines dropped to the barge. I heard a splash as the stern lines dropped to the water. The lights at the foot of the pier appeared before me, one by one, as the ship slid backward.

The bow cleared the barge and the ship drifted for a moment when the engine stopped. Then she started at dead slow ahead and the bow swung to port. The ship eased past the southern end of the T-head, all lights out, and within minutes it was nothing but a dark blob against the darker water.

I waited for an alarm, but nothing happened. The disco's thumping music was the only sound in the world. For five minutes, ten minutes, nothing moved on the pier. Now the ship was completely invisible, probably turning north past the tip of the island. Filled with elation, I hissed to myself once again, "Not yet, by God, not yet!"

It was a saying I'd first used when I once survived an engine fire in a single-engine plane over Chetumal, Mexico. I'd put the fire out by diving straight down at VNE, the never-exceed speed. After I managed to land at the Chetumal airport, I jumped out onto the tarmac and danced around the smoking fuselage, shaking my fists at the sky and shouting "Not yet, by God, not yet!"

The Mexicans who came to rescue me thought I was crazy.

It was a quick paddle back to the end of the lane, with the wind behind me, and a few quick slashes with my knife reduced the inflatable to a limp sack that I pushed out to drift away. I did the same to the other boat.

The lane was deserted. I hurried to the side street and turned toward the disco. It was 12:40, and the music was as loud as ever. I took cover behind a closed kiosk to spy on the guard shack.

The guards were talking to two girls at the foot of the pier, their shotguns slung over their shoulders. Damn, I realized, I should've hired a couple of whores to distract them. Well, it worked out anyway. The ship was long gone. The guards might not even notice until dawn. I walked up the street, then caught a taxi to the Holiday Inn and walked the two blocks to my hotel.

Raoul was watching a black-and-white Western, drinking a Moctezuma beer. We got our bags and checked out, and began the long drive through the primordial jungle that spans the base of the Yucatán Peninsula. We reached Chetumal shortly after dawn and crossed the border at the Hondo River.

We reached the Theodore Hotel in Belize City in late morning. It was a bright, breezy day; it felt good to be back.

Mr. Alemano's crew arrived that afternoon. I met them at the Prince George Hotel and briefed them on how they were going to get to the ship. The following day, the *Petro Chem IV* called from Turneffe Island and I went with Raoul to take the crew out. The ship sat still in the water, rolling in the swells. After the crews swapped places, within minutes the ship was under way again, steaming south toward an unknown destination.

Raoul delivered my crew to an abandoned shipyard south of Belize City, where we met the immigration man, dressed in civilian clothes, who laid the crew's passports out on the hood of his car and stamped them in quick succession.

I had made reservations for the crew for the next day's flight to Miami, with connections to their various homes. After I took them to the Hotel Belize and paid them off, Otto and I had a few drinks in the bar before I retired to the Theodore Hotel for the evening.

That was the last time I saw Otto. Ronald ran into Otto's Haitian girl-friend in Port-au-Prince years later, and she'd told him that Otto was very sick. Nobody's heard from him since.

I had to call Mr. Alemano several times to get my success fee; I hinted darkly that he was in no position to make me his enemy. The money arrived shortly afterward.

CHAPTER TWELVE

STEALING BACK THE *MAYA EXPRESS*

B Y THE SPRING of 2002, the shipping business was booming again, with no end in sight, and I was in the delightful position of having to turn work down. Karla graduated from high school with honors and went off to Louisiana State University to study interior design. My son Alex and I sailed around Lake Pontchartrain and camped on the deserted beaches that ring the lake.

One day I got a call from Michael Bono, who had been one of my students when I taught at Pope John Paul II High School in Slidell. "Remember me?" he asked.

"Course I do! You and Eddie Dardienne were my star pupils. What're you doing these days?"

"Practicing law. Eddie and I went to Tulane Law School together."

"Interesting coincidence," I said. "I'm practicing law myself."

"I know. That's how I found you."

"What kind of law do you practice?"

"Maritime. I took an LL.M. in admiralty from Tulane."

"That's what I practice. Exclusively, as a matter of fact."

He laughed. "Hard to believe, isn't it?" He got serious. "I have a business proposition."

"Shoot."

"I've been wanting to start a ship-repossession service. I've done a few repossessions as a lawyer, but we've always had a hard time finding people to do the operations. Would you be interested in the job?"

"Stealing ships out of port?"

"That's right. I read about you stealing the *Erika* out of the Dominican Republic. I knew you'd be the man for the job."

We met the next day at the Chili's restaurant in Slidell. I'd remembered

Michael as a tall, lanky boy with long black hair falling down over his eyes. Now, at thirty-four, he'd filled out and sported a neatly trimmed mustache and goatee. After reminiscing about our days at Pope John Paul II and talking about the other students in his class—I told him I'd given Jimbo Boyer flying lessons some years earlier—we sketched out a plan to form Vessel Extractions L.L.C.

Michael had practiced maritime law in New Orleans and Anchorage, but he was planning to move to San Francisco. He would be the company's business manager and I would handle operations. He was only in town for a few days. After he left, we collaborated by phone and email on a website and press releases, and waited for business.

A few jobs trickled in not long afterward, but we were able to resolve them without having to resort to extractions. A couple ended in lucrative business for my law practice, so I didn't mind. I was able to spend more time at home. But the years of absences, and my wife's ever-present fear that I would end up dead or stuck in a foreign jail, had taken their toll. In February 2004, our marriage came to an end, and she moved to northern Mississippi with Alex.

A few weeks later Michael called. A ship had been stolen in the Dominican Republic. The mortgagee, a Boston investment firm, wanted us to find her and deliver her to a jurisdiction that would recognize its rights.

The ship's owner had died suddenly; for a couple of months the ship was left at the dock without management. The Russian crew had been stuck on board with no money to live on and no money to get home.

A Colombian named Mario Vargas had chartered the vessel for the voyage to Rio Haina, Dominican Republic; when he learned that the owner had died, he persuaded the crew to steal the ship out of port without a clearance. Mortgage payments were overdue, and our client had already started looking for her, but by the time the investment firm learned that she'd been seized in the Dominican Republic, she was gone. With no clearance to another port, she could've gone anywhere.

I figured she'd gone to some lawless country where the thief could change her identity. So I called Ronald, who was living in Port-au-Prince, Haiti, at the time, and asked him if he'd heard anything about a ship called the *Maya Express*.

"The *Maya Express*!" he cried. "She's in Miragoane, Captain. She's at the old Reynolds Dock. I saw her there two weeks ago."

That wasn't as much of a coincidence as it seemed. There aren't many places in the Caribbean as remote as Miragoane; it has always enjoyed a reputation as an outlaw port. If I were looking for a port to put a stolen ship through a corrupt judicial sale, Miragoane would be the place.

"That takes care of finding her," I said with satisfaction. "If I come down in a couple of days, can you go to Miragoane with me?"

"He hesitated. "But, Captain, it's very dangerous to travel on the road. You know there is revolution here now."

"I heard about that. We can still get to Miragoane, though, can't we?"

"I don't know. The rebels have broken open all the jails and the roads are full of bandits. I haven't been to see my family since the revolution started."

"Can you find out what's going on with the ship? Are there any phone lines into Miragoane?"

"No, Captain, no phone in Miragoane. Somebody told me there might be cellphones there now, but I don't know anybody who has one."

"Okay, I'll call you back."

After some negotiation, Michael came to terms with the funding company and got a fat retainer. American Airlines had stopped its flights to Port-au-Prince, but Air France still had one a day from Miami. I called their reservations number and got on the next day's flight.

It was clear and windy when the plane landed. The airport was crowded with soldiers armed with assault rifles. They looked ready to use them. The street in front of the terminal was usually thick with people meeting passengers, but today, except for policemen and soldiers, it was almost deserted. Ronald was waiting with a small, sharp-faced taxi driver. We shook hands and I got in the back seat.

The streets of Port-au-Prince were eerily quiet. We had to take a detour through the hills because the government had barricaded the downtown streets. But by midafternoon we reached Carrefour, the immense slum that stretches westward from the capitol. We passed the remnants of a few barricades, where the traffic carefully negotiated the gaps in the piled-up rocks. Rusty steel rings lay in the street where tires had been burned. The driver gripped the wheel tightly. Usually talkative and jocular, Ronald sat without speaking as he scanned the street ahead.

There's only one main street running the length of Carrefour, and usually it's jammed with traffic. Today it was almost empty, and we made good time. We passed the Admiral Killick Naval Base, a collection of ramshackle buildings and a small pier with a decrepit patrol boat tied to it. I noted with satisfaction that the boat's engine hatches were open. It was out of service, which meant it wouldn't be able to chase the *Maya Express*.

The traffic came to a stop and a heavy mushroom of black smoke billowed up ahead. Our view was blocked by the gaily painted buses that Haitians call tap-taps. People started running past us, terrified looks on their faces as they glanced back.

Ronald spoke sharply to the driver. The man cut the wheels into the oncoming lane, which was empty, and rocked over the curb. There were gunshots from ahead, three, then two. Ronald spoke to the driver again, urgently, and the driver gunned the engine. Cars were trying to turn around all up the line. Black smoke poured into the blue sky.

We finally got turned around. I heard more gunshots as our driver swerved around a stalled car and kept going. The crowds on the sidewalk pressed themselves against the stalls to get out of the way of the careening cars.

We managed to get downtown without further incident. Ronald tried to convince the driver to take us through Carrefour on the coast road, but he refused. When Ronald pressed him, he shook his head miserably, trembling. Finally Ronald had him take us to the central bus station.

The station was less of a bus station than a wide, open area near the waterfront where buses from outlying towns meet the tap-taps that people can take to different parts of the city. Ronald and I got out and I paid the driver. We went from taxi to taxi, looking for one that would take us to Miragoane. Agreeing to pay two hundred U.S. dollars, twice the going rate, we finally found a driver who was willing to attempt it, a big, tough-looking man with only a thumb and little finger on his left hand. He had a Mitsubishi Montero with black-tinted windows.

We turned off on the coast road that parallels the main road a few blocks down the hill. It was rutted and potholed, and the car couldn't go more than about five miles an hour, but traffic was sparse and we were able to keep going.

At one point, where the road followed a shallow point that stuck out into the bay, I looked back at the city. I could see the entire Port-au-Prince waterfront and the houses on the slopes behind it. Pillars of smoke rose above the buildings, mushrooming into a haze that blurred the sun and obscured the tops of the mountains.

We reached the point where we'd had to stop earlier. Smoke was still drifting up from the roadblock; as we drew abreast of it, we could look up the cross street and see the debris that had been piled around it. A large tap-tap lay on its side, smoking, a thick crowd milling about.

We continued westward, past the pipes and tanks of a small oil terminal. Suddenly the driver jerked the car to a stop. A large crowd, some with sticks, came surging down a side street and spilling out on the road. "Turn around," I told Ronald. "Tell him to turn around."

But it was too late. "Get down!" Ronald told me. "We can't let them see a white man in the car."

I slipped down between the seats and buried my face in the floorboard. The shouts got closer. The car bumped forward. I heard heavy clangs as sticks hammered on the hood and roof. Ronald yelled something about Aristide.

Then the noise fell behind and the car gained speed, lurching over the potholes. I raised my head. The crowd swarmed over the road behind us. The road ahead was clear. "Jesus," I said, sitting up. "Everybody okay?"

"Everything okay," Ronald said.

"What did you tell them?"

"*Aba* Aristide. It means 'Down with Aristide.'"

"What if they'd been pro-Aristide?"

"Nobody pro-Aristide now," he said. "Nobody will admit it."

We reached the place where the coast road rejoins the main road, at the very edge of Carrefour, without further incident. Tap-taps lumbered westward, packed with passengers and stacked with bags and people on their roofs. We joined the procession.

In the next town, Gressier, we passed a burned-out police station with fans of black soot staining the walls above the windows. A white police pickup truck lay on its side; there were no policemen in sight. "What happened there?" I asked Ronald.

"All police gone now. They threw off their uniforms and ran up in the hills."

At the big army checkpoint outside Grand Goave, the police barracks were deserted, although not burned out, and the traffic sped past unhindered. The police station in downtown Grand Goave was also deserted, its windows smashed out. The same was true in Petit Goave.

"What about Miragoane?" I asked Ronald. "Are all the police gone there as well?"

"No, no," he said. "The Aristide police ran away, but Miragoane is a port. The foreign ships will not come if there are no policemen to keep the streets safe. The mayor hired some men and bought them uniforms. So there are police in Miragoane, but all they do is keep people from fighting. They are not Aristide men."

We reached the small mountain town of DeRousseau, where the road to Miragoane splits off from the road leading to Les Cayes and the southern coast. There it was business as usual, with tap-taps parked along the road waiting for passengers, and cars and motorcycles jockeying for space and honking their horns. Dust hung in the air and lay like volcanic ash on the abandoned cars and concrete traffic barriers.

We went to the Mirabeau Hotel in DeRousseau, the only hotel in the area with a functioning generator. Miragoane has no electricity of its own, and the plant in Petit Goave only provides electricity to Miragoane a couple of days a week. The Mirabeau consisted at the time—it has since expanded—of a small three-story building surrounded by large trees, with an open-air restaurant at the back. It is so open-air that it has no roof, and when it rains diners have to grab their plates and run to their rooms.

It was late afternoon by the time we got there. Ronald hired a decrepit old Toyota to take us down the hills to Miragoane. When we reached the old colonial church at the top of the last hill, I could see a large RO/RO carrier—a roll-on/roll-off ship that loads cargo by truck rather than cranes—tied stern-to at the Reynolds Dock on the other side of the two-mile-wide cove that shelters Miragoane.

"That's it," I said. "It's a RO/RO, and it's the right size."

Ronald asked the taxi driver something, and translated the man's answer. "He says the ship's been there two months. There were some Russians on board, but they're gone now. Two Dominicans are living on board."

"Guards, or just living on board?"

"He says they're guards. People say they're dangerous."

We reached the bottom of the hill, where the street makes a U-turn at the Chateau Caribe, a hotel and whorehouse at the north point of town. It was business as usual on the Miragoane waterfront, with two ships discharging at the dock and another three or four at anchor in the bay, waiting their turn. We inched past the police station. A couple of policemen stood in front, wearing khaki uniforms without badges instead of the traditional blue-and-red garb of Haitian police. They carried short-barreled pump guns.

We bumped and rattled along the narrow, rutted road around the rim of the bay and reached the old Reynolds Dock. From the 1960s to the '80s, Reynolds Aluminum had operated a huge bauxite mine here, and had built a large concrete pier to load ore for export. Then, after a spat with Baby Doc Duvalier in the early '80s, Reynolds had closed the mine and abandoned the pier.

The *Maya Express* was secured stern-to, with both anchors out forward and two ropes running from her stern to the pier. She was a large, high-sided ship, with a house forward and a stern ramp aft, about ten thousand gross tons and four hundred feet long. She had a general air of neglect about her. Ronald had the taxi driver park at the foot of the pier—the dirt was washed away and we couldn't drive up on it—and we walked to the end. The ship's stern ramp was down, showing a cavernous interior and a few cars still in the hold. With no electricity on board, the ramp couldn't be raised. The ship had carried cars on her last voyage, from Philadelphia to the Dominican Republic, and for some reason they hadn't all been offloaded.

A couple of Haitians were fishing on the pier. Ronald knew them—he was from the next town on the road going west, Bezin—and they told him there were two Dominican guards on board. The men had been selling car parts to locals, but the word in town was that they were dangerous men and difficult to deal with. Fortunately, no one had been shot yet.

We went to visit a friend of Ronald's, a fisherman named Jermaine who lived with his family in a small two-story frame house a few hundred yards from the Reynolds Dock. Jermaine spoke to Ronald, and Ronald translated. "He wants to know if you want to see the graves of the crewmen."

"The crewmen?"

"Two men died on the ship. They got sick and had no money for a doctor. The captain came to town and asked for help to bury them. Jermaine and some other men took their bodies off the ship and gave them a Christian burial."

"Does he know their names?"

Jermaine didn't. They were buried in a small cemetery a couple of miles to the west. He said a man with a van came shortly afterward and took the rest of the crew away. I learned later from a fellow maritime attorney that the Seamen's Church of New York had somehow learned of their plight and had sent a man down to get them home.

I told the fisherman that we would go to the men's graves later, and had him row me out to the *Maya Express* in an old fiberglass ship's lifeboat. I wanted to inspect the anchor chains and look to see if there were any other obstacles to getting the ship out.

Both chains were down, hanging slack into the clear green water, but except for the ropes stretching from her stern to the dock, I saw nothing else to keep the tugboat from putting on a towline and pulling her out.

Two channels lead from the Reynolds Dock to open water. One threads between a low hill called la Tête Américaine—the American Head—and a string of swampy islets called les Petites Filles, or the Little Girls. The other channel goes around the eastern end of les Petites Filles and runs past the town of Miragoane. With luck, the tug could pull the ship out by the western approach and stay away from town. The less attention the ship attracted, the better.

Later, Ronald had the taxi driver take me to the hotel, while he went to visit friends. It was a beautiful evening, with pink-and-purple clouds across the sky. The Mirabeau's kitchen couldn't serve anything except spaghetti, as food supplies had been interrupted by the riots and roadblocks, so I settled for that.

Ronald returned to the hotel about ten o'clock. "It's bad news, Captain," he said, sitting on the other bed. "The ship's been seized by the court in Anse-à-Veau. It's going to auction next week."

"What was it seized for?"

"Oh, it's monkey business, of course. It was seized by a man named Robert Franzy. I think he's from Port-au-Prince."

"Where the hell is Anse-à-Veau?"

"It's about thirty kilometers from here, past Petite Rivière des Nippes."

"Why didn't he go to court here?"

He smiled. "It's very hard to get to Anse-à-Veau. There are two rivers that have to be crossed. He did it so nobody would come to the auction."

"Okay, I'll have to report to our client in the morning. So there's still no telephone in Miragoane?"

"Not at the telephone office. I hear the port director has a cellphone."

"We won't be using his phone, that's for sure. Okay, we'll go to Petit Goave in the morning."

About midnight the generator shut down, but it was a breezy night, and except for the mosquitoes, it wasn't bad. The next morning, after some runny eggs and toast without butter, we caught a tap-tap to the telephone office in Petit Goave. As we were getting out, I heard guns being fired not far away. Ronald and I ducked and ran for the office door.

The people in the office were grinning and hugging one another. A man held a transistor radio to his ear, and the people who were crowded around him relayed the news to the rest. Ronald turned to me with a big smile. "Aristide is gone!" he said. "He left last night. We're free, Captain. Free!"

There was more gunfire from the street. "Rebels?" I asked.

"No, no," he said. "They're shooting because they're happy."

Finally I was able to call Michael. It was still very early in San Francisco, but he finally answered, groggy with sleep. I apologized and gave him the rundown. He said he would call the client in Boston, and asked me to call back in half an hour.

Ronald and I walked down to the Hotel L'Impératrice, a couple of blocks away, for coffee. Petit Goave is a very small town, smaller than Miragoane; most of its buildings date back to colonial times. A dozen taxi drivers sat on their motorcycles in front of the hotel. The people of Haiti are so poor, and gasoline so expensive, that motorcycle taxis are the most common form of local transportation.

When I called Michael again, he said, "The client says get the ship out before the auction. They're willing to pay what it takes. What can I do from here?"

"Call Barry Butler," I said. I gave him the number. "See if he can find a tugboat to tow the ship out. There's no way we'll be able to start the engine."

"Anything else?"

"Not for now. I'm going to Anse-à-Veau to check on the status of the lawsuit, so I'll be out of touch until this evening. I'll call when we get back to Petit Goave."

We drove back through Miragoane and took the western road to Anse-à-Veau. It was the dry season, and the SUV we rented was able to ford the streams, although the ford at Petite Rivière des Nippes was dicey. At one point, the car started to float, but the rear wheels found traction again and we made it to the other side with water sloshing over the floorboards.

We reached the beach town of Anse-à-Veau around 4 P.M. The justice of the peace court was in a small, whitewashed building with a rusty tin roof laid over hand-hewn poles. We decided it would be better for me to stay out of sight, so I walked down the beach to a kiosk with some tables and chairs around it. The ancient woman running the place opened a refrigerator lying on its back and pulled away some burlap sacking to reveal a rounded block of ice with beers and sodas packed around it.

I had barely finished my beer when Ronald came slogging across the sand. He'd seen the arrest decree and sale order, but he couldn't get copies because there was no copy machine in Anse-à-Veau. The sale order said that the auction had been advertised in the Port-au-Prince *Observateur* for three consecutive issues. It was set for March 8, three days away.

I looked at my watch. "Can we make it back to Port-au-Prince tonight?" I asked. "I need to make some arrangements. I don't want to have to do it from the Petit Goave phone office."

He stared at me. "Nobody travels at night. The jails are empty, you know. The rebels even let everyone out of the national penitentiary."

"So?"

"The roads are full of bandits. There are no police outside of Port-au-Prince. Maybe the new government will hire some policemen, but now there is nobody to protect us. My sister told me that two people were killed last night on the road to Les Cayes. Their car was stolen and their bodies were left on the road."

"Okay. But can we go back tomorrow morning?"

"Yes, I think there is enough traffic in the daytime. But we need a car with tinted windows. It is not good if people see a *blanc* on the road." *Blanc*—"white"—is the Creole word for "white person."

"Can we make it back to Miragoane tonight?"

He swallowed his beer in one long gulp. "Yes, but we must hurry. Even on the Nippes Road it is dangerous after dark."

When we passed the *Maya Express*, it was dark. At the Mirabeau Hotel, the high steel gate was closed and locked. Ronald yelled that we were guests, and the watchman reluctantly opened it wide enough for the car to pass.

The next morning we made it to Port-au-Prince. I took a room at the Oloffson and called Michael.

"The auction's on Thursday," I told him. "What's the word on a tugboat?"

"Nothing yet. I talked to Barry. He's checking around."

"Call him back and tell him we've got to have one here tomorrow night."

"Okay," he said dubiously. I lay around the hotel the rest of the afternoon, drinking cold Presidente beers—an excellent Dominican brew—on the wide verandah that serves as the hotel's dining room. Michael called just before dark to say that Barry had found a tugboat owner in the Dominican Republic who was willing to send his boat to Miragoane. The client had asked us to have the ship delivered to Nassau, Bahamas.

When a ship is sold at a judicial auction, there is a ranking of priority in paying off creditors. Normally the mortgagee, even the holder of a first preferred ship's mortgage, ranks below a number of other claimants, but in the Bahamas, the mortgagee's claim comes first behind court costs and crew claims. The Bahamian lawyer would have a seizure order ready for her arrival.

The arrangements for the tugboat were in place late that night. The *Angel Arguello* would arrive off Miragoane Point, about four miles from the Reynolds Dock, by 10 P.M. the following night. I would make contact by VHF radio under the assumed vessel name *Carib Trader*, and the *Angel Arguello* would be the *John Pierce*.

After supper, I went out on the balcony in front of my room. The city twinkled in the dark, with the lights of the ships at the port, far below, glittering against the black water of the bay. A full moon was rising into the clear sky, the worst possible scenario for the next night's operation, but nothing could be done about that.

The next morning, Ronald rented a SUV for the drive to Miragoane.

When we reached the Port-au-Prince waterfront and turned west toward Carrefour, I saw a U.S. Navy frigate at anchor in the bay, a couple of miles offshore, a long, gray silhouette bristling with guns and antennae.

"That wasn't there yesterday, was it?" I asked Ronald.

"No. It must have come in during the night."

"That's a complication we don't need," I said. "If they decide to interfere, they could catch us long before we got to international water."

We made it through Carrefour without incident. The burned-out taptap still lay on its side where the roadblock had been, but the stones had been cleared away. There was a government roadblock at the customs station near Grand Goave, with about fifty soldiers carrying submachine guns standing in the road. We had to get out of the car while they searched it for weapons, then they waved us through. The police stations in Gressier, Grand Goave, and Petit Goave were still empty.

While we were eating lunch at Miragoane's only restaurant, a tiny, ramshackle room with a half-dozen tables crammed into it, one of Ronald's cousins came in and took him outside to talk. Ronald appeared in the door and beckoned to me.

"There is a cellphone in Miragoane now," he said as we stood in front of the restaurant. "The port director has it."

"Damn," I said. "So he can call Port-au-Prince as soon as we start cutting the anchor chains. We'll have that navy ship on us before we can get out of Miragoane Bay."

A big tap-tap, a school bus with a brightly painted wooden body depicting Calvary scenes, turned the corner and blew its horn. We had to step up into the restaurant's doorway to get out of the way of its massive, dented bumper.

"And he can see the ship from his house," Ronald went on. "He lives in one of those houses on the hill above the Reynolds Dock. As soon as we start cutting the chains, he'll see the light."

"Christ. Do you think we can pay him off?"

He shook his head. "I don't trust him. He might take our money and then make the call anyway. You know who he is. Jean-Paul Gourrient. The *Cous I*."

I laughed. The *Cous I* had been a small, decrepit freighter owned by a mysterious Haitian named Henri. A few years ago, Jean-Paul Gourrient had had a load of cocaine stored in a moribund panel truck near his ware-house with a guard watching over it. The coke was supposed to go out on the *Cous I,* but the ship had been delayed and he'd had to leave the coke in the truck overnight.

Somebody in the neighborhood learned that there was a load in the truck and hired a local girl to cozy up to the guard. She persuaded him to leave the truck for a couple of hours of pleasure at the Chateau Caribe, the waterfront hotel-cum-whorehouse at the north point of town. While he was gone the neighbors descended on the truck and looted it. Everybody in the area had a few kilos squirreled away.

Jean-Paul was in a panic. The *Cous I* would arrive any moment, and his Colombian bosses would not be very understanding about the loss of the coke—it was worth millions on the street in Miami. So he went to his ware-house and put out the word that he would buy the coke back, no questions asked. All that day and night, people showed up at the warehouse with a kilo or two, sold them to him for a few gourdes, and slipped away. By the time the ship arrived the following day, he'd bought back all, or almost all, of the cocaine, and was able to load the ship.

I heard the load got through. But later the *Cous I* was caught in the Miami River with almost a ton of cocaine on board. The crew were arrested, but the mysterious owner was never identified.

While we were eating our lunch, I said, in English, "So what can we do about Jean-Paul?"

"I have an idea," he said. "You remember the old man we hired on the *Erika* to keep thieves off the ship?"

"Yeah, sure. Why?"

The *Erika* had called Miragoane many times under my command. I'd finally gotten tired of thieves stealing everything not welded down, so I per-suaded Ronald to hire an *houngan*—pronounced "oon-GAHN"—to cast a spell on the ship, or "put the powder on it," as Haitians call it. Word of the curse spread quickly, and for a while the thieves left us alone.

"My cousin says there's only one place where cellphones work here, because of the mountains. It's the soccer field up the hill from the Reynolds Dock. Jean-Paul has to go down to the soccer field to make calls."

"So we hire the *houngan* to put a spell on the soccer field?"

Ronald ducked his head and looked around quickly as I uttered the dread Haitian word for "witch doctor." "Don't say that word," he cautioned. "Yes, Jean-Paul won't dare go near it. I will need one hundred dollars to pay him."

It was an inspired plan. "Okay, you can arrange it this afternoon?"

"Yes, I'll go see him. He still lives up on the top of the mountain."

"Man, he was an old man fifteen years ago."

Ronald glanced at me. "He still has much power," he said. "All the powerful men like him"—Ronald wouldn't use the word *houngan*—"are very old men."

"And you'll make sure that everybody sees him put a spell on the field."

"Of course."

I gave him a hundred dollars and waited in a nearby bar while he went up the mountain to talk to the *houngan*. When he got back, we took a taxi to the Reynolds Dock and walked out to the end of the T-head. The high, white side of the *Maya Express* gleamed in the afternoon sun. A half-dozen Haitians sat at the end of the pier, dangling fishing lines with their toes. "The Dominicans are on board," one of them told Ronald in Creole. "The black one was on the back a few minutes ago."

Ronald yelled to the ship, and a few minutes later a burly Hispanic with close-cropped hair and a big brown belly under an open shirt came out on the stern ramp. *"Que veux tu?"* he yelled.

"We want to come on board," Ronald yelled in Spanish. "I have a gringo who wants to talk business with you."

The man studied me for a moment. "Okay," he said. "I'll come get you." He got in a dugout canoe tied to the stern and paddled across. We went on board with him and threaded our way forward between the abandoned cars. Most had their hoods up, with engine parts missing, and only half still had their wheels and tires.

We sat in the crew's mess. The man who had questioned me had a knife scar that puckered his upper lip into a perennial snarl. "Who are you?" he demanded of me in Spanish. "What do you really want on this ship?"

I stared at him. "Fuel," I said. "*Combustible.* What do you think?"

"Where is the money?"

I laughed shortly. "I'll have it tonight. You think I'm going to walk around this country with money on me?"

He looked at the other guard, a bony black man with matted dread-locks and bulging eyes. "What do you think, Julio?" he asked. "Maybe this gringo thinks he can steal our fuel."

"Don't be *estupido*," Ronald said suddenly, leaning over the table. "I know this man. He has a tugboat in Jamaica. If you don't want to sell him fuel, just say so. But don't make stupid accusations."

The Dominican laughed suddenly. "Okay, gringo, but you'd better bring the money. *Dinero Americano, comprende*?"

"Yeah," I said, getting up. "I *comprende. Vamanos,* Ronald."

The Dominican paddled us to the dock in the dugout and gave a friendly wave as we walked away. I had Ronald take me to Petit Goave, where I called Michael. He reported that the client's Bahamian lawyer had an arrest warrant for the ship ready as soon as it reached Bahamian waters.

A court cannot issue an in rem arrest warrant unless the ship is within its jurisdiction. This is one of the ways that an in rem action—with the ship itself as defendant—differs from a nonmaritime lawsuit. In the same way, an in rem sale by a court is invalid unless the res—the thing—is within the jurisdiction of the court at the time of sale. This was why we had to get the ship out before Thursday's auction.

I told Michael our plan—the ruse of buying fuel and Ronald's idea of hiring an *houngan* to keep the port director off the soccer field so he couldn't call the coast guard. "We do have another problem," I said. "It's going to take a while to cut through the anchor chains, an hour or more. Everybody on the hill will be able to see what we're doing. I'm afraid we're going to get a mob on the dock."

"Are you going to be there?"

"I don't think so. I'm too well-known in Miragoane. All it would take would be a single phone call to the airport and I'd be arrested when I tried to leave."

"Then where will you be?"

"I've found a house where I can surveil the dock. It's very close, only a few hundred yards away. As soon as the ship's gone, I'll take off. And Ronald has a friend who's a cop in Port-au-Prince. I'll get Ronald to hire him and a couple of his buddies to control the dock. It'll cost a couple of hundred each. But it will be well worth it."

Michael agreed. "Now, listen," I said, "and listen good. This is a really dicey situation here. If you don't hear from me by tomorrow morning, something bad has probably happened. I'm serious, Michael. Don't waste money trying to recover my body. The Haitians'll bury me here."

"All right," he said somberly, "but make sure you call me when you get to Port-au-Prince."

I got the tugboat owner's telephone number and called him directly. He told me the boat was scheduled to call him on the high-seas radio in about an hour. We ran through the procedure and our cover names for the VHF radio contact, and I explained how the boat should try to take the western channel in and out.

"Do you know if the Haitians have any patrol boats?" he asked. "I do not want my captain and crew arrested."

I thought about the U.S. Navy ship at anchor off Port-au-Prince, but I answered truthfully, "No, the Haitians don't have any boats that work. There's a small boat at the Admiral Killick Navy Base in Port-au-Prince, but I just took a look at it, and the engine hatches are up. They're working on the engines."

He was satisfied with that. I made sure the tugboat had a cutting torch and plenty of oxygen and acetylene, and we hung up. I went down to the room and brought Ronald up to the roof to call his policeman friend in Port-au-Prince. I planned to trick the Dominican guards into getting off the ship, but I needed some way to keep them from getting back on. When he finished his call, Ronald said that Abuel, his friend, and two other policemen would leave Port-au-Prince in a few minutes, and would arrive at Jermaine's house by nine o'clock.

Just before dark, we caught a taxi to the fisherman's house, where I waited while Ronald went to the Reynolds Dock to make final arrangements for buying the fuel. A strong wind was building out of the north; it would make the tug's job that much harder, as it would blow the ship toward the shallows as soon as the anchor chains were cut.

Ronald returned to report that all was arranged. He'd told the guards that we would go on board to pay them. But later, when the time came, he would tell them that the *blanc* was afraid to go on board at night, and if they wanted their money, they would have to come to the dock. We were pretty certain they would agree, rather than give up the thousand U.S. dollars we'd promised.

As the evening wore on, I got more apprehensive about the location of my stakeout point. There was only one way out of town, the narrow street that ran past the restaurant, and all anyone had to do to block it would be to roll some stones—never far away in that rocky land—into the street. Whether or not I was seen on the dock, any white man going through town would be automatically suspect. And in Haiti, *due process* and *probable cause* are words without meaning. They would just toss me in prison and throw away the key.

When Ronald returned, I told him I wanted to run the operation from town instead of the fisherman's house.

He nodded. "That makes sense, Captain. I was worrying about that. Abuel and his men and I can get out, but having you in the car would make it harder for us as well. But where can you go in town without people knowing you're there?"

"I'm going to try paying the captain of one of the ships at anchor to let me run the operation from his wheelhouse."

By then it was almost dark, and the ships at anchor had their lights on. The nearest one, also nearest to the Reynolds Dock, was the *Cabo Rico,* a small freighter with two cranes and a modern, squared-off house. A pale man with blond hair looked over the side as we approached.

The crew of the ship were all Russians. The captain was a middle-aged redhead with a bristly pink mustache, a big, gangly man in a loose muscle shirt and running shorts. I had some misgivings about letting him in on the plan, but I had no alternative. I told him what I needed and he agreed to let me use his wheelhouse to con the operation for four hundred dollars. I gave him two hundred dollars down and told him I would be back shortly before midnight.

Back at the fisherman's house, we waited for Abuel and his men to arrive. They got there about ten o'clock, in a white Nissan police truck. Abuel was a jovial man, about thirty years old, in a sport shirt and slacks. The other two were younger men, also in civilian clothes. Abuel carried an automatic in a nylon holster on his belt. One of the other men carried a similar service automatic, and the third carried a MAC-10 submachine gun on a leather sling, with two extra magazines on his belt.

Ronald and I made last-minute plans. I gave him six hundred dollars. "Don't let the Dominican guards go back on board to get their stuff," I told him. "Give them three hundred each to pay for what they've got to leave behind. But, Ronald, no rough stuff, unless they attack first. Is that clear?"

"Don't worry," he said. "Abuel is a professional policeman. He knows how to handle these things."

I laughed. Being a professional policeman in Haiti didn't necessarily mean that he wouldn't use excessive force. But at that point all I could do was hope nobody got seriously hurt. "Okay," I said. "As soon as the ship gets free and starts out, you and Jermaine come to the ship to get me."

Ronald briefed Abuel and his men, then they got in the truck to drive to the Reynolds Dock. The fisherman took me back to the *Cabo Rico*.

The ship's wheelhouse was dark, but the radar was on and the green light from the display filled the bridge. The captain was sitting on a stool by the port door as I went in. Under the press of the north wind, the ship was swinging to the south, putting the Reynolds Dock off her port stern. There was no electricity in town that night, and the only lights were dim candles in the windows. The police station, dead ahead of the bow, was completely dark. Ronald had told me that the impromptu policemen hired by the mayor probably didn't stay at the station at night, and it looked like he was right.

I turned one of the VHF radios to our agreed frequency, channel 72, and waited for the tugboat to call. The captain and I chatted while I waited. He was from Moscow and had graduated from the Russian Naval Academy. He'd served on Russian-flag ships until the collapse of the Soviet Union. He had a wife and three daughters crammed into a single-room apartment in Moscow, and considered them lucky to have that.

Shortly after eleven o'clock, the radio crackled and a Hispanic voice came on. "Motor Vessel *John Pierce* calling the Motor Vessel *Carib Trader*. Come in, *Carib Trader*."

"Come in, *John Pierce*," I said.

"I am crossing the reef now," he announced. I glanced at the radar. The Russian captain had set it at the twelve-mile range, but I'd forgotten to watch the display, and the tugboat had reached the opening in the reef unnoticed. Now it was a small, triangular blip just west of Miragoane Point. As we watched, the blip moved south through the break in the reef.

I scanned the Reynolds Dock with the ship's binoculars. All looked quiet. There were no lights on the dock or on the *Maya Express*. I called Ronald on his walkie-talkie.

"All okay, Captain," he said. "Tell me when to call the Dominicans."

"Go ahead. The tugboat will be there soon."

A few minutes later I could pick out the tugboat through the binoculars, steaming south with all lights out, a black spot against the silvery water, staying well away from town. It passed the anchorage and reached the western channel. Then a long time went by when it didn't appear to move. Finally, the captain came on the radio. "Cap," he said, "we're aground here. Trying to get off now. We can't find the channel."

I studied the tug's position. "You're too far west," I told him. "If you can get off, try going east. If you have to, go around the eastern side of those little islands."

"Roger, Cap," he said. "I think we're getting off now. Yes, we're moving now."

A few minutes later the tug disappeared behind the westernmost of les Petites Filles. I called Ronald. "The tug's there. What's the status on the guards?"

"They fell for it—they're coming to the dock. They're getting in their boat now."

"Okay, keep me posted."

I called the tug and told the captain to start cutting the chains. "We're backing up now, Cap," the master reported. "There's no light on the ship. Is everything okay?"

"All okay. Proceed."

Ronald called. "We have the guards on the dock. Abuel has them under control."

"Are they causing any trouble?"

I could hear his fat chuckle over the radio. "No trouble, Captain. Abuel and his men are very impressive, you know."

That MAC-10's impressive, I thought. I wouldn't make any trouble for a man holding one. "Anybody else on the dock?"

"Nobody."

"Okay, stand by."

A few minutes later, a great blue-white light bloomed from behind the westernmost island, at the bow of the *Maya Express*. I winced. The cutting torch lit up the entire rim of the bay, throwing hard shadows from the rocky outcroppings and illuminating the huge Reynolds shed that over-looked the dock. I checked my watch: Twelve-fifteen.

The radio crackled. Ronald said, "People are coming on the dock, Captain. How long is it going to take?"

"I don't know," I said. "Any officials?"

"No, just ordinary people. Everything okay for now."

The cutting went on. I glanced over the Russian ship's bow at the sleeping town. Nobody seemed to be paying any attention to the light on the other side of the bay. The police station was still dark.

"How does it go?" the Russian captain asked me. "It go okay?"

"Yeah," I said, "as well as we can expect for now."

"What all this about, eh?"

I nodded my head toward the *Maya Express*. "This is a stolen ship. We're taking it back. It had a Russian crew on board. Two of them died. They are buried here."

"What they die from?"

"Sickness and hunger. The rest are back in Russia."

"Ah!" he said angrily. "The world is very bad for Russians now. What we do, I ask? We do not want Russian government. We are slave to government. Why world think we are bad people?"

I lowered the binoculars and went up to him. "Captain, Russians are the most wonderful people in the world."

"Oh," he said, "I make apology. Very kind thing you say. But very sad about the men who die. Very sad for family."

"Yes," I said, "that's the worst thing about foreign crewmen getting stranded in these hellhole countries. They never come home, and their families never know what happened to them, what happened to their bodies."

The radio crackled again. "Captain," Ronald's voice said, "people all over here now. How long to get the ship out?"

"What are they doing?"

"They want to know what we're up to."

"Anybody fighting?"

"No, Abuel's keeping everything cool, but I don't know how long we can keep them on the dock."

"Okay, I'll check on the cutting and call you back."

I switched to channel 72 and called the tugboat. "How's it going?"

"Very hard work cutting these chains, Captain," the captain reported. "Almost finished with the first one now. Maybe another thirty minutes to cut the other one."

"All right. Keep at it."

I watched through the binoculars, but except for the light from the cutting torch, I could see nothing. The dock was dark. I scanned the road leading from town, but I saw no headlights.

Long minutes went by; the cutting torch continued to bathe the southern rim of the bay with light. Ronald called a couple of times, but I had nothing to tell him.

Finally the tug captain called to report that the second anchor chain had been cut. "We're hooked on now and starting to pull," he explained.

At last, I thought. I could see heavy white smoke pouring from the tug's stack. But the *Maya Express* didn't seem to be moving.

"The ship's still hooked to something," the tug's captain reported. "We're trying to find out what's holding it now."

A few minutes later he called back, agitated. "The ship has a cable to shore," he said. "It was underwater until we started pulling. I'm going to drop off the bow and go to the stern to cut the cable."

I signed off. "Shit," I said. "So that was their backup plan. An underwater cable." I called Ronald. "How's it going there?"

I could hear excited voices in the background. "Plenty people here now, Captain," he said. "Plenty problem. Some people want to get off the dock, but, em, right now they can't get off. I don't know how long we can hold them."

"Can you see some underwater cable?"

"Yes, Captain, when the ship moved away from the dock, I see one big cable come out of the water. But the tugboat is there now. I think it will be cut soon."

I was on pins and needles when the tug captain called a few minutes later to say that the cable had been cut. He was maneuvering around to the bow again. I watched through the binoculars as the tug's exhaust smoke turned white again. Now the *Maya Express* was moving. I glanced at the town. It was still and quiet. The buildings were stark and white under the giant moon.

I went out on the starboard wing of the bridge. My heart leaped into my throat when I saw the bow of the *Maya Express* turn slowly toward the north. The wind was blowing the ship south toward the shore. Now it was bow-on to me, a great white triangle above the mangrove islands.

Everything stopped: the ship, the smoke, the beating of my heart. The radio was silent. I strained my eyes in the binoculars to see movement, any movement at all from the ship, but everything had stopped.

It was my worst nightmare. With the ship hard aground, the tugboat would have to cut its towline and steam out at full speed. Ronald's men would have to let the crowd off the dock, and within minutes somebody would get to town and raise the alarm. I couldn't get out by road— my white face would nail me. But maybe I could make my way over the mountain to DeRousseau.

I ran into the wheelhouse and put the binoculars on the dashboard. I shoved two hundred dollars into the Russian captain's hand and rasped, "Thanks, Captain. I gotta go."

I ran out to the starboard wing. I couldn't wait for the boat. I was going to have to swim for shore. I threw my leg up to the gunwale and started to heave myself over, but for some reason I hesitated, and in that second I saw the shape of the *Maya Express* start to lengthen. The tug was still pouring white smoke into the night sky. I couldn't tell if it was moving, but the ship was turning, so it couldn't be aground.

I brought my leg down. The captain came out behind me. "What happen, eh? Some problem?"

"No, it's okay," I husked. "I think it's okay."

The captain handed me the binoculars. I trained them on the ship. The tug was definitely moving now, toward the east, with its black hull visible between the islands. The whole length of the *Maya Express* was turned broadside, trailing behind the tugboat like a great white elephant following its mahout. I called the tugboat captain.

"All okay," he reported, "but we must take the other channel. Too dangerous to take the western channel."

"Okay, Captain," I said. "Carry on."

I called Ronald. "What's the situation on the dock now?"

"We let the people go. No problem."

"What about the guards? Are they okay?"

"Yes, Captain. I paid them. They're already gone."

The tug and ship emerged from behind the Petites Filles and turned toward town. The two vessels came closer, and a few minutes later the tugboat chugged past the Russian ship, not a hundred yards away. The moonlight on the side of the *Maya Express* cast a bluish reflection over the water. Then they pulled ahead and came up on the town's northwest point, bathing the Chateau Caribe and the buildings around it in a ghostly luminescence. Even the police station was lit like a movie set.

The tug's engine throbbed heavily as it went upwind. Then it and ship were gone into the darkness, the ship's hull getting smaller as they steamed toward the break in the reef. I put the binoculars on the top of the running-light box and rested my forehead on the gunwale. "Not yet," I muttered to myself. "Not yet, by God, not yet."

The Russian captain tapped me on the shoulder. "You okay, mister?"

I raised my head. "Yeah," I said, "I'm okay. Now I've got to see about getting to shore."

He pointed. "Boat coming now."

I looked. The orange hull of the fisherman's lifeboat was pulling steadily toward the ship. When it came up to the foot of the Jacob's ladder, I thanked the Russian captain again, shook his hand, and went down.

Ronald had the fisherman put us ashore at the head of a lane between the police station and the Chateau Caribe. Both were closed and silent. We reached the street and turned right, in front of the station, but then we heard a squeal of tires as headlights turned the corner by the restaurant. A second set of headlights came behind the first.

It was the police truck, with Abuel and the policeman with the MAC-10 in front and the other policeman in back. The rented SUV was behind it. Ronald and I piled into the SUV. *"Allons-y,"* Ronald hissed out of the window, to the pickup truck. *"Allons vite!"*

The truck jerked ahead and made a hard U-turn in front of the Chateau Caribe. We followed it and both vehicles rocketed up the hill, our engines echoing between the silent buildings.

It was one o'clock when we reached DeRousseau. Nothing moved except a few emaciated dogs rummaging through the piles of garbage in the littered wasteland within the roundabout. It took a while to get the watchman to open the gate at the Mirabeau Hotel, but I finally got my bag and we headed for Port-au-Prince.

It was strange to see the road, so full of traffic during the day, now so deserted. No one walked along the shoulder, and the houses set back from the road were dark. We roared across the bridge at Lac Miragoane—I'd escaped death at the hands of an angry mob on this bridge many years earlier—and up the hills toward Petit Goave.

The town of Petit Goave was silent, but a few motorcycles weaved along the highway and jerked out of our way as the truck ahead blared its horn. The burned-out police station was still empty. We reached the other side of town and accelerated down the rutted, potholed road, the SUV's springs and shocks squeaking and clanging.

There was an impromptu roadblock ahead, made of piled-up rocks gleaming white in the truck's headlights. The truck skidded to a stop and we almost ran into it. The vehicles sat there for a moment, engines ticking over, as we scanned the vegetation on the sides of the road for movement. The dark bushes rustled in the wind.

The policeman in the passenger seat got out and cocked his submachine gun. He covered the right side of the road—the left side was more open, and held fewer places of concealment—while Abuel and the other policeman rolled some of the rocks out of the way. Ronald sat stiff and tense beside me, almost vibrating with fear. I held the door handle so hard my fingers hurt.

The policeman with the MAC-10 covered the two vehicles as they negotiated their way through the narrow opening in the roadblock, then he ran to the truck and jumped in. It roared up the hill with our driver about a foot behind. No shots followed us.

Grand Goave was as still and silent as Petit Goave. The blockade from the revolution had been dismantled, but the burned-out police truck still lay on the other side. We reached Gressier a few tense minutes later, and after that the beachfront posadas and restaurants that line the road outside Carrefour. A few cars appeared on the road, the first vehicles we'd seen since leaving Miragoane.

We stopped at the checkpoint on the outskirts of Carrefour. Abuel talked to the policemen manning the roadblock. They waved us on. Ronald said something cheerful to them as we passed.

We had to stop at a closed service station on the edge of town. The city was under a curfew until 6 A.M., and we didn't dare enter Carrefour until then. Soldiers controlled the city now, and they had a tendency to shoot at moving vehicles with no questions asked.

It was five o'clock. I stretched out in the SUV's backseat, and after a while I felt my breathing lengthen. I didn't actually go to sleep, but when the driver started the engine and put the car in gear, I had a fleeting moment of disorientation.

Sunrise bathed the sleeping city in a soft pink light. Traffic was light, and most of the roadblocks had been cleared away. Abuel's truck turned off in the center of town and we continued to the international airport, arriving at about 7 A.M.

I gave Ronald money to pay the policemen and the taxi driver. "You did a hell of a job," I told him as I hugged him. "I couldn't have done it without you."

"Yes," he said, "we did it together, my brother. God go with you."

But I still had to get through Immigration. I was the first in line at the booths, hoping to get through before the "bad-boy list" got distributed. In the old days, before Haiti got computers, the authorities would distribute a photocopied list of the names of people who were to be arrested if they tried to leave the country. I knew this because a friend of mine, who'd escaped from jail in St. Marc, tried to fly out and got caught that way. I'd considered going overland to the Dominican Republic, where they probably didn't get an updated list very often, but I wanted to get out of the country in a hurry and decided to take a chance at the airport.

Then I saw with a sinking heart that each booth had been fitted with a computer monitor. Finally, after all these years, Haiti had reached the computer age. The man in the booth waved me forward. I trudged up to the counter with a heavy heart.

He opened my passport and typed something on his keyboard. He studied the screen for a long moment, then stamped my passport and slid it across to me. Keeping a straight face, I headed for the baggage-screening station. Then I heard a rapping sound behind me. Reluctantly, with the blood draining to my feet, I turned.

The immigration man was waving me back. There was nothing I could do. I started toward him, but he shook his head and pointed past me. He was waving to a round black woman at the baggage-screening station. She started for him, and I managed to turn back and continue on. My feet felt as if they were trudging through quicksand.

American Airlines had resumed its flights to Port-au-Prince. The plane was already on the tarmac. Airline personnel took station at the exit doors and the passengers lined up to go out. Out into the early morning heat, up the long boarding ramp and into my seat, a few rows back from the door. I settled in and closed my eyes. I was in a middle seat, but I didn't care.

The plane filled and the door closed. Then two American Airlines employees, a man and a woman, came running across the tarmac carrying papers. My heart jumped in my chest. The truck carrying the boarding ramp backed up to the airplane and the stewardess opened the door. The man and woman came in and consulted with her. They checked the seat numbers overhead and looked right toward me.

I braced myself. I'm going to fight it, I told myself. If I make a fight of it, the American embassy will hear and maybe send somebody to the prison to check on me. The stewardess and the man and woman started toward me. I braced myself against the armrests and stuck my legs out, like a blowfish lodging himself in a coral reef. I'm going to scream bloody murder, I said to myself grimly. They'll have to get the cops to get me out of this plane. I ain't going under my own power.

But the stewardess stopped at the woman sitting in the seat in front of me and said something to her in Creole. The woman got up, got her bag from the overhead bin, and followed the man and woman off the plane. The door closed once again, the plane's engines whined to life, and we started a turn toward the runway. A few minutes later we were in the air and on our way to Miami.

A U.S. Coast Guard cutter stopped the tugboat in the Old Bahama Channel, but Michael had provided the owner with a packet of documents showing our right to repossess the vessel. After the master showed them to the boarding officers, the tug and tow were allowed to proceed.

As the tug approached Nassau, Bahamas, where the client planned to seize the ship for its claim, the tug's master called his owner to report that another tugboat had appeared and was calling him on the radio, saying it had instructions to take over the tow. We had arranged for a Bahamian tugboat to come out to international water, but this wasn't the same tugboat.

Michael checked with Barry, and we learned that our tugboat was just leaving the dock in Nassau at the time. Something was wrong. Michael advised our client, who advised their lawyer in Nassau, who called the Bahamian coast guard. A cutter soon discovered that the other tugboat had been sent by Mario Vargas in a last-gasp attempt to get the ship back. It would've worked, too, if our tug's captain hadn't checked with his owner before turning the ship over. The Bahamian cutter escorted the interloper back to Nassau and arrested the crew on suspicion of piracy.

We heard later that the president of the mortgage company, Victor Marks, had sent an email to his friends proudly describing a line-item expense in our extraction bill, "$100 for the services of one witch doctor." The story must've gotten around, because I was asked about it recently at a Maritime Law Association meeting.

"That really true?" the man asked me. "You really hired a witch doctor to keep a guy off a soccer field?"

"Course I did," I said indignantly. "We billed for it, didn't we?"

Some months after the extraction, the case went to trial. Mario Vargas appeared and tried to argue that our extraction had been illegal, that he really did own the ship. But the Bahamian judge summarily dismissed that claim and told him that he was lucky he didn't get arrested right then and there. The ship went to auction.

As it turned out, it was Vargas who bought the ship at the judicial sale. He put her into service as the *Dayana*. Two years later she sank off the coast of Panama; two crewmen died. The August 20, 2006, edition of *The Panama News* reported that "the ship's sailing patent had expired and the vessel had been found so unseaworthy as to only have a permit to proceed from the Dominican Republic to Venezuela for drydock repairs. . . . It was carrying a load of scrap metal from the DR to Colon when it sank."

In late August 2004, Captain Tiwali called me. Alex and I were out sailing, but I took the call on my cellphone. I could hardly hear him, so I turned the wheel over to Alex and went below.

"Jim Maher's disappeared," Captain Tiwali said. "He was flying from La Ceiba to San José, Costa Rica, and his plane disappeared."

"Jesus," I said, "I hadn't heard anything about it."

"It was a private plane. Jim and the pilot were the only ones on board. I just heard about it from Dolores. The Honduran air force is searching, and Cartones del Sud hired a plane to follow the route they were supposed to take, but so far nothing. It's been two weeks now."

I sighed. "I'm sorry, Captain. He was a decent guy."

"Dolores said he was carrying a lot of money."

"How much?"

"Something like half a million."

I whistled. "Man, that does make it suspicious. What about the pilot?"

"It was a charter flight. The pilot was Honduran."

"The pilot could've faked an emergency and landed somewhere, offed Jim, and disappeared into the sunset."

"There's been some talk of that," he said, "but so far no evidence. They just disappeared."

"Did the pilot contact Nicaraguan air traffic control?"

"No. He was supposed to call Tegucigalpa an hour after takeoff, but he never did. There was nothing from the plane after it left La Ceiba."

"Well," I said, "maybe somebody'll come across the wreck someday, if they really did crash."

No trace of Jim Maher, the pilot, or the plane was ever found.

In the spring of 2005, I was back in Miragoane, running a shipbreaking operation on some property I'd bought next to the Reynolds Dock. I and my partner, a hard-charging New Yorker named Don Delmont, had a contract with the Haitian government to cut up all the derelict ships in the country. I had a hundred cutters and assistants working for me.

I was living in a hut down the road from the breaking yard, a primitive arrangement with no running water, but I had a satellite dish that gave me Internet and phone communications with the outside world. One day I returned to the hut to find an email from Karla asking me to call her.

"Daddy," she said, "where are you?"

"Haiti."

"When are you coming home?"

"I am home," I said. "Nowadays, home is where I rest my head."

"Well," she said, "you have to come back to Louisiana next month. I'm getting married."

"What? You and Napoleon?" She'd been dating a wonderful young man from El Salvador named Napoleon. I'd figured they would get married someday, but I didn't realize it would come so soon. It was hard to realize that my flaxen-haired daughter was now twenty years old and a senior in college.

"Yes, Daddy. You've got to be here."

"Of course, sweetheart. What day is it?"

"May twentieth. At the rotunda in City Park in New Orleans."

"I'll be there," I promised. "Oh, my baby, I'm so happy. Give Napo my love and congratulations."

I called my partner in New York. "I'm taking two weeks off next month," I told him. "My daughter's getting married."

"What about the *Liberty Belle*?" he demanded in his nasal New York accent. "You have to cut that ship up next month."

"The *Liberty Belle* can wait," I said. "My daughter's getting married and I'm going to be there."

Two months later Karla was dead. She died suddenly of heart failure, a mitral valve prolapse. I don't remember much about the months after that. When Hurricane Katrina's floodwaters ruined my house and took all of my possessions, I hardly noticed. I lost my prized drum set, my Honda Shadow motorcycle, and my collection of some seven thousand books, but nothing meant anything to me.

Nonetheless, life went on. I closed the Haitian breaking yard and moved back to Louisiana. Owners and mortgagees still needed ships extracted. Clients needed monies collected and cargo-damage claims defended. The years continued in their inexorable march toward oblivion. More old friends died, and a few new friends grew close. Girlfriends came and went.

Today, in the spring of 2009, every day brings more flowers in the vines and bushes around my house, and the grass grows green and thick with clover. The boat traffic has awakened from its winter hiatus; speedboats, party barges, and long, sleek sailboats putter past my office.

Last night I stood on my dock and stared out over the shimmering water. A full moon bathed my boats in its light. It was an evening similar to the night I extracted the *Maya Express*. My bayou leads to Lake Pontchartrain, then to the Gulf of Mexico and the world beyond. From my dock I've sailed to Mexico, Belize, Honduras, Venezuela, and back. Always back, back to the place where I would lose my marriage, my daughter, everything I own.

Music drifted across the water from one of my neighbors' houses, as faint and affecting as music remembered from childhood. I took a deep breath. Music—and moonlight, and the scent of spring—are for the living. I hadn't wanted to live, but I had lived. And if I had to live, I had to work. I reached down to make sure I had my cellphone on my belt.

Soon it would ring, and I would go.

ACKNOWLEDGMENTS

*With special thanks to
Michael Bono and David Fisher.*

INDEX